THE DAYS OF THE SPACE BROTHERS

The interaction of humanoid extraterrestrial visitors with the people of Earth

Moira McGhee

Published by INUFOR — Independent Network of UFO Researchers

The Days of the Space Brothers

The interaction of humanoid extraterrestrials with the people of Earth

Copyright © 2020 by Moira McGhee. All rights reserved.
Printed in Australia. No part of this book may be reproduced in any manner whatsoever without written permission.

For information address:
INUFOR, PO Box 169, Katoomba NSW 2780, AUSTRALIA

INUFOR books may be purchased for business, educational, or sales promotional use. For information please write:
INUFOR, PO Box169, Katoomba NSW 2780, AUSTRALIA

INUFOR web sites:
www.independentnetuforesearchers.com.au
www.facebook.com/inufor
Email:
ind.net.ufo.res@bigpond.com

FIRST INUFOR PAPERBACK EDITION PUBLISHED IN DECEMBER 2020

ISBN 978-0-9587-045-0-2

THE DAYS OF THE SPACE BROTHERS

CONTENTS

	Introduction	1
1	The Early Contacts-Part One	9
2	The Early Contacts-Part Two	26
3	George Adamski	44
4	Adamski's World Tour	59
5	Rosemary and Millen	75
6	Fred and Phyllis Dickeson	89
7	Mr. X	94
8	The Radio Contacts	120
9	Contacts and Debates in Later Years	132
10	Aliens Among Us-Part One	150
11	Aliens Among Us-Part Two	167
12	Telepathy	185
13	More Contactees	192
14	The Scientists	201
15	Puzzling and Unusual Reports	213
16	Strange, Humorous and Suspect Incidents	229
17	UFOs-A Mysterious and Risky Pursuit	247
	Epilogue	277
	Annex A-George Adamski's Peace and Prosperity Program	279
	Annex B-Mr. X's Writings	282

INTRODUCTION

In this book I have concentrated on the 'heady' days of the early to mid-twentieth century when handsome, human-looking extraterrestrials were visiting this planet. Why were they coming to Earth? It is a complex problem, and we don't know all the answers. The 'Space Brothers', a group who most closely resemble humans, were always peaceful and friendly, interacting with us on a consensual basis.

When I speak of the 'Space Brothers', it is a collective term. According to the 'Ummites', who mainly contacted Earth's scientists, there was more than one group of alien 'humans' visiting and present on our planet. Although they may have come from different extraterrestrial societies, they all had 'good intentions'. It is not known if they were working with different agendas, or whether they formed part of an overall contingency plan.

Ancient societies' historical records never credit their sudden advances in culture, law, literacy, astronomy, architecture and civilization to their own efforts. In Mesopotamia, Egypt, the Andes or Meso-America, it is nearly always due to the 'Gods' who usually came down from the skies. Religious records describe 'Angels' who also come from the heavens above.

Over the last one hundred years their presence has been growing. In the early twentieth century, contacts were frequently accidental, often with children. In the 1950s it seemed as if the 'Space Brothers' were recruiting selected humans to spread their message to mankind. Also, certain families, whose genetic history may be connected to these visitors, have noted an increase in receiving information and knowledge through more frequent contacts.

Simultaneously, there was a growing movement for an 'alternative' lifestyle. Large groups of predominantly younger people, sometimes referred to as 'hippies', were gathering to promote world peace, civil rights, nuclear disarmament, and care for the environment.

Contacts did not always go as planned, and by the 1960s our visitors were much more circumspect in their activities. Perhaps this was not only due to other less pleasant aliens arriving here, but also because our own surveillance satellites and technologies were much more capable of detecting their craft.

There has always been evidence of some of the 'Space Brothers' living incognito among us, and giving assistance where possible. It is understandable that a more advanced and benevolent race would be concerned about the future of their human 'brothers'. The upsurge in their recent visitations commenced after the end of World War II. At that time humanity stood at the brink of a new age, not only with the introduction of new technology and communication systems, but also included the proliferation of nuclear weapons which made us capable of destroying all life on this planet.

Our first planes had taken to the air at the beginning of the twentieth century, and less than sixty years later we launched our first satellite. Only twelve years after that our astronauts first walked upon the Moon.

We were venturing into the cosmos, and possibly bringing our problems and failings with us. From an extraterrestrial perspective, perhaps our initial Apollo landings on the Moon were not a welcome sight. There are many unconfirmed reports of astronauts reporting unidentified craft on the surface. In later missions the TV connection on the side of the Lunar Module was eliminated, thus preventing vision of post-landing activities.

The Moon Landing program came to an abrupt end after Apollo 17. NASA proffered the ridiculous claim that this was due to a 'lack of congressional funding and public support'. *'Time'* magazine in December, 1972, was critical of the decision, even though some funds were to be diverted to the Skylab program.

We had trained astronauts and ground control experts, and our craft, equipment and techniques were perfected. The whole world was in awe of what the Americans had achieved and three additional missions had been planned and budgeted for. The team of skilled technicians, scientists and engineers was disbanded, and in later years there were even claims that some of the original film footage from landings was 'missing'.

We must ask the question; Why, when we had invested all that effort and billions of dollars getting to the Moon, after the early seventies, not one of us, not even the Russians, went near the place for about forty years?

Brinsley le Poer Trench, once married to my friend Millen, had some thoughts on why the extraterrestrials are here; *'Now we have made considerable advances, during the last two hundred years, in the field of technology, and despite our obvious shortcomings in other directions – (insane wars, cruelty to our fellowmen and animals, among many other examples) – they may be prepared to take a calculated risk. After all, we have been out of contact with other members of the galaxy for thousands of years. Possibly, they might consider we have been in isolation long enough, and that now is the time, before we once again destroy our civilisation, to make contact and give us assistance in making our planet a 'Grade-A' one.*

'......Perhaps they have decided to make open contact with us now, before we take war and skulduggery into space. Possibly, they may consider that, in spite of our failings, we have managed to stand on our own feet for a very long time, and now that we are on the verge of space travel, that this is the moment to introduce themselves.'

The views of theologians vary greatly, with some religions vehemently rejecting the concept of visitors from space, and others partly embracing the concept. In 1976, the *'National Enquirer'* ran an article on evangelist Billy Graham's opinions on the Space Brothers.

'He not only expressed a belief that there are other intelligent beings in the universe, but also added that they are creatures "…..who probably look very much like the average American. And I feel they have developed space vehicles capable of reaching Earth."

Billy Graham considered that intelligent beings like us, far away in space, are like us, God's creation. Having extensively studied the Gospels, he could find nothing that would change our faith in God if we discover life on other planets. It must be remembered that Billy Graham was well respected, had a following of millions, and most probably many contacts in the corridors of power – contacts who would be more 'in the know' than the average citizen.

There were numerous accounts of unidentified craft and saucers monitoring our atomic tests and also disabling our nuclear facilities and missiles. Jim Hickman described one such incident in the 2001 *'Australian UFO Bulletin'*.

Walter Cronkite, who related this incident to Hickman, was perhaps one of the best known and respected American reporters, and for many years was the CBS

Evening News Anchor. In the 1950s he joined several news reporters, on a South Pacific island, to witness the test of a new Air Force missile.

The group of journalists were kept at a safe distance from the temporary launch site, and told that photography of the event was forbidden; *'As Air Force guards, with guard dogs, walked around the perimeter, and the newsmen watched, the missile was fired up and about to be released. Just then, a large disc-type UFO appeared on the scene.'*

Cronkite said that it was a dull grey colour, about fifty to sixty feet in diameter with no visible means of propulsion. It hovered about thirty feet above the ground, and the Air Force guards and dogs raced towards it; *'It suddenly sent out a blue beam of light, which struck the missile, a guard and his dog at the same time. The missile was frozen in mid-air, about seventy feet from the launcher, as it had taken off. The guard was frozen in mid-step, and the dog frozen mid-air as it had jumped at the disc. Suddenly, the missile exploded. After that the disc vanished. The guard and dog looked all right, but were quickly taken away by medical personnel.'*

The guards ushered the journalists into a concrete bunker, where they remained for thirty minutes, before being brought out and addressed by an Air Force Colonel. He tried to claim that the disc was one of their own prototypes, designed to test the media's reaction to UFOs, but then forbade them to report on it! Neither Cronkite nor the other correspondents believed a word, not then or at any time since!

The extraterrestrials' intentional displays of their craft and occupants, plus contact with select individuals, may be designed to gradually disclose their presence, and their wish for us to live in peace. The limited integration of their agents into our society, to assist with scientific and government technical advances, are obviously intended to guide us away from our more dangerous discoveries and innovations.

In more recent years, have they been monitoring the increasing appearance and activity of conspicuously different aliens, who, without consent, abduct and interfere with humans?

Gordon Creighton, a respectable and highly educated British colleague, has written about an incident when he was a student at Cambridge University. In

April 1955, a fellow student and his girlfriend, whilst sitting in a cafe at Halstead in Essex, had overheard a conversation between two men. One appeared to be a physicist, and the other from British Naval Intelligence.

At first the discussion centred upon UFOs, which they thought had come from another Solar System. They mentioned their incredible speed and soundless propulsion systems, and how they prompted research into centrifugal and other possible technology.

Gordon's friends listened to the conversation with increased interest. The two men thought that smaller craft, like those seen in World War II, were from a parent ship, orbiting out of sight. Only six weeks earlier, at about the end of February 1955, five UFOs had landed in England, and although some were unmanned, others had occupants who looked very much like us.

Contact had been established with the visitors, who were scientists, and 'intensely curious'. It was thought that some of these 'scientists' might have mingled with our general population. Although the two men speculated on whether these visitors may stage a peaceful invasion in the near future, they felt that they might have only come to investigate the atom and hydrogen bomb explosions which it seemed were having far more effect in outer space, than we, in our enclosed atmosphere, had realised.

The contention that we have retrieved extraterrestrial craft, which have crashed on Earth, is still disputed by some 'experts' who even deny the much documented incident at Roswell in 1947.

In 1959 Norma Gardner was dying of cancer, and made some startling statements regarding her 1955 employment as a civilian at Wright Patterson Air Force Base in the USA. She claimed her job was to catalogue over one thousand items retrieved from UFO landings, and included parts from a crashed disc. Everything had been meticulously photographed and logged.

She also claimed to have seen two discs in a hanger, and the removal of humanoid bodies. She had to write up the reports on some of them, who were autopsied.

She treated her breach of security as a 'death-bed' confession. *"Uncle Sam can't do anything to me when I'm in my grave!"*

Beings from other parts of the galaxy are obviously monitoring our society and the physical state of Earth. Our lack of care for the planet, and the development of more sophisticated weapons and technology, along with our early ventures into space, must also be of prime concern.

Perhaps the Space Brothers early efforts to influence our behaviour were not as successful as they had hoped. An interesting report, published in *'Spaceflight'* 1973, is the transcript of a message supposedly picked up on radio by researchers.

"Earth creatures are now beginning to venture out into space. This activity must be viewed with concern, as these creatures are potentially dangerous. They have very imperfect understanding of, and control over, their emotions, and are consequently extremely unpredictable and unreliable.

"In addition, they are very quarrelsome and exceptionally stupid. For instance, they have a money system which is based on, and indeed encourages some of their worst instincts, notably selfishness, greed and lust for power. The same system effectively and drastically slows down every effort these creatures make to improve their living conditions and increase their knowledge – including space research.

"Earth creatures seem incapable of working together on a large scale for the common good. On the contrary, there are endless stupid quarrels during which large numbers may be killed and maimed by their own species, often using exceptionally brutal and cruel methods.

"Efforts are being made to instil some measure of cosmic responsibility into these creatures, by telepathy and other means, but so far these efforts have met with little success, as the stupidity, ignorance and complacency of these creatures is almost beyond belief. Meanwhile, there is a grave danger that the species will become extinct, either owing to unwise exploitation of natural resources, leading to deterioration of the environment, or to self destructive wars. Although one regrets the disappearance of any species from the Universe, it has to be admitted that this particular species is at the moment one of Nature's less successful experiments.

"For the time being, efforts will continue to prepare this very backward species for cosmic co-operation. In view of the unpromising material, it must be some considerable time before any tangible results can be expected."

Nearly fifty years have passed since this broadcast was intercepted, and we must be a disappointment to the Space Brothers. Yes, so far we have ceased nuclear testing and avoided an atomic war, but in the interim there have been countless brutal wars and massacres. Caring for the ecology of our planet has been token, with thousands of animal species becoming extinct, and global warming rising by the year.

Why do these space visitors conceal their presence and interactions with the people of Earth? One good reason is that there is no single leader, representing the planet, with whom they can liaise to gain public recognition and acceptance.

In 1995, Steven Greer MD, the International Director of CSETI, put another thought very succinctly; *'ETI's enigmatic and elusive behaviour may be understood as human-protective when viewed from their perspective; a war-torn, aggressive, nuclear armed and disunited Earth civilisation must not receive further potentially harmful technologies until a lasting world peace and unity is achieved, and international human goals become peaceful, cooperative and unified in nature. Such a transformation will then indicate a readiness for a fuller contact and exchange between humans and ETI. We must respect and accept ETI's control and wisdom in this regard.*

'Notwithstanding the protective limits mentioned above, ETI is apparently desirous of expanded contact with humans, and is open to voluntary, human-initiated contact and exchange. There is strong evidence to suggest ETI has been systematically introducing themselves to human civilisation for the past forty-five years or longer, and that such contact has steadily deepened and intensified over this period.'

What concerns me is Dr. Greer's reference to 'ETI' – 'extra-terrestrial intelligence', which can encompass all manner of visitors, both good and evil. Whilst the 'Space Brothers' apparently had good and honourable intentions, this trusting analysis cannot be said of others, including biological-type entities created and driven by artificial intelligence.

This leads me to revealing what some contactees said the Space Brothers had told them. There was another reason for them coming to Earth. A reason which was so confidential they could not divulge it. Some close contacts of the Amicizia may have learned the secret, which we have discovered, in later decades, may be a horrifying reality. One of the 'Akrij-W56' alien visitors told Stefano that they were in conflict with a dangerous CTR artificial intelligence, the *'contrari'*, which were a danger to both them and Earth; "The CTRs are the result of a W56 experiment that has run out of control. They are robots, in the full sense of the word, even if centuries ago they began as a biological reproduction."

In 1978 the CTRs attacked and destroyed most of their creators' W56 bases, and while the majority of the Akrij departed Earth by 1986, they promised that they would return. Some have remained integrated in our society, and maintain smaller bases elsewhere on the planet. Since then, reports of flying saucers with beautiful blond haired emissaries have been almost non-existent.

The references to the CTRs also became much more meaningful in later years, when hapless victims reported unpleasant abductions by the taller 'greys' with large heads, skinny bodies, black wrap-around eyes and no visible reproductive organs. Stefano added that he was told it would be difficult for us to discriminate between a natural being and a biological robot, and these entities, (Extraterrestrial Biological Robots – or EBEs) are trying to understand how to bridge the difference between themselves and us. This certainly would explain the behaviour of the 'greys', and makes sense of their interest in genetics, and human reproductive and biological material. I suggest these beings are not really interested in helping us and have 'control' as their ultimate goal.

My late friend and colleague, BUFORA's Betty Wood, summed up her opinion of the entire situation; *'The sentimentalists, (and I must admit to some leanings myself here), are still hanging on hopefully to the 'Space Brothers' idea – those gentle humanoids of the 1950s, who are so rarely reported nowadays. Have they given up in despair, and left us to the not-so-tender mercies of beings who are not so benevolently inclined? Beings who, with their attendant weirdo robots, don't appear to give a scrap about the feelings and sensitivities of the people they grab for some undignified medical or genetic experiment. Rather like some of us, with animals! Chickens coming home to roost, maybe.'*

CHAPTER ONE

THE EARLY CONTACTS – Part One

Many types of Visitors are reported by contactees. Whilst some aliens have distinctly oriental appearances, I am most interested in the fair, or sometimes dark-haired, Caucasian-looking humanoids – as described by witnesses in this book – the information they impart, and the possibility of genetic manipulation or enhancement. The contactees insist these beings and their craft are as physically real as we are.

Much has been reported about crashed flying saucers during 1947. I am also interested in the years before and after this. After many years of research I am convinced by the evidence of humanoid type visitation and influence upon many countries, during those earlier decades. Many times these were accidental encounters with children. Perhaps they were more innocent, less questioning, and probably less likely to be believed by their own parents, let alone the authorities.

A commonality in many of these accounts indicates fair-haired humanoids in charge, with smaller creatures performing assisting roles. I have always considered the possibility that these little entities are biological worker robots, as distinct from the taller 'greys' frequently reported over the last forty years.

Some witnesses claim multiple meetings with extraterrestrials as human as we are – just more evolved and with advanced telepathic abilities. These witnesses report being told that these Visitors had been coming to Earth since ancient times. There are many hypotheses, with really no way of knowing which, if any, are correct. Modern day reported contacts certainly go back one hundred years or more.

Days gone by
There are many UFOs cases recorded well before the modern surge of reports which began in 1947. As early as 1790, a landed craft and occupant was reported in Alencon, France. At 5am on June 12th, a group of witnesses, including the mayor, a physician and other local authorities, reported seeing and enormous globe which crashed on top of a hill, starting a grass fire. The villagers rushed to put out the flames, and were startled when a 'sort of a door'

opened, and a person, 'just like them', came out. He was dressed in an unusual manner, with clothes which adhered completely to his body.

After muttering some incomprehensible words, the stranger fled into the woods, after which the object exploded, leaving nothing but some fine powder. Police inspector Liabeuf investigated the incident, and noted in his report that no trace could be found of the mysterious man.

UFO reports from the early twentieth century are of great interest because we had little *known* aerial technology at the time. While I am unsure about many 'airship' sightings from the beginning of the 20th century, no conventional explanation can account for a report made in 1927, by Russian explorer and author Nicholas Roerich. Roerich was fascinated by reports about, and with finding, Shambhala (Shangri-la) – a mystical realm where powerful, spiritual lords were rumoured to reside.

During his August 1927 expedition, Roerich and his party saw a fast-travelling metallic, disc-shaped object at high altitude over the Himalayas. He documented this in his book, *'Altai Himalaya'* in 1929. One of Roerich's companions, a Tibetan lama, put a spiritual connotation on the event, because at the time of sighting it was a clear day, and they'd been watching a large black eagle flying overhead.

Roerich described the UFO as a huge oval object, with a shiny surface, and one side brilliant from the Sun. It moved quickly north to south. When overhead it changed direction from south to southwest, and quickly travelled out of sight.

(I have also wondered about the myths regarding ancient Atlanteans retreating to little known parts of the Himalayas, and some contactees, such as Adamski, going there to learn Tibetan 'secrets'.)

Belize – Central America

One of the earliest twentieth century cases involves a simple farmer called Raul, who lived in a village in Central American Belize. In 1919, when he was only nine years old, he encountered some strange visitors in the nearby forest.

At first they asked him about the care and traditional use of native trees and plants. Later, they would take him on board their hidden 'space ship', where he would teach other children, 'who were clearly not of Earth', more about agriculture. Sometimes he would stay for a couple of days, sleeping with the children in dormitory type accommodation.

It appears that much of the environment on the aliens' planet had been destroyed, and they lived underground in huge caverns. Apparently the visitors returned there from time to time with new plant life.

His contacts continued for the rest of his life. The visitors treated him with respect and curiosity, especially as he aged, as they had never seen wrinkles before! By the time he reached his nineties, Raul was training a young lad in his village to take his place.

After Raul's death, researchers discovered that he had left a box containing 'dozens of gold bars' for the youngster's education. His mother stated that the boy had also started disappearing without a trace, sometimes for days on end.

Albert Coe
In his book *'Alien Base'*, Timothy Good describes the experiences of Albert Coe in Canada. In 1920 the teenager was on a canoeing trip in the remote Ontario wilderness, when he had a chance meeting with a possible humanoid alien, a blond-haired young man, whom he rescued from a fall down a cliff. Coe helped the man back to his 'aircraft', which was 'parked' downstream. He was surprised when he saw it. It was a twenty-feet round silver disc on a tripod. He also found a torn bandana with blood on it, indicating a physiology similar to ours. Later meetings, extending over five decades, revealed the young man's race. They were 'Norcans', who had migrated to the Solar System following a natural disaster on their own planet, and later interbred with humans. Some details (which are extensive) are suspect, and involve living on Venus and Mars.

Part of the information Coe received was that 'Norcans' had infiltrated human society since 1904 to observe and evaluate our progress. (Coe claimed his 'friend' masqueraded as an engineering student – he had seen him later, in a suit and tie at a city restaurant.) Humanity was on the verge of discovering nuclear power, which could have disastrous consequences for our planet.

Unfortunately, Coe did not publicly disclose his encounters until 1977 – long after the atom was first split. Although healthy scepticism is required, we cannot dismiss Coe's claims out of hand. We know that the extensive use of nuclear energy carries the inherent danger of serious accidents, which could damage the Earth for tens of thousands of years.

Norman Massie

MUFON Colorado reported a US case from Wayne County, Illinois. In June 1923, maths teacher Norman Massie was only 10 years old. He had just let his parents' horses out into pasture, and was closing the gate, when he saw a metallic object, standing on three legs in the field. It had lights all around, and a domed top that looked like melted glass. Massie approached to within fifty feet and watched five men who were inside. It may have been difficult to estimate, but he said they were at least four feet tall, with blond hair.

"I got close enough that I could hear them talk...One guy sat in a chair and the others called him 'Commander'. Four others made trips back and forth in the ship. I didn't know what was going on until the end, when one of the men said that 'the repairs had been made'. In a minute, it came to a hovering position, and the tripod legs telescoped up into the belly. It went straight up about two hundred feet, and whizzed off to the west like a bullet."

Obviously Norman could hear the men speaking to each other in the English language. If these beings were from Earth then someone had an advanced technology of which we knew nothing!

John Cole

John Keel reported on an incident, near the small town of Gem, West Virginia, in May of 1924.

In those days, an aeroplane was a rare and exciting sight, and when a farmer thought he saw one crash in the forest it was big news. What puzzled him was its enormous size – 'as big as a battleship' – and the fact that it was noiseless and didn't appear to have any wings.

The sheriff organised a search party, which included the local 'newsman', John Cole. Within hours they found the wreckage in a small clearing. Cole was surprised that they were not the first on the scene.

The downed craft was indeed 'mighty big' – at least seventy-five feet long – and it filled the whole area. It looked like the fuselage of one of today's more modern planes, with windows, but no wings, tail or propellers.

There were already five or six men standing near the wreckage. They were all just over five feet tall, and slightly oriental in appearance - darker skin, with high cheekbones and slanted eyes. While some were dressed in shiny 'coveralls', the others were wearing black business suits and ties, unusual attire for the middle of the forest!

They were all talking in a strange foreign language, and looked startled when they saw the sheriff and his search party. The men in coveralls ran into the wreck, as if trying to hide, and some of Cole's colleagues raised their guns, thinking they must be spies.

One of the men in suits spoke English, and said everything was alright, and nobody was hurt. He would call into town later, and make a full report. There was nothing else the sheriff could do, as no crime had been committed and apparently nobody was injured.

Before their curious search party reluctantly withdrew, John Cole noticed something metal on the ground. He called it a 'thingamajig', and picked it up, covertly putting it in his pocket.

The sheriff and his team went back to town, and Cole, tired from his day hiking through the forest, went straight to bed. At about 3am, he woke to somebody pounding on his door. He opened it to be confronted by a man whose appearance was identical to the strangers at the wreck that day - a little taller, but the same dark skin and slanted eyes.

He was now wearing what looked like a US army uniform, and didn't mince his words; "You picked up something today! We need it back!"

Cole went inside, took his 'souvenir' out of his coat pocket, and went back to the front door; "Is this what you mean?"

The stranger just grabbed it out of his hand, and walked off, without saying a word. Cole looked out the door, and couldn't see a horse or car in sight. How had the stranger got there, let alone managing to track him down?

A couple of days later he went back to the clearing in the woods. It was empty, and the enormous wrecked craft and 'people' were gone. All that was left was the crushed grass and bushes.

The Crimean Peninsula

In 1920, during the Russian Civil War, the Red Army was also not exempt from unwanted 'visitors'. Ukrainian researcher, Dr. Anton Anfalov, has researched an unusual case involving a mobile Red Army group going, in a cart wagon, along a road in the rugged mountains of the Crimean Peninsula

They saw a lighted area at the side of the road, and a dome shaped object on the ground. Several people, at least six feet tall, were nearby. They were dressed in what looked like 'chainmail' suits, and assuming they were the enemy, the soldiers prepared to fire upon them with their 'Maksim' machine guns. A bright flash of light blinded them all, rendering them unconscious on the ground. When they recovered, the strange craft and unusual entities had all disappeared.

The Rankin Family

In the 1930s, a family of four watched as an unusual craft landed in their garden in Greensboro, North Carolina. Sisters, Katherine and Mary Rankin, along with their parents, were amazed as the forty feet wide object sat on the ground, outside their house, for several minutes.

It was a dark colour, shaped like a child's top – wide at the centre, and tapered towards its edges. Through a 'window' they could see that it appeared to be 'hollow' inside. The head and shoulders of an occupant were visible, and he seemed to be responsible for operating this strange machine. This 'pilot' was wearing a dark, tight fitting outfit, and had some kind of head-cover or helmet.

They watched through the window, and after a while, it lifted straight up into the sky, and as it moved quietly and smoothly away, it seemed to have the ability to both hover, and move horizontally and perpendicularly.

At the time, thinking no-one would believe them, they said nothing. It took several decades before the sisters, by then both retired from school teaching and nursing, to confirm the event.

Often people in responsible positions, mindful of their reputation, wait until after retirement before divulging their experience. Researcher Robert Bartholomew unearthed the following report.

A retired Canadian church minister, who still preferred that researchers did not reveal his identity, told of a life changing event in 1932. He often experienced visions when he had to make important decisions, but this time it was a lot more than a vision.

He lived 150 miles north of Toronto, and one night as he was walking down the main street, everything suddenly it lit up, 'brighter than the sun at noon'. He could see white lights surrounding a 'round cloud' with 'etched' or 'scalloped' outer edges. A light streamed down like a laser beam, and the young minister turned around to see someone standing beside him. It was a young man with radiant blue eyes, golden hair, and a similar colour suit.

'He smiled and told me my real work would be training...in that city. He said to remember the cottages in the rear of the Mansions are as important as those who dwell in the mansions...'

The minister mentioned seeing the 'laser beam' on later occasions, and obviously had further experiences he did not wish to discuss.

Leo Dworshak
Leo waited until he was 83 before divulging his contact with the Visitors, in his 2003 book '*UFOs Are With Us – Take My Word*'. In 1932, Leo, then a twelve-year-old farm-boy in Killdeer, North Dakota, USA, saw a large spaceship land in a nearby valley on several occasions. The seamless craft, at least as big as their barn, was a light blue colour, which allowed it to blend-in with the sky. It had flashing coloured lights on the outer shell, and rotated in a complicated way, with the inner and outer bands going in opposite directions.

At first, he encountered what seemed like an invisible force which stopped him moving too close to the spaceship. After several trips to the landing spot, he and his seven-year-old brother got to know several men from the craft, which they were eventually allowed to enter. Inside it had living quarters, and what appeared to be a movie screen showing pictures "of a place or process we could not fathom."

The men were five to six feet tall, similar in appearance, with short light brown hair, light beige complexions, and blue eyes with dark pupils. They spoke fluent English and German and told him that they were from another galaxy. Their people had been visiting Earth for thousands of years, and at that time twelve of their group were living on the planet to monitor human activity – it was part of their 'responsibility'.

Leo observed: "They were so ordinary looking in one way – but so exotic in another. If you dressed them in ordinary clothing, you would pass one of them in a strange town without blinking an eye."

Leo had spasmodic contact with them. As the years went by Leo aged, but his 'friends' did not! (This is an interesting anomaly. Recent genetic research indicates that degeneration of our genes contributes to the aging process. Some Visitors indicate they undergo a 'regeneration' process from time to time, which may explain their increased longevity and youthful appearance.)

Leo entered the Navy in 1941, and his brother Mike was killed in Korea. In 1962, with his three daughters and two friends present, they all saw the ship land. He had wanted to take his companions over to meet the occupants, but they were so scared they just watched, at a distance, for about thirty minutes.

On 21st October 1963 Leo again visited his friends on the landed craft. Two of them welcomed him and explained their activities had become more difficult. For the previous three years humans had been trying to detect and capture one of their ships.

"Your science and technology have advanced enough to pose a threat to our ships, as well as to the entire planet," they said, and went on to explain that even if provoked, they would only respond in self-defence if our military threatened their lives by trying to damage their ships.

Leo observed; "These great men willingly took the time to speak to two grubby little farm kids in North Dakota, and changed our lives forever."

Howard Menger

This has always been a controversial case, and most details can be found in Menger's 1959 book *'From Outer Space to You'*.

Menger was born in 1922, and like many of the contactees in the early days, was only a youngster, just ten years old in 1932, when he claims to have experienced his first contact. He was living in Highbridge New Jersey, and he and his brother sometimes saw bright shiny objects in the sky. On one occasion, a disc shaped object, about ten feet in diameter, landed in a field where they were playing. There seemed to be a larger object hovering in the sky above. As the two boys cautiously approached the larger craft disappeared and the smaller disc took off from the ground at incredible speed.

One day, while alone in the countryside, he met a beautiful lady, sitting on a rock by the brook in a nearby forest. She spoke to him about having come a long way to tell him he had a mission in life. There was no craft involved in this incident, but it had a profound life-time effect on the young Howard. Many times he returned to the spot, hoping to meet her again. It must be remembered he was a young pre-teen boy at the time, and about to experience puberty and the feelings and emotions that accompany it. Perhaps she had become an obsession, and this can explain the profound effect the encounter had on his thinking and later life.

In 1942, during World War II, he joined the army. By the time he was posted to Camp Cook in California, he had a wife and new-born son in Abilene, Texas. While Howard was at the camp, a man in khaki army clothing approached him, and identified himself as being one of the space people the beautiful woman had told him about over ten years before.

Soon after, he was posted to Hawaii, and transferred to Battalion Headquarters, where he had access to a jeep. One evening he got a strong impulse to drive out to a series of caverns, a few miles away. There he met another beautiful 'space lady' who passed on more messages to him and his proposed role in later life.

In April 1945 his unit was sent to Okinawa, where he had a couple of lucky escapes until he was hospitalised with shrapnel in his eyes, which sent him blind. A woman, with a soft spoken voice, visited him during the first week. She did not identify herself, and indicated he was the only person she was visiting.

She assured him his sight would be restored, and gradually it did come back. When he got to see his visitor, whom he suspected of being one of the space people, she was an attractive woman in an army nurse's uniform. Just before his release from hospital, she made the mysterious comment that he would soon meet someone very interesting. He never saw her again.

Later, after returning to camp, Howard went back out to the caves, where he met and spoke with another man. Although he was unarmed, and dressed in army uniform, he confirmed that he was not from this Earth, and his people would continue their contact with him in the future.

In 1946 and 1947 he met the visitors again, this time when they landed their craft in designated remote fields. In 1953 and 1956 there were further contacts. His space friends explained how they were working with many people in this part of the world, and enlisted his help to buy them clothes, get suitable haircuts, and advise them on local customs so they could more easily blend into the community.

During one meeting, he went on board their stationary craft, and he asked if the voice coming over their radio was from another planet. He was advised that it was from different parts of Earth, where they were in constant contact with various contactees.

Later in 1956, he was taken for a short trip on one of their ships. Due to their telepathic abilities, the visitors knew it was something he had been wanting for some time. They then asked Menger to invite certain witnesses to accompany him to the landing field. It seemed they eventually decided he could be trusted to help them spread their message, which was essentially the same as other contactees. 'A great change would inevitably take place on Earth as a result of the wasteful wars, torture, and destruction brought about by the 'misunderstanding of the people'.

It was about this time his 'friends' suggested he meet with George van Tassel, and Howard Menger started giving lectures as well as interviews on 'talk-back' radio programs. In 1958 he sponsored the 'First Annual East Coast Interplanetary Spacecraft Convention' in New Jersey. Over one thousand people attended, to hear him talk about the 'benevolent Space Brothers'. Other speakers sometimes deviated more into the occult.

He also developed a sudden musical ability, as if the notes were being 'channelled' to him. (Something in common with M. X, Desmond Leslie and other contactees.) He even released a record *'Authentic music From Another Planet'*, which was reasonably successful.

There were some aspects of Howard Menger's reports which caused doubts in researchers' minds. One was his decision to divorce his first wife, and marry Connie (Marla), a woman who reminded him of the "girl on the rock' whom he had become obsessed with when he was ten years old.

Another was his assertion that he had been taken on trips to the Moon. The first time he merely saw pictures on a screen, similar to the claims of George Adamski. The second trip involved actually alighting at a Lunar Base. Unlike Adamski's claim of vegetation, Menger described a terrain similar to the one we know, and claimed the 'space people' had bases under camouflaged 'domes'. (A possibility that, even now, we cannot easily dismiss.)

Suddenly, in the early 1960s, he retired from the UFO field, and tried to recant all his previous claims. Nobody knew why there was such an abrupt turn-around. Although he may have invented or magnified some events, there were a few witnesses willing to come forward and corroborate others. Some investigators felt he was intimidated, but he would not offer an explanation.

Whilst he had supposedly retired from public scrutiny, Menger spent a lot of time experimenting with electronic devices designed for harnessing free energy to build flying saucers. Jim Moseley recalled that when Menger attended a UFO convention in the 1970s he 'blew out all the fuses in the hotel with one of his contraptions.'

He once suggested he may write another book which would 'settle lingering doubts and create more of a public sensation than anything revealed in the past.' He never did write that book, and died in 2009 aged eighty-seven.

Humanoid 'neighbours'
My friend and colleague Margaret Fry, a long-time Welsh ufologist, has documented early extraterrestrial incidents in the United Kingdom. They record the activity of 'humanoids', during the 1930s and early 1940s. It then begs the question; were the authorities aware of, or complicit in these interactions?

In 1934, in a rural farming area of South Wales, young Ruth went to play with her friend who lived nearby. She saw 'soldiers', dressed in tight green-grey suits and armed with 'ray guns', pushing the children with their 'rounded-up' family ahead. When Ruth tried to intervene she was pushed along with the others to a 'big silver caravan' behind the trees. She kept tugging on one soldier's leg, saying: "Leave my friends alone!"

Ruth remembers being taken into a room with lots of people, and when her friend's family said she was not one of them, the soldiers put her back outside. She went back home and told her parents, who naturally didn't believe her. Later that evening they went over to the neighbours' two houses and found them empty – both families had disappeared.

By 1943, nine years later, Ruth had moved to an even more rural area. She used to talk to gypsy children who lived in caravans on the Common, and would take them food. One day she realised all the gypsies had gone, however she saw a much larger silver 'caravan', which was like a long silver disc. It was similar to a helmet with rows of windows and very bright lights. At first, she thought the owners must be very rich, and walked across the field to get a closer look.

As Ruth approached, a man and woman came towards her. They were wearing the same green-grey boiler suits and carrying ray guns as she had seen in 1934. Ruth was afraid, remembering what had happened to her neighbours before, but they took her into the caravan and shut the door behind her.

Ruth was taken to see a taller, good-looking 'man'. She could distinctly remember a very ornate ring he was wearing. She called him 'Khan.' He told her they were from another place or galaxy. He reminded her of the incident when she was a small child: "You were with your friend and her family who were 'ours'; we programmed you then for the first time."

They told Ruth they wouldn't harm her, but she wept as she recounted the procedures they performed. As with many other female abductees, contact did not stop there, and continued in later life.

When Ruth was twenty-one she went parking with her boyfriend in a field near the ocean. It was a clear night. Suddenly a mist began creeping up around the vehicle. They saw some bright lights, but thought these were from ships at sea. Ruth vaguely remembers being lifted from the car, and her boyfriend followed a little later. They 'lost' two hours and afterwards edged their way around the mist to find the road was clear. Ruth's boyfriend was not happy to find the duco on his brand-new car ruined, with many circular rings on the rear. They drifted apart soon afterwards ...

Some recollections of this encounter are vague, but Ruth recalled other parts very clearly. There had been some form of examination, before she was taken to see the Khan. She remembers him talking about anti-gravity, and telling her an 'anti-matter' world existed near his solar-system. One also existed alongside ours, and to interfere with it could destroy the whole universe.

She had since married, and although she recalled a subsequent incident, she could not remember the details, and her husband refused to discuss it.

In *'UFOs Now and Then'*, I discuss the contact history of Leonard and his family. Leonard's father, who was born in 1930, had an English mother, (born in Chile), and an American Indian father, who was part of the Hopi Nation. In

1939, when Leonard's father was just a child, he had always been a sickly youngster, and rather a burden to the tribe.

It is not known if the tribe had abandoned him, but one day he was alone, and he started walking until he came to an old oak tree. He sat under it for ages until two tall beautiful people came up. The man and woman were both blond, and at first he thought they were Germans.

He felt a hand on his shoulder, and they said; "Come with us, we will heal you."

His father didn't feel scared, and followed them to a 'spaceship', which looked like a traditional 'saucer' on three legs. He followed them up a ramp, and once inside, it took off at a fast speed. He could see through the walls and the Earth was disappearing behind them.

He was reasonably sure that Mars was their destination. The craft orbited then went down into a tunnel below the surface. When he alighted, he was greeted by normal people, wearing three different types of military uniforms. They all spoke English, and he assumed some were from the US and Britain, and was unsure about the third. There were also other different alien races present.

His father couldn't see this base from above, but once inside he could see the sky through the roof. It was similar to a one-way mirror. The rooms were like compartments, and the floor glass. He was healed of his disease, and remembered having blood on his ears and nose. When they brought him back to Earth and his family, the visitors told him they would come back for him much later in life.

Once an adult, he migrated to Australia, and got married. The visitors kept their word, and he and his family experienced more friendly contacts and interaction. He recently passed away in Sydney, and had lived well into his late eighties, without a recurrence of his childhood illness.

Udo Wartena
Australian investigator, Warren Aston, conducted excellent in-depth research into the case of Udo Wartena, who in 1940 was a thirty-seven year old of Dutch origin. At the time he had a mining claim, near Canyon Ferry Lake, in the forest at the base of Boulder Mountain, in Montana USA.

One mid-morning, in May, he encountered a disc-shaped craft, hovering above a nearby meadow. It was a dull, stainless steel colour, thirty-five feet high with a diameter of one hundred feet, and several portholes. It continued to hover, just above the ground, and a man descended from a 'stairway', which had extended downward from part of the hull.

He was nice-looking, young and strong with white hair and clear, almost translucent skin. He wore a grey coverall, with a matching cap on his head. He walked towards Udo, who also moved forward to meet him. The man was not a mirage or in any way ethereal, as he shook Udo's hand firmly, and spoke in slow English.

At first the stranger apologised to Udo, saying that they had not known anyone was in the area, as it was not their custom to 'interrupt' or allow themselves to be seen. After explaining he had stopped his craft to take on water, Udo was allowed on-board where there was another plainly-dressed, slightly older man, who also had white hair and the same translucent skin. They told him that they were both several hundred years old! Udo's impression of these visitors was that they were men – "just like us and very nice chaps."

They explained their ship had its own gravitational field, was powered by electromagnetic forces, and could travel faster than the speed of light. They discussed their technology in great detail, but refused to comment on any religious aspects of either their or our civilisations.

Like other such incidents, the visitors said they came from a far and distant planet which had been monitoring our civilisation for some time; including living with us incognito. One of them told Udo; "As you have noticed, we look pretty much as you do, so we mingle with your people, gather information, and leave instructions or give help where needed." They also qualified this with the comment that they cannot interfere in any way.

Before they left, Udo was invited to go with them. He was tempted, and sometimes he wondered why he declined. He later recalled that two years earlier a young man had gone missing, without trace, in that area. Perhaps he had met with the same Visitors and accepted their offer.

Udo said that as he was leaving the ship, the men suggested that he - "tell no-one, as nobody would believe me at that time, but in years to come I could tell about this experience." He said after he left, and had walked a couple of hundred feet away, the ship rose straight up. It cleared the trees, circled slightly, then went straight up, and was soon out of sight. All that remained was an area of crushed grass, where the 'stairway' had rested.

Udo never spoke of the incident for over thirty years, not even confiding in his wife. It was only shortly before his death, in 1989, that he first told his two closest friends.

In 1985, the *'Flying Saucer Review'* published an interesting case which was investigated by Dora Bauer-Lammer.

On June 3rd 1942, a twenty-eight year old American housewife, whom she called 'Mrs T', was travelling from Minnesota to Michigan. There were five adults and one child in the car, and since they had started off at 8.30pm, by the time they reached Wisconsin, at about 2am, they decided to pull over. They needed a rest, and wanted the driver to get a little sleep.

Suddenly 'Mrs T' noticed a strange light beaming down over the car. It was coming from a 'lilac' coloured, fifteen to twenty feet diameter, disc shaped object, hovering silently, about one hundred feet overhead.

Suddenly the car started moving, with the craft above keeping pace. The car's headlights were not on, and 'Mrs T' tried to speak to the driver. She got no response, and his head and arms were resting on the driving wheel. He and everybody else seemed to be asleep.

The car travelled along the main highway, and then veered off into a more deserted area away from the city. It went down a rough narrow road, and entered a wooden gateway, into a cow pasture, coming to a halt in front of a windmill and old water trough. 'Mrs T' could still not wake the driver, and thinks she must have laid back and also gone to sleep for a couple of hours.

When dawn was breaking, at about 4.30am, everybody woke up, and didn't know where they were and how they had got there!

I will recount the next incident in 'Mrs T's' own words; *'It was about midnight on August 27th 1942, about three months later. I suddenly found myself on the road going northwards from our farmhouse. I heard the dogs barking, and was impressed to go on....I came to the side of a creek, about a quarter of a mile from my home, and noticed a light, as bright as day, shining down from the treetops. Slowly I kept walking on, as if guided by some unseen hand.'*

She looked up and saw a strange man, who looked to be in his mid-thirties, approaching from the other side of the narrow creek. He had a round face, wavy, sandy coloured hair, and greyish–blue eyes. He reached across the water, took her by the hand, and greeted her by name. 'Mrs T' recalls saying; "I have been looking forward to meeting you for a long time."

He replied, in a soft, low voice, and asked if she remembered seeing him before, and 'Mrs T' said not to her knowledge. He looked at her from head to toe, and she suddenly realised, to her embarrassment, that she was barefoot and clutching tightly onto her blue nightgown.

As he took out a small pad and pencil, and started writing something, she could hear other voices coming from the area where the bright light was shining. About fifty feet away she saw a dome-shaped craft underneath the light. A young girl, with long blonde hair, was sitting on a large rock near the water.

The man looked at 'Mrs T' and said; "You may leave now, but tell no-one of your visit here with us tonight."

She got back home at about 2am, and feeling rather dazed, sat on the edge of the bed. Her husband, whom she thought was asleep, rolled over and asked her where she had been for the last two hours? She looked down at her feet. They were covered with dust and sand. She knew it hadn't been a dream.

The next day her neighbour remarked that the dogs' barking had woke her up at about 2am. When she looked out the window, she saw someone walking down the street. 'Mrs T' still needed convincing this really happened. She took her daughter, and drove out to the spot she recalled being at the previous night.

In the dirt were the prints of her bare feet, along with the prints of a man's heavy soled boots. The big rock was there, but no sign of the girl, only a well-trodden area of brown dried grass.

Twenty-three years later, on July 24th 1965, there was another unexpected incident. It was about 2am, and 'Mrs T' and her family were all awakened by the sound of beautiful music, which appeared to be coming from outside their house. It continued for a long time, and they just lay there, listening.

When 'Mrs T' eventually looked out of the bathroom window, she could hear low voices and laughter. Suddenly there was a flash of light, and a humming noise 'like a swarm of bees taking off'.

"It was like the minute I got up, and was about, it all came to an end."

Early next morning, they all walked behind the house to see what, if anything, had been there the previous night. There, on the ground, was a twelve feet diameter burnt brown area, as if something had been hovering above. All around it the grass was trampled, as if by heavy footsteps. For a few days her eyes seemed to have been affected by the bright flash of light – something which had not happened after seeing the bright light of the landed craft all those years ago.

There were a couple more incidents in the following years. One, which was of concern, happened on October 31st 1969. 'Mrs T's' children were returning from a Halloween party at a neighbouring school. They saw a huge object overhead, which followed them as far as the railway tracks. It disappeared, but when they arrived home, there was a bright light over the house. It remained overhead for a short while, then disappeared into space.

Researchers know that there is more to these encounters, but 'Mrs T' was adamant that up until this report, she had kept her promise to the mysterious being not to reveal her experience to anyone else. Even though so much time had passed, she would still recognise him instantly if they ever met again.

CHAPTER TWO

THE EARLY CONTACTS – Part Two

America was not the only place where the Space Brothers were quietly meeting with the people of Earth.

Gosta Carisson

In 1946, twenty-seven year old Gosta Carisson was employed as a gamekeeper in southern Sweden. One night he saw a bright light coming from a wooded area, and thinking local teenagers may have started a fire, he went to investigate.

He found a fifty feet landed disc, with eleven human-like occupants. They were all good looking, with dark brown hair and 'beautiful teeth and eyes'. Each wore a strange tight fitting 'skin-suit'. They told him that they were from Sirius B, and hadn't been to our planet before.

Apparently their craft had collided with their mother-ship, damaging one of the twelve quartz rods which powered their craft. Two of the crew had been killed in the accident, and they had landed on Earth to dispose of their bodies and replace the damaged rod.

Over the years he had regular contact with these visitors, and although most communication was telepathic, they taught him the medicinal value of certain plants and pollen. With their help he invented a machine to extract the pollens.

He agreed not to divulge the alien source of his discovery until after the year 2000. After this he became very successful, and retired a millionaire after selling his business to a large pharmaceutical company.

Elizabeth Klarer

Although their motives are debatable, the Visitors are essentially similar to us, both in physical form, emotions and psychology. Their paranormal powers seem to relate to humans on a fundamental level. If they have 'had their wicked way' with female abductees, I'm not sure if this is manipulation for scientific purposes, their own sexual needs, or perhaps genuine emotional attachment. I am aware of cases where 'love' seems to be an important factor.

The South African case involving Elizabeth Klarer remains controversial. Born in 1910, Elizabeth claims her first contact with a flying saucer occurred when she was seven. She was sent to Oxford, England for her education, but returned to South Africa and worked for the Air Force intelligence there during World War II.

This case was investigated by researcher Cynthia Hind, who knew Klarer personally. In 1957 Elizabeth was staying with relatives on a farm in the Drakensberg Mountains near Durban. She was out riding in the hills and saw a strange craft overhead. Before it shot off, out of sight into the clouds, she noticed there was a man standing inside, watching her.

Sometime later, she felt compelled to go back to the area, and found the same man waiting for her beside the landed craft. He was tall, and extremely handsome with slightly slanting grey eyes. Elizabeth claimed his name was 'Akon', and although he was from another planetary system, they fell in love. Their relationship eventuated in her becoming pregnant, and going to his planet where her son 'Ayling' was born. Klarer was unable to adjust to the atmosphere there, and returned to Earth, leaving Ayling to be raised by Akon.

Elizabeth wrote two books *'Beyond the Light Barrier'* and *'The Gravity Files'*, and addressed many prestigious gatherings in several countries, including America, Russia, Europe and the House of Lords in Britain.

She spoke of Akon's craft more as a living entity, calling it 'she', and said it was constructed from natural cosmic energy. Elizabeth also mentioned a huge 'mother ship' about five miles in length that hovered some distance from the Earth. She described the occupants as "human, slightly taller, better looking, more considerate and gentle, and living far, far longer than us on planet Earth. They are more advanced, technically and spiritually."

One interesting comment, that Elizabeth made during an interview, was that Akon's people consisted of a civilisation over seven planets. This corresponds with the information given to Mr. X (see Annex B), when the visitors told of their society encompassing seven planets.

Cynthia claimed that, despite publishing her love story, Elizabeth was not an attention seeker, and presented as an attractive, intelligent and softly spoken lady. She was, however, paranoid that the Russians were spying on her, possibly to seize Akon when he visited. Elizabeth also claimed ongoing contact with the

South African Air Force (SAAF), a fact which had some limited verification from a witness, who said that when Elizabeth was too elderly to go on horseback, the SAAF used to fly her to Flying Saucer Hill where she would meet Akon.

Elizabeth died in 1994, and although her story was treated with a great deal of scepticism, an interesting event in 1992 caused some to re-evaluate her story: Connor, the owner of a lodge below the mountains, told of how one day a tall, blond, handsome man came in looking for Elizabeth Klarer., whom he was supposed to meet there. He seemed a little strange, with "good features and high cheekbones" and spoke perfect English.

The landlord had never heard of her, and after the stranger walked out to the car-park, his wife urged him to follow, to see if they could do anything else to help. When he looked out the man had literally "vanished" which was not possible. A week later, when Elizabeth arrived and booked into the hotel, they told her of the man looking for her. She showed them a photo of a sculpted bust of Akon in her book. Connor and his wife immediately recognised him.

George Van Tassel

George van Tassel was a very colourful ufologist during the 1950s. He was born in Jefferson, Ohio, in 1910, to a middle class family. He entered the field of aviation in 1927, at the Cleveland airport, where he gained his pilot's license. He spent three years gaining experience in the early aircraft industry, and went on to hold a variety of responsible positions with Douglas Aircraft Company in California. In 1941 he became the personal flight inspector for Howard Hughes in the flight tests of experimental aircraft. From 1943 to 1947 he was the flight test safety inspector for Lockheed's 'Constellation' aircraft.

In 1947 he bought some land in the Southern Californian desert, and leased, from the US government, an adjacent abandoned airstrip, known as Giant Rock Airport. George van Tassel and his family moved in, and planned to turn it into a 'dude ranch' and stopover for weekend aviators. He had known the previous owner, Frank Critzer, in the early 1940s. Critzer, a rather eccentric miner, had hollowed out a simple abode, of several rooms, under the Rock. Van Tassel and his uncle were well acquainted with Frank, who told them that when he started to dig under the Rock, he had stumbled upon some unusual glass-lined tunnels, which went down deep underground. In 1942, Frank was killed there when his stash of dynamite exploded during a confrontation with local sheriff deputies.

Whilst the underground home was no more than a hovel, it supposedly had some paranormal aspects. The local Indians claimed that the 'Great Stone' was part of their 'holy ground', and through the ages they had contact with extraterrestrials on a regular basis. The Indian tribes from all around would gather there every year, and only the chiefs were allowed to go close to the Rock. Native American society had a history of visitors from space, and some spoke of energy vortexes, where they could commune with their ancestors from the stars. Soon, Van Tassel also began experiencing 'strange psychic messages from extraterrestrial spaceships.'

On August 24th 1953, there was a full moon, and like many people in the desert, Van Tassel slept under the stars. At about two in the morning, he woke to see an ordinary looking man standing about six feet away from the bottom of his bed. Van Tassel sat up, and asked the stranger who he was and what he wanted.

He replied, in very precise English; "My name is Sol-Gonda, and I would be pleased to show you our craft."

Van Tassel could see a hovering craft, about one hundred yards away. It was about eight feet off the ground, and a four feet diameter spot of sand underneath appeared to have turned a golden colour. He stepped into the circle, and was immediately raised up into an opening in the bottom of the disc. Sol-Gonda followed close behind him.

They stepped onto a deck, which was about eighteen feet in diameter and ten feet high, and comprised what appeared to be the 'cab' of the vessel. There were three other 'crewmen' present. They were all wearing similar suits of tight fitting tops and pants made from some form of knitted material. He was later told that their uniforms adapted to all temperatures, keeping them hot or cool dependent upon atmospheric conditions.

From then onwards, all communications were telepathic. Every time Van Tassel thought of a question, he would immediately receive a reply. He was told he was on a 'scout' ship, which was only used for observational work. Sol-Gonda introduced him to the other three men, and showed him their various instrument panels etc.

After a tour of the craft, they left the ship, and Sol-Gonda walked Van Tassel back to his bed outside the Giant Rock. He and his 'scout ship' quickly disappeared as they shot off into the sky.

Van's new space friend had asked him if he would like to do something to help mankind, to which he replied he would do everything possible to help his fellow humans. He was then told about their larger cigar-shaped vehicles, which were thirty six miles long and one mile wide, completely self contained, and used on their longer journeys in space. The members of the craft could 'walk through' a device which re-energised and rejuvenated them, making it possible to live much longer lives. Sol-Gonda gave him the plans and specifications for the equipment, and the building required to house it.

Van Tassel first built a small model of what he called 'The Integratron', and preliminary tests with mice proved successful. He then started constructing a full size building, situated on a ten acre plot about three miles from Giant Rock - the exact spot specified by his space friends. The structure itself was a non-metallic dome, thirty-eight feet high and fifty-eight feet in diameter.

Of course, this was all going to cost money which he didn't have. In 1953 he founded a science and philosophy organisation, which also incorporated electromagnetic research. He generated further support by holding an annual 'Giant Rock Interplanetary Spacecraft Convention', the first of which occurred in 1954. He also held meditation groups of up to fifty people in the 'cavern' under the Rock, however he tended to drift into more paranormal aspects as time went by.

Construction of the 'Intergratron' commenced in 1957, and despite twenty-five years of work by Van Tassel and his friends, was never fully completed. The site was sold shortly before his death, from heart failure, in 1978.

Most researchers concentrate on his 'Integratron', however, I think his greatest contribution was to enable the message of the Space Brothers to be conveyed at his Giant Rock Conventions, which continued for many years. It provided a platform for individual contactees, such as George Adamski, Daniel Fry, George Hunt Williamson, Howard Menger and many others who were able to share their information with a much larger audience. Was this the Space Brothers' devious plan all along? We will never know!

Van Tassel himself wrote several books, and gave numerous lectures revealing the Space Brothers' message. He was also featured on hundreds of radio and television programs.

Some Italian Cases

The 1962 *'Flying Saucer Review'* published an article from the Italian Magazine *'Domenica della Sera'*, (translated by Gordon Creighton), where Italian engineer, Luciano Galli, said that one July, in the late 1950s, he met extraterrestrials who took him for a ride in their craft. In keeping with most of the witnesses at the time, Galli had conscious memory of the event. The use of hypnosis didn't occur until decades later.

Galli was a modest man, and head of a small workshop. He was walking back to work from lunch, and when he reached the blind alley where his business was located, a dark coloured car pulled up in front of him. A tall, dark man, with a friendly face, normal features, a moustache and very dark eyes, got out and offered him a lift. He had seen this man, who wore a business suit and spoke perfect Italian, several times around the town, and once, when he tried to speak to him he suddenly disappeared. Galli described him as having 'a face like an angel in plain clothes'.

There was another man in the car, who never spoke, and after Galli got in, they travelled fifty-seven-kilometres from Bolgna to the Croara Ridge, where there was a shining grey flying saucer hovering about six feet off the ground. They all entered the ship via a metal cylinder which 'came out'. Once aboard he could see what he described as a pilot's cabin with instruments and panels all around.

They seemed to be flying through space until they arrived at what Galli described as a giant dirigible, at least six hundred metres in length. (I assume this was a 'mother ship'.) At one end were six openings – each opening divided into six smaller 'cubicles' – out of which small flying discs were seen coming and going. Once inside the large craft, Galli could see about four to five hundred men and women, all very friendly and good-looking, walking around or standing in the hangers. They all wore overalls of some silky or shining plastic material.

"This is one of our spaceships", his companion said, and proceeded to give him a brief tour of some of their amenities. Afterwards his companion took him back to their original 'transport' disc, and they returned to the same spot on Croara Ridge. The entire trip had taken just over three hours.

Some researchers tried to discredit this report, as he claimed the visitors told him that they came from Venus. Considering many other contactees were, for some reason, told this falsehood, it appears that the Space Brothers were deliberately misleading us.

New Zealand *Xenolog',* Number 107, details a 1952 report from near Mt. Etna, in Sicily, Italy. The witness, Eugenio Siragusa, was waiting for a bus, early one morning in Martyr's Square, Catania, when a white, mercury-coloured, luminous object appeared in the sky. As it zig-zagged and rapidly descended towards him, he could see it resembled a spinning-top.

When it hovered overhead, a brilliant ray left the object, and "completely pierced me!" At that moment, his fears turned to 'indescribable serenity'. The ray shrank back into the craft, which then moved left and right in an arc across the sky before disappearing. For the next ten years, his personality changed and he developed extrasensory perceptions, and telepathy;

'When I pulled myself together, I rapidly discovered, more and more, that something extraordinary had happened to me...Ever since then an inner voice began to instruct me on geology and cosmology. It opened my mind to the mysteries of Creation and of my former lives. This re-dimension of my existence was possible thanks to continued ESP, contacts which were established between certain extraterrestrials and myself. This extra-sensory perception was continually developing within me. It lasted eleven long years before I could actually physically meet my extraterrestrial instructors.'

One night in 1962 he felt compelled to go back to nearby Mount Etna. As he was driving up towards Mount Manfre, it felt as if his car was being guided up the mountain by some superior force. He stopped his car at the side of the road, and as he walked along the path he saw two silhouettes on top of the isolated hill. They were two tall, well-built men, with long blonde hair and 'soft' features. They wore silver space-suits, with gold armlets around their wrists and ankles, a luminous belt and a strange metallic chest-plate.

At first, he was terrified, but one directed a green beam at him, from an object he had in his hand. Immediately he felt a sense of calm, and the men spoke to him in Italian, saying: "We have been waiting for you. Record in your memory what we are going to tell you."

He was given a message to pass on to our leaders, similar to what other contactees of the day had been told: We must stop our warlike tendencies, especially nuclear weapons, and practice justice, freedom, love and fraternity to all. They mentioned being part of an 'Intergalactic Confederation', and said the 'Cosmic Counsel' condemns the people of Earth for their inhuman behaviour. Eugene heeded the message and dedicated the rest of his life to furthering their aims.

He had several other meetings with his mentors, who reiterated their messages, alluding to us ignoring previous missionaries being sent from highly evolved humanoids several light years away.

Siragusa's mission was to quietly spread their message by recruiting other contactees. They avoided the publicity of lectures or public meetings, and carried out their mission quietly and effectively.

There is a curious and unusual twist to the ending of this case. On July 4th 1978, Eugenio Siragusa died. At 10.30pm that same night, Italian Naval Officer Maurizio Esposito, along with two Italian Air Force sergeants, Attilio Salvatore and Franco Padellero, were walking near Mt. Etna.

They noticed three red lights in the sky, and when one broke off from the rest, they jumped into Salvatore's car, and headed to the spot where the object had seemed to land.

They found a saucer, resting on the slope below the road. Standing next to it were five very tall, human type beings, with blond hair and 'beautiful' features. They were wearing what appeared to be black, tight fitting 'flight suits'. They climbed up the slope until they were only about ten to fifteen feet away from the witnesses, then smiled and nodded before making their way back down to the disc.

Esposito and his companions could not move, as if immobilised by some unknown force. They felt so disorientated that they didn't wait for the craft to leave, and sped off back down the road. Were Siragusa's space friends bidding a final farewell?

Armando Zubaran Remirez

Rafael Palmeros wrote about an interesting case in *'Samizdat'*: One night, in January 1954, Armando was driving from Mexico City to Acapulco, where he hoped to arrive by sunrise. During the trip he suddenly felt very lethargic, and pulled over to the side of the road.

A bit further ahead he could see a strange, brilliantly lit, saucer type object, with several men gathered around it. They had long, fair hair and were wearing overalls with wide belts. Before he realised what was happening, he found himself escorted by the men and walking towards the craft.

As they took him inside he could hear a buzzing sound in his ears, and he turned and asked why were they taking him on board? The man, who appeared to be the leader, said; "You are neither the first nor the last earthman to be chosen for testing. Our task, slow that it may seem, is designed to persuade. We choose the likeliest, most malleable persons for contact, so that they might better transmit our message."

Armando was given a tour of the ship, and he was surprised to see, on one wall, a screen that showed every detail of his own life. He was full of questions, most of which his hosts answered. They did not reveal where they had come from, but said that they travelled through space using a gravity repulsion system.

After a while, Armando suddenly realised the craft was no longer on the ground, and they were travelling in space. When they reached an altitude of 40,000 kilometres, the captain took Armando to a porthole, and pointed out the Earth below. He asked if they were going to their 'home-world', but was told this was not feasible, but perhaps it would be possible in the future.

As they orbited our planet, the crew and Armando had breakfast, and he noticed, despite being given a normal meal, the others only seemed to drink a type of fruit juice. The Captain then told him about life and society on their home planet.

He said their average lifespan was two hundred and fifty years, and spoke about their philosophy, religion and history. There was equality between their occupations, and children and the elderly were given special consideration. Commerce was a matter of collaboration, rather than competition, and their leader was 'The Master', or 'Beloved Number Nine', who had been in control for three thousand of our earth years.

They then returned Armando to his car beside the road. He was confused, but excited, as he completed his trip to Acapulco, which only took him ninety minutes instead of the usual six hours.

Fifteen years later, in January 1969, just outside Mexico City, he stopped to pick up a young hitchhiker. After he got in the car, Armando realised he was one of the space people from fifteen years ago.

Armando later reflected upon his experience; *'God willing, the teachings of Christ, like those of Beloved Number Nine, will be chosen by humanity as a guide to keep it from stumbling upon the obstacles of the darkness in which we dwell. I hope that man's desire for conquest is fulfilled, not in subduing, but expanding our knowledge of other worlds, with the aid of our space neighbours, and that our pioneers may travel beside them in their ships to worlds of joy and happiness.'*

Further south, throughout the continent of South America, residents from many countries were reporting strange flying objects, and often stranger occupants.

John Keel discussed a case from 1957, which Gordon Creighton had translated and reported in the *'Flying Saucer Review'*. In late August, an Argentinean Air Force plane spiralled out of control and crashed near Quilino. It fell in a remote spot, and it was going to take some time to bring in the salvage equipment. In the interim, the Air Force dispatched three men to guard the wreck.

On the evening of the 20th August, two of the guards had gone into a nearby town for supplies, and the third was relaxing in their tent. Suddenly, an eerie, high pitched hum permeated the air, and he stepped outside to investigate.

Hovering directly overhead was a huge, luminous metal disc. He was terrified, and reached for his pistol, but seemed to be transfixed and unable to draw it from the holster.

'The young man heard a soft voice coming from the humming object. It addressed him gently in his own language, and told him not to be afraid. Then it went on to tell him that it was an interplanetary spacecraft and that a base for such craft had been installed in the nearby province of Salta, (an area where UFO sightings had been constantly reported).

'We intend to help you, for the misuse of atomic energy threatens to destroy you.'

Before the craft shot up into the sky and disappeared, the voice went on to say that soon the rest of the world would know about them. It is not known if the UFO was in anyway involved with the original plane crash, but the young Argentinean guard's report was taken seriously. Within two days, his commanding officer released a report to one of Argentina's largest and most respected newspapers *'Diario de Cordoba'*.

Walter Rizzi

It was well over forty years ago when Walter Rizzi first spoke of his contact with extraterrestrials. When I heard about this case I was a little sceptical, but I recalled that friends from Italy and other European countries telling me about the 'Friendship Clubs', in the 1960s, where they and others assisted aliens living incognito amongst us.

During WWII, in 1942, Italian serviceman Walter Rizzi was posted to the Gadurra airfield on the island of Rhodes in the Eastern Mediterranean. He was an interpreter for both the German and Italian High Commands, alternating between the two. Without any other duties, he enjoyed a lot of free time and movement.

Walter felt sorry for the local population, who lived in extreme poverty. A young, pitifully thin, little Greek girl used to come nearly every day, begging for a piece of bread or some sustenance. He would go into the officers' mess, and get some food for her, with extra for her parents and an 'old man' who lived up in the mountains.

He was curious about the 'old man' and it was some time before she confided that he was a hermit who never came down into the valley. She was the only one who spoke to him or knew where he lived. After a few weeks the little girl took Walter up the mountain to meet this mystery man.

In Walter's words – *'I was startled by his appearance. He was almost naked, with skin like paper maché, a long beard and hair, with very black eyes which glowed like beacons. I felt his gaze pierce me right through, as he raised his hand in greeting. – and said - "You are good" - in Greek.*

Walter spent a lot of time with the old man – sometimes two or three days at a time. The hermit taught him many things, including an ancient Greek prayer which would purify his spirit and exercise a positive magnetic influence.

'Once a month he went into complete isolation and remained like a statue for two days. He said he travelled in space, and told me that there was an infinity of other planets, very far from our solar system, which were inhabited by creatures very different from one another. He predicted that I should meet some of these beings from outer space, who would give me a glimpse of certainty and a more concrete idea of life in the universe. I asked him to tell me something more about my future, but he replied that my conscience was already on the path of light, and I should concentrate on the prayer he had taught me.'

After the war, Walter returned to his beloved Dolomites, and by 1968 was working as a representative for a Bolzano firm, covering the whole area of South Tyrol. One Saturday evening, at the end of July, he had a date with a Dutch girl, who was on holiday in the Badia Valley. At about midnight she returned to her hotel, and Walter decided to cross the Gardena and Sella Passes, and make his way to his aunt's hotel at Campitello in the Fassa Valley.

'The weather was not very good, and I seldom saw a star in the sky. There were always dense fog-banks, and more than once I had to stop because I couldn't see ahead. Once or twice I nearly went off the road, so I decided to stop at the first possible place and sleep in the car.

'After the Gardena Pass, I found a sand-dump at the side of the road, and decided to stop there. I lowered the tip-down seat, and settled down to sleep. It must have been about one o'clock, and I was a bit tired and sleepy.'

Suddenly Walter woke with a start. He could smell something burning, and thought it must have been his car. He jumped out and checked everything, but his Fiat 66 was not on fire – everything was in perfect order.

'I noticed below me, on the opposite side of the road, about five hundred metres away, a strong light shining through a gap in the fog. It looked like an illuminated hotel terrace, but - "Hell!" - I said to myself, "There are no hotels or houses around here – nothing at all!" I knew the area very well, and had passed that way hundreds of times

'In a moment of clear visibility, I saw an enormous object, bathed in a strange white light. My heart started pounding, and in that instant I remembered what

the old hermit had said to me all those years ago. I was convinced that this was the moment that he had prophesised.'

Walter got his torch and went down the slope at the edge of the road, making his way towards the large object. He felt his heart pounding in excitement as he neared a beautiful silver saucer. It was about fifty metres in diameter, and resting on three thick legs, about two metres above the ground. Everything was bathed in a fleecy white light, with an intense smell of burning.

'As soon as I got within three metres of the disc I felt suddenly 'blocked', as if my body weighed a thousand kilos. I was unable to move and had great difficulty breathing. The glass dome on top was brilliantly lit, and I saw two 'beings' looking down. On the right there was a 'robot', about two and a half metres tall, with three legs and four arms, holding the outside of the disc and turning it around.'

A circular 'trap-door' opened on the underside of the craft, emitting a violet and orange light. A man, about five feet four inches tall, emerged. He was dressed in a close fitting suit and a glass helmet.

'He approached and raised his right hand in the same way that the hermit had greeted me. I cannot describe my feelings as I looked at that creature with the beautiful eyes; it was a strange, gentle sensation. I felt as free and light as a feather, and was perfectly calm as I gazed at him.

'Despite the glass helmet reaching to his shoulders, I could see he looked very much like 'us', and I asked him in Italian where he came from. No sooner than I had framed my question, the answer was already in my mind, as if I had always known it.'

The planet they had come from was very far from our galaxy, and ten times the size of Earth, with two suns – one large and the other much smaller. Whilst their vegetation and animal life are, with some differences, similar to ours, their days were longer and the nights shorter.

On their planet everyone is equal and they do not work. Everything is automated, and they live on fruit, cereals and pills, with additional apparatus which generates energy. There are 'creatures', like monkeys, which do menial jobs such as cultivating and harvesting fruit and vegetables.

Walter could clearly see the man's features, and light olive skin. His hair was very short and light brown in colour, and almost looked like 'fur'. He had beautiful eyes, wider apart than ours, and slightly oblique, with the whites being light hazel and the irises a greenish-blue. His pupils contracted and dilated continually, like those of a cat. His nose and lips were small, and at times Walter noticed small, white regular teeth.

'I noticed the top of his head was bigger than ours, and was told that it was because his brain was double the size of ours; simply by means of thought and the emanation of waves they can do things that we cannot even imagine.'

Walter asked many questions, and although he did not hear the 'being's' reply, the answers appeared in his mind, as if by telepathy. He noticed when this 'being' emerged from the disc and came towards him, his walking gait was slightly different to ours, and his body proportions slightly different. He told Walter that whilst many of their organs were similar to ours, there were some differences, and the liquid which runs in their veins is not the same composition as our blood. Further, they have very powerful muscles in order to withstand the strong atmospheric pressure on their planet.

'I was continually struck by the beauty of his eyes, and wanted to ask 'him' if 'he' was a man or woman. His eyes twinkled for a moment and he explained, with a smile, that he was neither, and that their system of proliferation was not mating like animals.'

Walter was standing very close, but on the couple of occasions when he reached out to touch him, he was impeded by some invisible force. In the meantime, the robot was repairing something on what appeared to be a two metre rotor on the outside of the disc. The being explained that the rotor enabled them to enter the atmosphere of the planets they are visiting, and where they attempt to remain for a specific period.

'In space they travel in the 'main disc', which is outside any magnetic field, using another source of energy. It has the same shape, but is very big, with a diameter of, I think, five kilometres. It is fitted with ledges for smaller discs, much as the one I was privileged to see, or a number of very small discs, without equipment, which are used for exploration purposes. They have a system of magnetic propulsion with no speed limit in any atmosphere, and are immune from temperature and other conditions.

'On the main disc, hundreds of people can live as if on their own planet. They have an inexhaustible supply of energy and everything else that they need. I asked him what defence weapons they had, to which he replied that they could disintegrate anything, even at enormous distances.

Walter asked him why they didn't give us the benefit of their technical knowledge? He said it was impossible for them to interfere with the evolution of any other planet, and spending any length of time in our Solar System would age them prematurely.

'At this point I asked him if he believed in God, and he said that God is everywhere – in us, plants, stones grass and nature – everything that exists.'

Walter noticed that the robot must have finished what he was doing as he moved to the centre of the disc, and when an orange light came on, he seemed to fly up and board the craft. The other individual, inside the dome, waved and Walter realised that it was probably time for them to go.

'I was so upset that I should never see him again that I started to cry, and asked him to take me with them. It didn't matter if I never returned. He explained that no-one from Earth could ever remain with them – much less travel in their spaceships.

'He made a sign of salutation, his hand raised as before, and I felt some unknown force push me away from the disc. The 'visitor' went below the disc and disappeared in the luminous circle. The white light dimmed, and I watched from about thirty metres away. The craft gave off a violet/orange light, made a noise like a circular saw, and rose a few metres when the feet folded in.

'The light changed to white, and there was a whistle that I thought would shatter my eardrums. The disc began rocking, as if in salutation, rose slowly to about three hundred metres, then suddenly shot away at a terrifying speed.'

Walter made his way back to his car, and pricked himself with a pin to make sure he wasn't dreaming. He drove to his aunt's hotel, and the next morning started making notes and sketches. His cousins made fun of him, and the reaction of more serious minded people persuaded him to keep the entire experience to himself.

Three weeks later he returned to photograph the landing area, and the marks of the three legs which had sunk into the ground. He noticed the grass had grown to three times the height of that surrounding it. Two side-effects that Walter experienced was his watch, which had stopped and never worked again, and the loss of his hair. He went totally bald, however after three months it grew back again.

Friar Giuseppe Madau

In September 1948, Giuseppe Madau was an eighteen year old novice living in a religious residence at Oristano, Sardinia. In those days there was no television, they were not allowed to listen to the radio, and he had never heard about 'flying saucers'. One afternoon he was saying his prayers while taking the dog for a walk in the countryside behind the seminary. He was taking his time, as the dog was very old, and nearly blind.

He looked up and saw a strange craft hovering above a tree about thirty metres away. From his vantage point, it looked like a 'huge, metallic cylindrical platform', or disc, with a transparent dome above. Two white, human looking young men came out and gestured to Giuseppe to come over. He was too scared to go, and seeing his reluctance, the beings got back into the craft, which emitted a powerful beam of light and started to rise back into the sky.

Suddenly he felt himself and the dog, rising into the air, and unable to move. He was terrified, and prayed to 'Holy Mary' for help. He then heard a woman's voice, remote and from somewhere unknown, saying to 'let him go'! He found himself and the dog back on the ground, but when he raced back to tell his friends, they wouldn't believe him.

In 1974, when he was a missionary to Zambia, Friar Madau saw another strange craft when boarding a plane. It brought back memories of the 1948 incident, and he detailed the two events to Italian investigator Gianfranc Esposti.

This was not the only case of a startled witness inadvertently being lifted into the air by a saucer. In *'Contact Down Under'* I discussed a 1956 case in Hughenden, Central Queensland.

'Loretta', who was only twelve at the time, was walking across an open paddock at 4.30pm, when she heard a soft hum. A 'force' across her back and shoulders lifted her off the ground, and the next thing she remembers was being in a large room.

She could see two men, dressed in 'silver-white ski-suits' standing with their backs to her. They appeared to be operating a control panel which faced a large wall-screen showing a full colour outline of a galaxy. The two men said nothing to a confused Loretta as she looked around. She felt enormous pressure on her head and neck, and must have lost consciousness again.

The next thing she knew she was back in a different paddock, with a huge, eighty metre diameter saucer-shaped disc hovering just over her. It took off, ascending back into a bank of clouds in the west. Two hours had passed, and she didn't tell her family, or anyone else, until much later in life. There hadn't been any witnesses, and she was hesitant for fear of ridicule.

She had no conscious memory of what transpired during her time on the craft, and the investigators decided against any hypnotic regression.

South America
Other researchers have heard from witnesses repeating the same cautions that Alan had expressed to Dan Fry. Gordon Creighton, of *'Flying Saucer Review'*, translated a 1957 newspaper article from Argentina; an Air Force guard had an encounter with a flying saucer. A disembodied voice spoke to the guard from the craft, saying they were here to help, as our misguided use of atomic energy threatened to destroy us.

The same year a similar message came from Dr Joao Guimaraes of Brazil. In 1957, this Santos Catholic University professor had gone to Sao Sabastiao as part of his duties as a professional military advocate. He finished his dinner, and just after 7pm he went for a walk along the beach.

He sat down on the shore, and peacefully gazed out to sea. Suddenly, a jet of water, similar to a waterspout, appeared in the stretch of ocean between Bela Island and Sao Sabastiao. At first he thought it might be a whale, but soon realised it was some kind of 'pot-bellied' machine, moving in the direction of the beach. It was disc shaped, about sixty feet wide and eighteen feet high.

When it arrived, it threw out what looked like a landing line, with 'spheres', not buoys, attached. Two normal looking human beings jumped out and walked towards him. They were both nearly six feet tall, with long fair hair and clear youthful complexions. They were wearing green one-piece garments, which narrowed towards the neck, wrists and ankles.

At first Guimaraes was a little apprehensive, but he asked the strangers if their craft had met with an accident. They did not answer, despite him posing the same question in several different languages. At that stage he sensed that they were inviting him on board, and could only conclude that this must have been a telepathic communication. (Later on, these beings used articulate speech.)

At first he hesitated, but then felt an overwhelming desire to know what was inside. The two visitors escorted him to the craft, and helped him up a ladder into the entry hatch. Once on board, Guimaraes saw a third crew member in the illuminated compartment. He was able to ascertain there were other compartments in the craft, but he didn't get to see them.

The craft rose into the air, and he could see, through the portholes, that at one stage they had left the Earth's atmosphere. During the trip, which took about forty minutes, he got the impression that these craft were investigating our planet and its inhabitants.

The humanoids advised him not only of the danger of nuclear weapons, but also of scientific experiments being conducted with flagrant disregard for the possible consequences, including damage to our atmosphere.

When they returned him to the beach, they made an appointment to meet him again, in August 1957. At first, he confided in no-one, but soon word got out, and the when the Brazilian Air Force heard about the rendezvous, they planned to send some jet fighters. The professor decided not to go. It would be a breach of faith if he were to contribute to any unwelcome situation for those beings who were so considerate towards him.

CHAPTER THREE

GEORGE ADAMSKI

Whilst George Adamski claimed UFO sightings from 1946, when he had taken several photographs, it seems he had been in contact with these entities long before, but never wrote about this or spoke of it publicly.

Adamski's childhood still remains a bit of a mystery. He was born in Poland in 1891, and when he was two years old, his family migrated to New York City in the US. His father died when he was a child, and he and his mother were quite poor. His family were Catholics, and for a short while he served as an altar boy, but soon abandoned formal religion. He also kept contact with a younger brother, who became a priest in later life.

When he was still fairly young, a mysterious family friend financed and arranged for him to travel to Tibet to study with Buddhist 'Masters'. (Perhaps it is co-incidental that Tibet is said to have a long association with aliens; some close to Adamski suggest he was being prepared for his 'mission'.) Further, Fred Steckling, one of George's close friends and colleagues, said that Adamski's mother also had 'experiences'.

(Glenn Steckling, an airline pilot and Fred's son, firmly believed in extra-terrestrial visitors. In 1992 he told the *'Sunday Telegraph'* that he had seen several of them in his time; "I saw them as a child, with my parents, and I've seen them mingling with crowds at talks and conventions. Occasionally they will speak up during a debate and inject some thought or information to send us in the right direction – a little bit like tutelage."

Fred also said that one of his alien contacts worked for several years on Earth, often doing menial jobs, with both rich and poor people, and in many different environments.)

In 1913 Adamski joined the US Army, and served with the 13th Cavalry on the Mexican border. In 1917, he married his wife Mary. He worked as a painter/decorator for the government at Yellowstone National Park, and later spent a year with the National Guard, stationed at Portland, Oregon.

George and Mary moved to California, and in 1926 settled at Laguna Beach. In the early 1930s they moved several times, finally settling on a small property on the road to Mt. Palomar Observatory. By then, Adamski had founded an organisation called the 'Royal Order of Tibet', conducted educational philosophy courses, and delivered many lectures on Los Angeles area radio stations.

Having spent time studying with mystical practitioners, Adamski published his first book *'Wisdom of the Masters of the Far East'* in 1936, and continued lecturing on Eastern philosophy. An enthusiastic amateur astronomer, George also lectured on 'space ships' and authored a little-known book, *'Pioneer of Space'*. It is believed that Lucy McGinnis, who had been his loyal, unpaid secretary since 1945, was actually also the 'ghost-writer' of this book.

Adamski was certainly no paragon of virtue. Jerome Clark wrote a very interesting article regarding Ray Stanford's teenage memories of George, whom he met in 1956.

Stanford liked him, and despite George's heavy drinking, was impressed with his artistic abilities and the paintings he had done in his spare time. Ray visited several times, and never forgot the last conversation he and his brother Rex had with George in 1958.

Adamski expressed dislike for President Roosevelt for lifting Prohibition, and admitted that his 'Sacred Order of Tibet' was a legal excuse to make wine, and have a bootlegging business on the side.

"Listen, I was able to make the wine," George said. "You know, we were supposed to have the religious ceremonies. We made the wine for them, and the authorities couldn't interfere with our religion. Hell, I made enough wine for half of southern California. In fact, boys, I was the biggest bootlegger around. Then that Roosevelt come along and knocked out Prohibition. If it hadn't been for that man, Roosevelt, I wouldn't have got into all this saucer crap!"

(This left Stanford in doubt about Adamski's claims, but he knew, and trusted, George Williamson who confirmed all the events in the 'desert encounter'. Williamson's wife, Betty, also testified as to everything that happened. That day, they and the Baileys had a rendezvous with George, Lucy and Alice on a road out of town. She also mentioned how Adamski wasn't sure where to go, and it was her husband, George Williamson who knew the pre-designated desert 'meeting' place, and gave directions along the way.)

Friends and colleagues had helped renovate Adamski's property, and he was also thrilled by the donation of two large telescopes. From there, he photographed UFOs in the 1940s. Some critics tried to dismiss these photos as fakes, but Rosemary Decker came to his defence, saying that she had seen the negatives and prints before his trip to the desert in 1952.

"Also, my Uncle Bill owned a property near some acreage that Adamski and his colleagues had. He told me he had seen various original negatives of Adamski's spacecraft at the same time they had been photographed. He assured me that he also considered them to be genuine."

Rosemary Decker's research interests started early in life. She enjoyed amateur astronomy, meeting like-minded enthusiasts and was a friend of George Adamski long before his famous meeting with Orthon in the desert in 1952. She took advantage of Adamski's access to larger-than-average telescopes to view the wonders of the night sky.

In 1946, George, whilst observing a meteorite shower, had photographed a large spaceship. Not long after, three military officers from Arizona, were enjoying some refreshments in Alice Wells' cafe. George got talking to them when the subject of flying saucers was raised. There was some argument about whether they existed or not, when one spoke up and said;

"It's not as fantastic as it sounds. When you're standing nine feet away from one of these things, you really do know what you are looking at."

The officers told Adamski and his friends that they couldn't talk much, but they assured them that space craft were coming. Remember, this was months before Kenneth Arnold's report, and the alleged crash at Roswell. At the time, Adamski said he was unsure, but kept an open mind.

In 1949 several military personnel came into the cafe. They were having a meal before going on to the Palomar Observatory, to ask them to photograph objects that were travelling through space. George asked if he could volunteer to do the same with his smaller telescopes, and he was shown the area of sky to concentrate upon.

After several attempts he managed to take a couple of pictures, which were apparently 'lost' by the laboratory he had been told to entrust them to. After that, he kept the originals and sent copies to Captain Ruppelt at Wright Field, Dayton, Ohio.

He was further convinced and encouraged when, in 1951, Walter Winchell, the famous reporter and commentator, stated on a nation-wide radio broadcast, that space craft were landing in the desert, about thirty miles from Mount Palomar. Apparently, they had been seen by staff at the observatory, and 'beings' alighted from the ships and walked around, before getting back on board and taking off.

We know that George Hunt Williamson, having received undisclosed messages from ham radios in Arizona, travelled with the Baileys to California. A few weeks before, they had spent a couple of days as Adamski's guests at Palomar Gardens. Early in the morning of 20th November 1952, they met up with Adamski, Lucy McGinnis and Alice Wells near the border.

It appears that Williamson was actually giving the directions, and they drove together to the foothills of the Coxcomb Range, a desert area with sparse vegetation. They stopped and ate a picnic lunch, and suddenly all seven became aware of a large, silver, cigar-shape craft in the sky. It was moving silently towards them when several Air Force planes appeared, and it shot off into the space.

Adamski asked to be driven closer to the foothills, where he took his cameras and set up his telescope. His colleagues moved a small distance away, but George was still in full view. Soon, a small circular craft, about thirty-five feet wide by twenty feet deep, appeared just above the foothills. When the Air Force had left the area, it came down, just hovering above the ground, before departing.

A young man appeared, at the entrance to a ravine between two hills, and after some initial hesitation, Adamski went out to meet him. He looked very human in all features except for his fair hair, which was longer than currently fashionable. He had grey/green eyes, was of average height and wearing a dark brown jump-suit with a wide belt or band around the middle.

Conversation, at that time proved difficult, as the stranger did not appear to speak English, but communication was established by gestures and scrawling with sticks in the sand. Not knowing his identity, George called him 'Orthon', and soon realised this man was indicating that he came from another planet.

George had practised and taught telepathy for many years, and found this useful in his communications with the visitor. The main message that he understood was that Orthon's people were concerned about our testing of nuclear weapons.

During their meeting, Orthon also indicated that his shoe prints on the ground were somehow important.

After a while, Orthon turned and pointed up behind the nearby low hill. The saucer had returned, and it was time for him to go. Adamski walked with "Orthon' back to the craft which was hovering just above the ground. His shoulder was accidentally caught under the flange, pulling his arm upwards. Orthon snatched George out from underneath, and in doing so, cut his hand, which bled red blood, just as with any other human being.

George was sure he saw a second person in the hovering craft, and after Orthon entered he could hear voices talking in an unusual, unknown language. The disc departed, and Adamski made his way back to his excited colleagues. My friend and colleague, Rosemary Decker, was present to witness their animated reports when they arrived back at Palomar.

Orthon had not let Adamski take his photo, saying it would allow people to recognise him, but before he left, he took one of Adamski's film plate holders with him. In December, a saucer appeared, and when it was about one hundred feet away from George and other witnesses, the plate holder was dropped back to earth with a film showing unusual markings inside.

George and Betty Hunt Williamson were anthropologists, and always travelled with a supply of Plaster of Paris. After the encounter, they had made a number of casts of the footprints left by Orthon.

There were several attempts to decipher the imprint markings made by the soles of the footwear, and the symbols on the film negative. It appeared the solution lay with the combined symbols from both artefacts. In South Africa, Basil Van den Berg made the dubious claim that he was helped by a 'visitor' to determine that the code was apparently a 'perfect plan for the construction and motivation of a UFO.' In 1962, Prof. Marcel Homet said that he had matched the strange symbols to identical ancient rock engravings found in the Amazon Basin.

In the following weeks there were a few mentions of the incident in the local press, but world-wide publicity didn't occur until after the publication of his first co-authored book *'Flying Saucers Have Landed'* in 1953. While some detractors doubted Adamski's desert encounter, Project Blue Book's Special Report No. 14, noted that on 20th November 1952, an Air Force pilot reported an unidentified craft in the general vicinity of Desert Centre, California.

Adamski did not have to wait long for his next contact. In February 1953, whilst in Los Angeles, two men approached him in the lobby of his hotel. Both were 'tallish' being nearly six feet in height. One had black wavy hair with dark brown eyes, and the other slightly shorter man had sandy hair and greyish/blue eyes. They were both wearing business suits, and gave him the same hand signal that had been used by Orthon. Since they didn't give their names, he decided to call them 'Firkon' and 'Ramu'.

As they drove him off in their car, George realised that they both spoke perfect English. One explained; *"We are what you on Earth might call 'contact men'. We live and work here, because, as you know, it is necessary on Earth to earn money with which to buy clothing, food and the many things that people must have. We have lived on your planet now for several years. At first we did have a slight accent, but that has now been overcome. As you can see, we are unrecognised as other than Earth men.*

"At our work and in our leisure time we mingle with people here on Earth, never betraying the secret that we are inhabitants of other worlds. This would be dangerous, as you well know. We understand your people better than most of you know yourselves, and can plainly see the reasons for many of the unhappy conditions that surround you......We are permitted to make brief visits to our home planets. Just as you long for a change of scene, or to see old friends, so it is with us.

"You are neither the first nor the only man on this world with whom we have talked. There are many others living in different parts of the Earth to whom we have come. Some, who have dared to speak of their experiences have been persecuted – a few even to what you call 'death'. Consequently, many have kept silent." They considered that once his book was published, it would encourage others from many countries to write of their experiences.

They drove to a remote spot where, on the ground, a soft, white glowing disc was waiting, along with Orthon. After their reunion, George realised that Orthon was also speaking perfect English. They all boarded the small 'scout' ship which took them to a 'mother ship', which was about two thousand feet in length, and hovering above the atmosphere.

When Adamski commented on its size, he was told that there were ships several miles long. He was given a tour of the craft, and some of the technology was explained, although he was warned not to describe it, or some of the information he had been given, to anyone. Afterwards he met with a much older 'space' gentleman, who seemed extremely wise, and emphasised that they were concerned that our nuclear bombs could destroy Earth's balance in the galaxy.

"Our main purpose in coming to you at this time is to warn you of the grave danger which threatens men of Earth today. In your first meeting with our brother, he indicated to you that the exploding of bombs on Earth was of interest to us. Even though the power and radiation from the test explosions has not yet gone out beyond your Earth's sphere of influence, these radiations are endangering the life of men on Earth. In time, a decomposition will set in, that will fill your atmosphere with the deadly elements which your scientists and your military men have confined into what you term 'bombs'.

Before George left, Orthon told him that he had been under observation for some years before he decided to contact him. He also admitted to their use of 'ham' radio operators to contact certain people, and added; "You were chosen to meet with me in the presence of witnesses to confirm your experience. We wanted the truth of this meeting to reach as far as possible. And we commend the staff of one of your newspapers which proved brave enough to publish the first account."

Firkon drove Adamski back to his hotel, and let him out at the door. It was now just after 5am, and he had been away nearly seven hours. He firmly believed his new friends when they told him that they had come from Venus, Mars and Saturn. Either they lied, or had advanced, environmentally protected bases on those planets.

Two months later, on 21st April, Adamski was sitting with his newspaper in the lobby of the same hotel, when Firkon arrived. They drove out to a slightly larger 'scout' ship, and to a different mother ship, where he was given another tour, and shown their science laboratory, and much of their advance technology, including tiny 'spy' discs, similar to our drones in later years. He was also shown misleading holographic type screen views of the Moon.

George didn't see Firkon and Ramu again until early September, when they ate together at a Los Angeles restaurant. They spoke about the many contacts, they and people from other groups, have made in almost every nation in the world;

'We do not enjoy the secrecy with which we have to make such meetings. We would far rather be welcome to come and go, and to visit with your people as we do with those of other worlds. But so long as our visits are not understood, and are therefore made dangerous for us and for our ships, we will have to continue with the present caution.'

A few weeks later, Ramu met Adamski outside a Los Angeles restaurant, and they again went back to the mothership where George had philosophical discussions with the 'Master'.

In August 1954, he was taken on another visit to one of the larger craft. This time it was to farewell Firkon and Ramu, who were returning to their home planet, although it appeared that Orthon was remaining on Earth. Before George left the ship, and was taken back to his hotel, he was shown holographic images of cities on Venus, which he totally believed.

George's last trip was in April 1955, when he claimed to have photographed another saucer through the porthole of the craft he was on. This picture, unlike his earlier photos taken near Palomar, has been discredited by many experts.

Adamski detailed all these later experiences in his second book *'Inside the Spaceships'* which was published in 1956. It was most probably 'ghost' written by his friend Charlotte Blodget who also wrote the 'Introduction'. It did not receive the same seal of approval which was accorded to *'Flying Saucers Have Landed'*.

Many found George's claims difficult to accept. All who knew him believed that his early photographs and contacts were authentic. His later trips to the 'mother ship' were, unfortunately, not independently witnessed, and his conversations with the 'Master' were extensive and almost identical to the philosophical dogma he had been preaching and writing for years.

He once said; "To have a healthy and prosperous society, that which causes the most trouble must be removed. As we all know, this stigma is poverty in the midst of plenty. It is the cause of sickness, crime, and the many evils that we know.."

He was not the only contactee expressing this opinion. At the same time he was communicating with Orthon and the Space Brothers, Dutch businessman Adrian Beers rescued a different type of alien being from his crashed ship. When he asked the space visitors for information on advanced technology he was told;

"The last thing you need is technological information to increase the gap between your intellectual development and your almost non-existent social development. Carry on playing with your Mars probes for the moment, as half your world's population lives in poverty and hunger. The only information you need lies in the field of societal standards."

In the early 1950s there were sometimes conflicting reports coming out of Palomar Gardens, when groups of amateur astronomers and other interested people gathered regularly. Some later tried to gain publicity by making dubious claims.

One was a gentleman called Jerrold Baker, who arrived at Palomar Gardens in December, 1952. He claimed to have been an Air Force Instructor, and after his discharge in October 1952, he went to California and 'began assisting the Professor in his work.' He claimed that, along with Adamski, he sighted and photographed a flying saucer flying at low altitude near the property.

In 1956, George Adamski's version of the events differed greatly. He said that he had been corresponding with Baker and another man, Karl Hunrath for some time. Both men seemed to be intelligent and scientifically minded. Then the situation changed; - *'I received a letter from Hunrath saying he was on his way out to see me. In late December 1952, he arrived at Palomar Gardens, bag and baggage, with intentions to stay indefinitely, but no money to pay for his expenses.*

'Jarrold Baker also arrived under similar circumstances, late one night in December 1952. He was also still there, behaving as one of the family, helping himself to everything freely and in abundance, but without money to pay for anything.'

Palomar Gardens depended upon a small power plant. A day or two after Hunrath arrived, he told Adamski that he and a fellow 'scientist' called Wilkinson, both from Wisconsin, had invented a magnetic machine that could produce all the electricity they needed. He wanted to have it shipped to California, and then casually noted that it would also not only attract saucers, it would bring them down!

When Adamski remonstrated that it may also affect the planes in the area, Hunrath said; "Who cares, we want the saucer!"

After Hunrath started trying to order everyone around, and Alice Wells reported that he had been taking their mail from the local post office, Adamski asked him to leave, which a very aggressive Hunrath did, taking Jarrold Baker with him. Fearing repercussions, Adamski and Alice advised the FBI of the situation. Hunrath then 'disappeared' along with Wilkinson. In 1954 Jarrold Baker visited Adamski, and told him he thought Hunrath may be across the border in Mexico.

In the early 1950s Adamski's wife was terminally ill, and their friend Alice Wells offered to help nurse her, and provided new accommodation at a residence on her property at Palomar Gardens. Mary subsequently died in 1954, and George later moved further up the mountain to Palomar Terraces.

Rosemary Decker, who was present at Palomar Gardens, in 1952, when Adamski and the six excited witnesses returned from the Desert Encounter, reminisced about her long friendship with George Adamski, and how she enjoyed her regular visits which occurred later during the 1950s: *'It was fairly easy to make the visits to his place, as I lived only an hour's drive from the locale, Palomar Gardens, which was at the 3,000 foot level of Palomar Mountain. He held an informal Open House on most Saturdays and Sundays, and the mountainside yard was pleasant most of the year.*

'Anywhere from forty or fifty people would come to discuss their UFO sightings with each other and with George. He replied to questions good-naturedly, or simply related his own experiences, and philosophised. George thoroughly enjoyed being heard!

'Occasionally, guests would report their own close encounters. Very few of them ever publicised their own contacts, and so I learned early that the vast majority of early contacts, or even the later ones, were never made public.'

In 1958 George also spoke about his meetings at Palomar Terraces; "People come and go constantly. On the first and third Sundays of each month, between the hours of 1pm and 4pm, it is my custom to talk with the public at my home – give a lecture on topics of interest and answer questions.

"Space travellers occasionally are amongst these guests, and there have been times I did not recognise them, nor did they identify themselves until some time later. It is rare for my closest associates to recognise these space people, even though they meet and talk with them. They are human like ourselves, with no outstanding features which would distinguish them from people of Earth."

He later spoke of one occasion when, whilst sitting around the dinner table, they heard a light knock on the door; "It was raining very hard at the time, and when we opened the door, a tall fine looking man stood there asking for me. He looked no different than any other earthman. He asked to come in and sit with us at the table. No car was in sight – how he arrived I do not know.

"His opening question was the type anyone would ask and from there we proceeded with space discussions that went on for at least an hour. From his conversation we concluded that he was not an earthman, for some of his answers he gave could not have been read in any earth literature about space."

Adamski felt he was definitely a spaceman, but the others present expressed doubt. It was only later that his thoughts were confirmed when he met this same man in the company of the 'Brothers'. He explained; "Only one answer exists to the recognition question. That is a blend of consciousness, as you did with me that evening, for in consciousness we find truth, and not in the mind."

Saucer activity in the area continued. Timothy Good wrote about a report from ex-Marine Alan Tolman, who worked for the Douglas Aircraft Company. In about 1955/56 he was visiting Adamski, and sky-watching through the six inch Newtonian telescope. He saw a blue streak shoot across the sky, and when he looked up, saw an elliptical glow behind a grove of trees.

"I walked towards the craft, and as I got closer I could hear a soft, pleasing 'hum' sound. At about a hundred yards from the craft I heard people that had just come out of a restaurant, down the hill from George's house, yelling loudly, "There's a flying saucer on the ground." From the restaurant parking area, the people had an unobstructed view of the craft."

The saucer's intensity and hum increased, and it silently shot straight up and disappeared into the night sky. (I wonder if the short landing and quick take-off, in close proximity to Adamski's house and the restaurant where people were gathered in both, was to pick someone up or drop them off? We will never know, however a witness called Henry Dohan claimed that Orthon lived on and off for about three years in Vista California, spending much of his time with Adamski.)

Rosemary Decker usually counselled contactees, and advised them that the Space Brothers did not expect them to take on any Adamski type onerous missions. They should work within their own spheres; "Actions are like a pebble being thrown into a pond – the ripples can spread far and wide."

'Most contactees I became acquainted with found ways to express appreciation by doing something to benefit our troubled planet. Many of the Palomar visitors formed lasting friendships. A number of careers were switched; writers changed their themes; holistic healing was explored; teachers at all levels, up to university, broadened the scope of the courses they taught. This quiet, but profound, movement is still on-going – not only among those pioneers who still remain with us, but among contacted people today.'

Desmond Leslie

George Adamski certainly had an increasing group of supporters, but if it hadn't been for Irish eccentric Desmond Leslie, his message would not have spread world-wide.

Desmond Leslie was born in 1921, to a titled family, whose aristocratic estate was the Castle Leslie in County Monaghan. His father, Sir Shane Leslie, was a poet and author, and related to Sir Winston Churchill.

During World War II Desmond was a dare-devil Spitfire pilot, but after became more unconventional, and followed his family's occult and paranormal leanings and interests. He spent much of his time in the British Library, studying ancient mythology, history and mysticism, including various esoteric movements and philosophies.

Eventually, in the early 1950s, he wrote a book on the subject, discussing ancient astronauts twenty years ahead of Eric Von Daniken's *'Chariots of the Gods'*. The manuscript was rejected by publisher after publisher, until Leslie read about Adamski in an American newspaper article. In 1934, as a schoolboy, Leslie had seen a UFO from his boarding school window, and after the war, he had formed a firm friendship with Lord Dowding, who had held the position of Air Chief Marshall during the Battle of Britain. Sir Hugh Dowding also held a firm belief in extraterrestrials visiting Earth, and with his encouragement, Leslie wrote to Adamski.

George Adamski offered him, free of charge, the entire story of his desert encounter, including the photographs he had previously taken. In 1953 he posted it off to Leslie, who delivered a completed manuscript to publisher Wayne Girvan. The first half was Desmond Leslie's 180 page chronicle – *'The Flying Saucer Museum'* – plus Adamski's 'scout-ships' photographs and the first draft of his account of meeting 'Orthon' in the Californian desert.

Wayne Girvan, didn't see much future for the two manuscripts individually, and decided to complete and publish their joint effort as a combined book – *'Flying Saucers have Landed'* – in 1953. It became an overnight success, helped in part by a couple of controversial radio debates Leslie had with scientists and astronomers on the BBC.

Desmond Leslie's articulate arguments, and wicked sense of humour, only added to the publicity and interest in the book. In one interview he was asked; 'Why don't they land?' He was quick to reply; *'Their ship would be impounded for evasion of custom duties. Their clothes would be torn off and sold as souvenirs. They would be denounced as saboteurs, Anti-Christs, disturbers of the peace, emissaries of Satan, and the rest......We can only conclude that our planet has a bad name in the stellar year books and travel brochures: like those signs in the roads running through the jungles, which caution the tourists not to tarry or leave the safety of their cars. 'Warning – Do Not Land on Earth. The Natives are Dangerous.'*

While Desmond Leslie went on a lecture tour, to promote the book, astronomers and scientists were publicly condemning it, which only added to the controversy and soaring sales of *'Flying Saucers Have Landed'*.

He first met George Adamski in person, when he visited him for three months in California in 1954, and stayed with him several times after that. During his stay he witnessed several lights in the sky, and once saw a 'golden disc', about fifty feet away.

Desmond disputed the rumours that George was arrogant, and claimed to be the 'only contactee', in fact, quite the opposite. He said; "Desmond, I just happened to be one of the first. But many others are going to meet these ships on the ground, and talk to their crews as time goes by. In fact, if you get back to Europe by October you'll find it already starting."

Desmond was used to being ridiculed, and was surprised at the response he received from some young US Air Force pilots who were present during one of his stays at Palomar Gardens. They had just come from a 'UFO Identification

Course', which was apparently 'all hush-hush and secret'. Desmond asked them what classifications they used. Did they call them 'spots before the eyes', 'light inversions', 'lenticular clouds' etc.?

"Heck no!" they said. "They had models, and actual photographs, and they classified them: Scout ship, Mother ship, Carrier types."

"You mean they've used the names from our book?' Desmond gasped.

"Sure thing!" the Airmen laughed. "And they've got pictures of some flying saucers you've never seen, but be careful who you repeat this to. It's all highly secret."

He met with several of the contactees, but publically denied meeting with the Space Brothers. In private correspondence to family or trusted friends, he said that whilst with Adamski, he had met with the 'visitors', who reiterated their concerns over our use of atomic weapons.

Desmond Leslie was always a flamboyant character, but few knew he was also a gifted author, film director, musician and composer. In 1958 he published the novel, *'The Amazing Mr. Lutterworth'*, in which the principal character is an extraterrestrial, who whilst on Earth, has an accident which causes amnesia. He cannot remember who he is, or what his mission was. Some researchers believe Adamski inspired him to write this tale. Who knows?

After the 1953 publication of *'Flying Saucers Have Landed'*, George Adamski was the subject of world-wide attention. Not all of his experiences were pleasant.; *'Shortly after I was visited by three men, two of whom I had met previously, but the third was a stranger. It was he who took the role of authority, demanding certain papers I had, for one thing. Some of these I gave him, and was promised their return, but this promise was never kept.*

'Since I did not exactly understand to what he referred, I did not give him some of my important papers. There is no need denying that I was frightened. Before they left I was told to stop talking or they would come after me, lock me up and throw away the key.'

'......Although there could be some influence of this kind coming from space, so far no evidence is showing up that could be interpreted to the effect that space men are trying to hush up people on this earth.'

It isn't any wonder that the authorities were not happy about the 'Space Brother' doctrine Adamski was promoting and preaching to his followers. He spoke of one equal society where there was no religion or money. Everyone lived in peace and love, with work, property and possessions being shared. This was happening in the middle of the Cold War, and the government naturally suspected that George had communist leanings.

Adamski said that in 1954, in New York, he was approached by a stranger who offered him $25,000 cash to sign a statement saying his portion of *'Flying Saucers Have Landed'* was fiction. He naturally refused.

A similar event occurred in Detroit, in 1957, following the publication of *'Inside the Spaceships'*. Two men approached him when he was alone, with no witnesses. They would not tell him their names, or whom they represented. They had a 'stack of bills', and this time the offer had gone up to $35,000 if he retracted his claims.

This was probably much more than he would have received from the publisher from the sale of his books, and he wondered how many genuine contactees were not able to resist temptation.

CHAPTER FOUR

ADAMSKI'S WORLD TOUR

Following the publication of *'Flying Saucers Have Landed'*, 'Adamski Correspondence Groups' were instigated in many countries. George would send them the occasional 'lecture tape', but it is now known that his letters, 'Question and Answer' sheets and Telepathy Course notes were all written by his loyal secretary Lucy McGinness.

(Desmond Leslie had noted that Adamski did not have a good command of written or spoken English. Later, it was established that most probably his books, *'Flying Saucers Have Landed'*, *'Inside the Spaceships'*, and *'Flying Saucers Farewell'*, were rendered first-hand to a succession of female assistants including Lucy McGinnis, Charlotte Blodgett and Alice Wells, and that they were his actual ghost-writers. However, C. A. Honey claimed that for several years, he was the ghost-writer for Adamski's published material, including most chapters of *'Flying Saucers Farewell'*.)

Many of George Adamski's growing band of 'followers' wanted to meet the space visitors themselves. In a 1956 private letter to one, he wrote; *'You have been wanting to be met and assured by the Brothers. Do you know that you have not been? I am always sceptical of those who claim personal meetings with identifications at the first contact, unless of course, there is a space craft in the picture at the time. This has happened on many occasions.*

'But according to those with whom I have had meetings, they do not reveal their identities unless the Earthman recognises them first by his own inner feeling. If this takes place, and if it is right for them to identify themselves, they will respond with a mental thought. Otherwise, they might visit with you, many hours, and many times, without identifying themselves.

So it is up to you folks, each one to be alert at all times to your inner feeling, hunches, or whatever you may call them. There will not be anything conspicuously different in their personal appearances. And remember that over-anxiety creates a tenseness that can act as a barrier to your 'feeling' alertness.'

He was also critical of some 'cults' which had recently sprung up; *'According to the Brothers, "Ashtar" is a spiritualistic character without reality in fact.*

'Ashtar messages' are coming from mediums, automatic writers, and people who are sincere in desire, but without understanding, and who open themselves mentally in the hope of contacting the Brothers. Such messages are sent to us from many parts of the world.

'You will find divisions, such as 'those who believe', or those who have 'raised their vibrations'....Specific dates are given for dire events to take place, along with specific places in many cases. We have even received messages where 'Ashtar' has introduced Jesus Christ, George Washington, Patrick Henry etc. with praises for America, warnings about America's acts, warnings against Russia and other places, and many such things. The Brothers, who are living human beings like you and I, never do such things, nor do they say such things.'

In New Zealand, the Dickesons, and other researchers and groups, from around the country, spent most of 1958 arranging, and raising the finance for George Adamski's 1959 tour of New Zealand. Later the Australian groups also participated in the project.

The cost was a little prohibitive, as Lucy McGuiness, his secretary, had insisted on First Class air travel. The New Zealand groups had planned on accommodating George in their own homes, but Lucy insisted on hotel accommodation the whole time. In Adamski's defence, he never asked for, or received any kind of payment or a speaker's fee. The organisers of these large meetings kept all the lucrative entry fees, and were only required to cover George's travelling and hotel expenses.

Adamski claimed that wherever he went he met 'space people' who looked completely human. He wrote to the tour organisers that he fully expected to meet these 'Space Brothers' on his travels, but the encounters would be discrete so as not to identify them.

Rosemary Decker once explained to me George was correct - the Space Brothers always accompanied him on his tours, and would meet with him late at night or early in the morning. They may be detected by intelligence agencies near a private home, but not so much in the environment of a city hotel, or in the crowd at a large lecture theatre.

Tony Brunt wrote in his book *'George Adamski; The Toughest Job in the World'*, that 'the boys' had checked out the New Zealand organisers before his arrival.

'It was not so much the sightings in the sky that tantalised his supporters, but his assertion that he met the space people regularly and furtively in everyday society, especially when he was on the lecture circuit.

'One of the New Zealand tour organisers got a shot at George's undercover escorts. She was waiting for him at Auckland airport on his return on a flight from a southern city. "I noticed two good looking men, with fair hair, disembark from the plane among the passengers and walk across the tarmac," she said. "They could have been brothers, but I didn't pay too much attention, apart from noticing that they smiled at me as they approached the gates.

"George was the last person off the plane, and when he got to me he said excitedly – "did you see de boys?" By the time they got into the terminal the men had disappeared – to her great regret.

Stan Seers, president of the Queensland research group, said that Adamski had confirmed that 'the aliens' were keeping a close watch on the tour arrangements, to make sure that everything went smoothly, and that they had actually visited him while he was in New Zealand.

Fred Dickeson, from the South Island group, wrote in his diary that when he picked George up one morning, he looked very happy and mentioned leaving the hotel at 6am that morning for 'a walk around the Bay'.

Although the visit was publically hailed as a great success, behind the scenes there were many problems and a great deal of controversy. Adamski first toured the North Island, giving talks at a number of centres where his large audiences were very interested in what he had to say. He then travelled on to the South Island, where Fred Dickeson was his guide.

Wherever he appeared, there were two slightly aloof men in dark suits who attended all the meetings. They sat at the back, as if keeping an eye on all that was happening. This gave rise to the belief that they were 'security people'. Fred Dickeson was suspicious, and initiated a conversation at the Christchurch meeting.

"How are you finding it?' He asked.

"Quite interesting," one replied with a slight smile.

What they didn't see were the two young blonde people, who quietly came in, and stayed out of sight behind them, after the lecture started. They always departed, just as mysteriously, before the end of the proceedings. Very few people noticed them, but those that did believed they were the 'Space Brothers' who reputedly always followed Adamski on his travels. One woman, who treated him like a cult guru and attended all the lectures, had noticed the same two people getting off every plane Adamski had arrived on. They would quickly disappear into the crowd. When questioned about it, he would just laugh it off.

Whilst in Wellington, on the North Island, George was having supper with a few devotees in a private home. His host, 'Mr L', stated that he had not seen any space people and if there were any about, he would recognise them.

George then told 'Mr L' that he had indeed actually met and spoken to two of his 'space escorts' when he was acting as doorman at the Wellington lecture; "They asked you if you thought the meeting would be a good one. You were not alert enough to twig." Much to his embarrassment, 'Mr L' then remembered the funny and very subtle questions they had asked him.

In Christchurch, on the South Island, problems started to occur. Five minutes before the projectionist was due to show the lecture slides, he demanded extra money, or he wouldn't work.

In Timaru the meeting was noisy, and there seemed to be an element in the audience that was trying to create trouble. Fed Dickeson was sure that the South Island meetings were deliberately being interrupted by 'outsiders' who had been 'bussed in'. Just before he was due to go on to Dunedin, the projector lens went missing, and a replacement had to be found.

The Dunedin meeting itself turned into a shambles. The hall lighting was wrong and the film had been incorrectly loaded into the projector. Precious time was wasted putting things right. Instead of writing their questions on a piece of paper at the break, some of the crowd started shouting out all at once. By the time order was restored it was nearly 10pm and they had to vacate the premises.

When Adamski was due to return to Auckland, to catch his flight to Sydney, and the Australian part of his tour, Fred Dickeson called at his Dunedin hotel to take him down to breakfast and then on to the airport. George was very shaken, looking startled and dazed. He said that two men in suits, had visited him previously that morning.

Just after 6am there had been a knock on the door, and George had opened it, wondering why Fred had come so early. Two men in the corridor had quickly pushed past him into the room, and cornered him between the bed and the dressing table. He could not reach the phone, which was on the other side of the bed.

They stood there for several seconds before one said; "You don't have your bodyguard with you now! It's a good thing you're leaving today, or we would have made it really difficult for you. We can't keep the crowds away from your meetings, but we can create disturbances like last night. You are lucky to get out of here alive - we don't want your sort here!" Their appearance and New Zealand accents left him in no doubt as to whom they were.

Fred called Jim, his Dunedin colleague. They and George agreed not to call the police, as any investigation would disrupt the scheduled flight plans to Australia for the lecture tour there. Adamski made both written and taped statements before he left.

Adamski visited many States in Australia. He lectured in Perth and Melbourne, and also made a private trip to Tasmania. His appearances in Sydney were not without their problems. Some members of the Sydney UFOIC group, were not totally supportive, and suggested he was perhaps exaggerating his story and a 'glory seeker', revelling in the publicity. Andrew Tomas, the editor of their *'UFO Bulletin'* counteracted this by publishing an article by Elizabeth Fry soon after. She had met Adamski in 1957, and detailed other sightings which tended to support the basic facts of his claims.

In regards to 'glory seeking', she quoted him saying; "There have been many more contactees, but usually they have more sense than I, and have kept their mouths shut!"

In Queensland the Brisbane City Hall was packed. It was obvious the disruptions were planned in advance. Noisy people were running around holding paper plates, painted green with faces on them. Some were dressed in bed-sheet robes, complete with antennae. Eventually, George had to leave the stage.

Whilst in South Australia, researcher Fred Stone, who had arranged and financed much of the tour, accompanied George Adamski during his stay. The Australian groups were paying for all Adamski's expenses, and Fred was far from happy with his guest's behaviour. He was not the altruistic 'saint' he was expecting.

Firstly he demanded to stay at an expensive hotel, and not the one which had been booked. The hotel of choice 'wouldn't have him', but he did eventually agree to an alternative venue. As it was, Fred commented that Adamski's whiskey bill was almost as much as what his hotel cost.

Fred soon twigged as to why he had demanded the first hotel. One of its guests was a 'mystery woman' called Elise, who was supposedly the daughter of a Dutch shipping tycoon, but George kept hinting that she had come from Saturn. (Apparently, when he was in Austria, he showed her photo to people as a 'visitor' from Saturn!)

Elise followed Adamski all over Australia, and the relationship was far from platonic. When Fred drove the couple around Adelaide, he claimed they were kissing and hugging, and 'other things' went on in the back seat!

Near the end of the South Australian leg of the tour, George was scheduled to give a lecture just outside of Adelaide. That morning he refused to do it, saying he was too tired. Fred lost the hall hire fee, and had to refund all the pre-purchased tickets. He was astounded when Adamski then, on the same night, went and lectured at another place for a rival group who had not been involved in, or contributed to the costs of the tour.

Adamski left for Asia and Europe, and his first visit to the United Kingdom. As well as his lecture commitments throughout the country, he appeared on the BBC's *'Panorama'* program together with astronomer Sir Patrick Moore. He also met Lord Dowding, who chaired a public meeting in Kent.

Many are unsure about a claim he made of meeting a 'spaceman' while travelling on a train to Weston-Super-Mare. He found a man sitting in his reserved compartment, and they became engaged in conversation. George said; *'To my amazement, he was a spaceman working as a scientist on projects for the British government! He, and countless others like him, are working in various scientific projects for every government in the world.'*

He then moved on to Holland where there was much speculation as to whether he had visited the Royal Palace, and met with Queen Juliana and Prince Bernhardt.

Adamski arrived in Switzerland on 23rd May 1959, and Lou Zinsstag, who was his hostess and translator, noted that he already looked very tired. She commented that on his first morning in Basel, he suddenly perked up. Two of the 'boys' had visited him in his room at 9am. He told her the same story during the week, and Lou was a little sceptical. The hotel manager and porter both confirmed that several men had visited in the mornings, but never more than two at a time.

His initial public lecture, which Lou had not organised, took place the following Sunday. Due to poor management it was not the success they had anticipated.

His second lecture, in Zurich, proved disastrous. There were three hundred students among the audience of seven hundred. They clapped, stamped, sang and hollered after every sentence. Pleas for order and silence went unheeded, and the students began throwing fruit at the platform and the audience.

In a futile attempt to regain control of the meeting, the planned film was started. This caused the 'rowdies' to use children's trumpets and crackers in further disruptions. When a beer bottle was thrown, hitting a woman on the shoulder, the police turned on the lights and closed the meeting.

After the problems which had already occurred in New Zealand and Australia, it is obvious that these disruptions were not localised incidents. They had been skilfully planned and implemented on an international level.

Lou said that George had remained remarkably calm during the incident, but he was not well, and she was glad that the next morning he decided to cancel the rest of his tour. His voice was badly irritated due to giving lectures over a prolonged period, and a doctor had warned him his lungs were already weakened by an infection, and he risked pneumonia if he continued. He returned to the U.S.A. via his friend and colleague Hans Petersen in Denmark.

Although Adamski's World Tour in 1959, added to his fame and success, many of his supporters were left disillusioned and disappointed.

Fred Stone, from South Australia, later wrote; *It was undeniably obvious that this man was not expounding the same 'doctrine' as he had done when he first hit the limelight. In fact, one could hardly recognise many of his actions and the statements and themes of his public and private talks as one in the same. It was the conclusion of a host of people that 'George had changed'.*

Fred also noted that Adamski had distorted many facts, and his lectures deviated greatly from what he had said and written after his first encounter in the desert. Unfortunately, this opinion was shared by many other loyal followers, including the Dickesons in New Zealand.

In 1962, George made the astounding claim that at the end of March, he had been the first human, in seventy-five thousand years, to represent Earth at an Inter-Planetary Conference on Saturn. He reported leaving in a craft from a U.S. Air Base, and being away for a week. The journey supposedly only took nine hours, and the conference was held over a period of three days.

He detailed incredible cities, architecture and countryside, and the proceedings from the Conference. He also claimed that after his return to Earth, he went to Washington D.C. to deliver a message to a government official. It is a fact that he did go to Washington, and appeared on a couple of radio programs. As for the remainder of his 'Saturn adventure' – it does seem rather dubious!

Nearly everyone confirmed and believed in his reports in *'Flying Saucers Have Landed'*, but his later visits to other planets and attending Interplanetary Conferences did stretch his credibility. Desmond Leslie, although George's friend to the end, had some doubts; *"To assess the validity of his claims is still difficult. I am personally completely satisfied that his photos and early contacts are completely authentic, and will in time be proven by later events. Some of his claims take a lot of swallowing.'*

In 1962, Lucy McGinnis also parted company with George. She was quoted as saying; "The task for which we were brought together is now finished." We can only speculate as to the real cause of the split. He was so distraught he asked the Dickesons, in New Zealand, and others to write to her and insist it was her 'duty' to carry on the work.

The Dickesons said; "Dear Lucy, whom we all love and respect, and who, after all, gave seventeen years voluntary service. No, his accusations were certainly not in keeping with the work. This gave us an uneasy feeling that all was not well at Palomar, and we could not accept his statement, nor could we write to Lucy in the manner requested."

In 1979, Timothy Good interviewed Lucy McGinnis, who confirmed witnessing the meeting in the desert twenty-seven years earlier. In keeping with the gracious lady everybody considered her to be, she made the following comment; *"He wanted brotherhood – that was the depth of his philosophy. He was a very kindly man, but he had a tremendous ego, and anybody that ever listened to him knows that – it couldn't be hidden. But he was deeply sincere. I think he was picked out because he had the courage to go out and speak. There have been many others who have been picked out. But they've been afraid...."*

Eventually, along with other friends at Palomar Gardens, Rosemary Decker felt compelled to withdraw her support for Adamski, despite their long association. She confirmed the desert encounter, and his later meetings with the Space Brothers, but added: "Yes, he was contacted, although his ego was inflated beyond a safe point, and he subsequently suffered the consequences. He developed a great fear of undercover security agencies, and ignored the warnings and advice given by the Visitors. We were all concerned about his well-being, and grew very worried about his later ego trips and false claims, but he was not reachable by reason."

It must have been devastating for George Adamski when, in 1964, Lou Zinsstag also distanced herself from him and his remaining supporters. Lou had once seen UFOs in the sky, and she had an interesting discussion with Carl Jung, who was her Mother's cousin. Although he preferred to keep an open mind on the subject, in 1958 he told her about a close friend from the U.S.A. who was a high ranking army officer and a well known university professor. Jung believed his description of a personal, and most impressive sighting of a metallic UFO, which had lasted for more than half-an-hour.

Until 1964, Lou had always supported and defended George. She had a perfectly understandable counter-argument to Adamski's frustrating habit of evading certain questions, and changing the subject when pressed by followers and audiences. The Brothers did not want any knowledge of their advance technology being leaked to a planet heading towards-self destruction.

He had told her that he had entered an agreement with the visitors not to betray certain identities, information or technology. If he breached this stipulation he would immediately lose his connection with them.

Timothy Good may have stumbled on this very reason as being why Adamski, in later years, started making ridiculous and unbelievable claims. In 1963, Timothy's good friend, Joelle, became friends with a small group of people who were working with extraterrestrials on scientific matters. These people, who admitted to being 'visitors', were perfectly normal in appearance, and confirmed that they belonged to the same group Adamski was involved with. They said that once he began revealing sensitive details they started feeding him disinformation.

Alice Wells stayed faithful to the end, and in the years following Adamski's death, continued, along with Hans Petersen, promoted his work through 'The George Adamski Foundation'. Desmond Leslie said of her; *'Alice Wells was also an amazing lady. You never had to tell her or ask her anything. She knew. She'd pick up your thought and answer it in advance."* Alice passed away in 1980, and Fred Steckling took over her role in the 'Foundation'

George Adamski's reputation was also sullied by some of his followers, who started assuming the role of gurus, and making all kinds or pseudo religious and political claims and statements in the Space Brothers' name.

CA. Honey

George was lost without Lucy's help, and he announced that he was handing over the correspondence part of his work to C. Honey, as he planned moving to Mexico, and was going to concentrate on teaching.

This new arrangement didn't last for long. Many of Adamski's 'followers' disliked Honey's actions and pronouncements, and in 1963, accused him of 'trying to take over'.

After what was obviously an acrimonious parting of the ways with Honey, George Adamski had this to say; *'Yes, I accepted his offer to help me after my secretary left, but the space people that I work with were not in full accord with my choice. However, they allowed me to proceed as I did, but they placed him on probation. And they have been observing his actions, even though he did not know it.*

'I did make the statement that I was going into the field of teaching, and he would be my representative in the USA, but I have never made the statement that I would leave the space program. In fact I am more active in that now than ever before......Mr Honey now insinuates that I am under a hypnotic spell, and

not capable of handling my own affairs, so he appointed himself to save me and the program.'

George went on to complain that Honey was, without permission, advertising his, George's, copyrighted 'Telepathy' course as his own, for five dollars a month.

In another public letter to all his correspondents, he elaborated even further regarding the problems with Honey; *'Whether he had contact with the space people or not, I cannot say. But I definitely know that he has not had a contact with the group that I work with. For this group did not come here to cause trouble with our people and cause confusion among the workers. And the group he claims he is working with does these very things, as you can see.*

'I did not sanction 'The Origin of Religions' which G.A. Honey published in the Newsletter. The Space Brothers did not come here to impose a new religion upon us, or to change the one we may have. The publication was contrary to the Brothers' wishes. They came here to alert us to the changes in our system, as well as proving to us that we can travel in space, which we are undertaking to do.

'At present we are in a major transition stage, and I will be given information by the Space Brothers from time to time. They are the same ones I made contact with some eleven years ago, who have served the men of Earth so well....They have warned against other hostile space visitors who are confusing many people, either by impressions or direct contact. All space people are not benevolent.'

In 1964 a very disillusioned South Australian, Fred Stone, had this to say; *'Over the past eighteen months or more we have warned people not to place too much faith in George Adamski, as he was only human....We repeat that in our opinion George was given a task to do, and having fulfilled it, took unto himself more than was intended, and the build up of public acclaim was too much for the psychological background and fed his ego which he let run amuck. He has repeatedly contradicted himself, and turned about face in his loyalties.'*

Fred was also critical of George's growing friendship with Laura Mundo, a rather whacky American 'devotee', turned self-appointed and self-opinionated 'ufologist', who claimed to be preaching the Space Brothers' message. George had previously no kind words to say about her five years before, when he was in Australia. Fred thought that George was not being guided too well by his contacts.

In 1961, George sold his home at Palomar Mountain, and moved to Carlsbad on the Californian coast. He and Alice spent another Christmas with Maria Cristina de Rueda and friends in Mexico. Even then, there was no mention of Lucy being present, and Cristina mentioned that he and Alice would be most welcome as permanent residents in their community.

Maria had written an excited letter to her friends in 1960. George had spent Christmas of 1959 with her, and before he left she held a gathering at her home to show the movie pictures he had taken of flying saucers whilst in the country.

'During the exhibition of the movie, a person entered, who remained standing behind the others, and who went away as soon as the conference ended. I can only tell you what the others, among my husband, told me...they saw him from very near. They say he was a very white man, almost transparent, with very beautiful blue eyes and hair with threads of gold. Later, Mr. Adamski told me that it was Orthon, and that he had been in my home that night.'

In April 1962, Adamski announced his intention to leave California; *'I have just returned from Mexico where I spent the holidays. I looked at several places in the Guadalajara area that would lend themselves nicely to the continuation of the Brothers' work.'*

He had been considering this move for five years, and it was mainly prompted by further nuclear testing by the world's major powers, and the possibility of a major war. This, of course, never eventuated, and while he and his colleagues took several holidays in the Guadalajara area, he never made the proposed move.

On February 26th 1965, shortly before his death, George Adamski was staying with his close friend, Madeleine Rodeffer and her family, in Silver Springs, Maryland. (Madeleine had also reported having a series of encounters with aliens living in the Washington DC area. In a later interview with Timothy Good she confirmed that sometime in 1959/60 Adamski was taken to a military base in California to meet with Eisenhower.)

Madeleine and George, in the presence of other witnesses, took an 8mm colour movie, from her front yard, of a 'classic' craft making a series of manoeuvres in the sky. Madeleine claimed that, although they are not discernable on the footage, she could see some obscure human-like figures looking through the portholes. They all had cropped hair, and appeared to be aged in their twenties.

That film, which has rarely been in dispute, was authenticated by an optical physicist and other specialists at Kodak-Eastman. Madeleine later had a meeting with some members of the U.S. Senate Committee.

George Adamski, the Catholic Church and Meeting the Pope in Rome.

In 1963, Adamski made another trip to Europe. When in the UK, he caught up with Desmond Leslie, and met with Lord Dowding and Earl Mountbatten. He eventually made his way across the Continent to Italy.

It has always been a contentious assertion that Adamski had a private meeting with the Pope when he was in Rome. Lou Zinsstag, his Swiss colleague, detailed the incident in a letter she wrote in 1965. As George had passed away, she felt able to detail the events which occurred in his later trip to Rome during May/June 1963.

'I had accompanied George to Rome already in 1959, and I still remember his urgent wish to see the Pope, Pius, in a private interview. This aim, however, was not achieved in 1959. I was also afraid that, in 1963, George was going to be disappointed. He arrived in Basle with Mrs. May Morlet from Antwerp, and as his mind was firmly set on going to Rome, she and I agreed to share the expenses, and to let him try his luck again, this time with Pope John XXIII.

'George told me that he was pretty sure to be received, and that he was to hand a personal message to the Pope which he had received from the Brothers in Copenhagen a few weeks earlier. He also said that he was to be in front of St. Peter's Dome on Friday, 31st May, at 11 o'clock.

'We took him there in time. When we arrived at the stairway leading up to St. Peter's, George looked around and within a few seconds he said; "I can see the man, wait for me on the same spot in an hour's time."

'He swiftly walked away from us, through the crowd, towards the left side of the Dome's entrance. I had looked to my right, as I had expected him to be admitted through the gate where the Swiss Guards are posted. Yet George

walked to the left, where I noticed, for the first time, a wooden door, some hundred metres away from where we stood. The door was slightly ajar, and the figure of a man was standing beside it, apparently looking out for someone.

'........When an hour later we met George again, all doubts were due to vanish. His face was radiant with joy, and his brown eyes shone like two precious topazes. I shall never forget this.

"I have seen the Pope", he said slowly, but triumphantly with his deep voice. "He spoke to me, I gave him the message, and he gave me his blessing. So you see, after all, we have accomplished something. Our trip was not in vain."

'The interview had lasted only a few minutes, he told us, but afterwards he had spent a considerable time with the man who had received him. I asked him if he was a spaceman. He said; "Yes, I think so, at least I got the impression."

'He seemed to be a close associate of the Pope, a kind of grey eminence, he said, and he knew a lot of things. George also stated that the Pope was not lodged in the rooms indicated to the people in the press, facing St. Peter's Square, but that the bedroom windows went toward the Vatican gardens....George also added confidentially that he did not think the Pope was a dying man, and that very evening the Roman papers told about the good day the Pope had.

......'It was at lunch the next day when George suddenly took from his breast pocket a kind of plastic wallet, very small and with a most singular inscription beneath a transparent insertion. It was written with a pen in letters I had never seen. They were certainly not Roman, nor Gothic, nor were they Russian, Chinese, Japanese or Arabic. Beneath this inscription was the date of the interview, written with Roman block letters in English.

'When George opened this wallet we sat spellbound. A most beautiful golden medal, with the Pope's head on it, was embedded in the modest wallet. It looked like an ecumenical coin to me, or it might have been older. I took it in my hand, and was astonished at the weight of it. It was certainly pure gold, at least in 18 carat, if not 22. (Being a goldsmith's daughter, I know exactly what I'm talking about.) This coin would cost between 200 and 300 Swiss francs at least. George could certainly not have bought it. He never carried any money around and he did not even know the differences between the currencies, and he had never been in the streets without us.

'.......For the first time it dawned on me that George Adamski was a missionary of some kind, although he had never introduced me to his innermost secrets. It is not for me to judge if he was able to fulfil this mission completely, and if he kept to the standard set by his specific task until his very end. But I do know that he was expected, and received by John XXIII three days before the Pope died on Whit-Monday, June 3rd 1963. I am therefore inclined to believe that there were other important meetings, in other important buildings, as he had told me.'

In 2007, *'Nexus Magazine'* published an interesting article by Cristoforo Barbato, who interviewed a Jesuit priest in 2001. This priest claimed to be a member of the Vatican Intelligence Agency, the Servizio Informazioni del Vaticano, or SIV.

He said that the Nordic aliens were 'flesh and bone', and although they were highly evolved to a technological and spiritual point, they still had bodies. They professed to have discovered the Catholic Church, and the message of Christ, and offered to co-operate for the good of humanity.

This assertion convinced Pope Pius XII to collaborate with them in determining the character of international social and political situations. Pope John XXIII inherited this support, but always kept it secret, referring only to 'angelic intervention'. Pope Pius had already made an agreement for collaboration between the Nordic aliens and the Holy See, but Pope John had reservations about trusting these beings.

Barbato's Jesuit priest went to elaborate on Adamski's visit to the Vatican in 1963; *"Adamski really met the Pope. The assignment that the aliens commissioned to Adamski was to try to attain a final agreement with the Pope, who was dying. He went to St. Peter's just once to meet the Pope, who at that time had already decided that the Church ought not entertain any further direct contact with these aliens, even if they were positive. Furthermore, John XXIII found it unacceptable to reveal this relationship to the Christian populace."*

Barabato was told that the alien's 'gift' was a liquid substance designed to alleviate the illness which afflicted him. The Pope did not drink it, and before he died shortly after, made the following determination, which ended direct contact between these beings, and the Pope and his successors; *'The Space Brothers might surely conduct positive and benevolent activities toward humanity, but they should operate autonomously and distinctly from the*

Church, and, in general, from human activities, with prayer, actions according to the law of God and, in particular, under the direction of the Holy Spirit.'

Given the importance of Adamski's mission, and the religious politics of the time, one must note Adamski's joyful version of events when relating them later to Desmond Leslie. Further, both his parents, his brother and his wife Mary, had all been devout Catholics. Adamski may have drifted away from religion, however his days as an altar boy must have instilled a life-long reverence for the church and the Holy Father.

He said he didn't know what was in the sealed package, and upon receiving it the Pope's face lit up, and he said; "This is what I have been waiting for." Although George was not aware of the contents, he thought it contained instructions, advice and suggested agenda for a second Ecumenical Council, which may have provided input from the 'Space Brothers'. Some people have suggested that the 'Space Brothers' had already infiltrated the Catholic Church, and had a 'fifth column' in very high positions. We may never know the truth of this, or what was really in that sealed package, and the circumstances of the Pope's death a relatively few hours later.

The Jesuits and the Vatican have always been very active in the areas of scientific research, and their centuries old Pontifical Academy of Sciences has included some of the most famous scientists of the times. The Vatican Observatory, situated at the Pope's summer palace at Castel Gandolfo, also owns other large astronomical facilities and radio telescopes around the world, including one in Arizona.

In 1967 Jesuit priest and scientist, Segundo Benito, was an internationally recognised astronomer, and director of the Adhara Observatory, at San Miguel, Buenos Aires in Argentina, He had photographed several UFOs, and had this to say about extraterrestrial visitors; *'Unidentified Flying Objects do exist. They are craft manned by living beings from another world. These alien beings are currently studying the Earth and its inhabitants. Sooner or later they will establish formal contact with mankind.'*

He went on to conclude that God had created intelligent life throughout the Universe: *'In our galaxy alone, there are more than one million planets where life as we know it could be sustained and where rational beings could have developed fabulous civilisations – and remember, our galaxy is only one of millions in the Universe.'*

CHAPTER FIVE

ROSEMARY AND MILLEN

The two most influential UFO researchers/investigators in my life have been Rosemary Decker and Millen Le Poer Trench. I was privileged to call them close friends. Both were highly intelligent, but never sought the limelight and often worked quietly behind the scenes, contributing to many studies, and supporting others who had experienced troubling contact or abductions. They promoted the idea that aliens were present on this planet in ancient times, and that mankind is partly a result of alien genetic engineering and modification.

They also had a more secretive side, some of which I have only discovered in recent years. Both were in contact with humanoid 'Visitors' on Earth during the mid-twentieth century, and I suspect facilitated their activities here – spreading the message of mankind's need to improve its ways, and adopt safer technologies, before we destroy ourselves and this planet.

I don't believe it was by chance that Rosemary was present at Palomar when Adamski and his six colleagues returned from that famous desert encounter with Orthon. She witnessed, at the time, their excitement and testimony.

I was exceptionally fortunate, Rosemary stayed with me when visiting Australia, and we corresponded for nearly thirty years. She imparted so much information in the hundreds of letters I received.

Rosemary Decker
Rosemary was born in New York, into an old birthright Quaker family, on 9th June 1916. She was raised in Chicago, later moving to Oregon for a short time, and then to California for the rest of her life.

She was well educated and a gifted author and artist. Despite gaining a PhD she never used the title 'Doctor.' Rosemary devoted most of her life to being an educator, specialising in, and writing a book about, teaching children with learning disabilities. She also had strong spiritual values, and quietly performed much charity and social work.

Rosemary's family was technically minded, although they varied in their support of her UFO work. Some were fully on-board; others more sceptical, possibly due to the politics of their workplace and employers. One was an electrical engineer within a large corporation; another in the Navy in the District of Columbia, yet another, a physicist and university professor.

She rarely divulged her own experiences, and once commented; "I learned quite early in childhood to keep 'mum' about it, though I suspect my father had some experiences himself, and was equally quiet. He did recognise it, and in a kindly way warned me, when in my teens, against ever permitting myself to be exploited by the unscrupulous...Glad I heeded his counsel!"

She married, had two children and afterward became a divorced, solo parent. In her later life, some of her 'kin by marriage' confided they'd had close encounters of their own.

Rosemary and George Adamski
Rosemary enjoyed amateur astronomy, meeting like-minded enthusiasts and was a friend of George Adamski long before his famous meeting with Orthon in the desert in 1952. She took advantage of Adamski's access to larger-than-average telescopes to view the wonders of the night sky. Rosemary also pointed out, that in order to diminish Adamski, *'TIME'* magazine erroneously reported George as working at a 'hamburger stall'. This was not true; Adamski and his wife were temporary tenants who rented accommodation behind cafe premises owned and operated by Alice Wells at Palomar Gardens. Adamski's wife, Mary, was ill, and Alice helped nurse her until she died in 1954.

Throughout her life, Rosemary embraced the study of space and maintained a strong interest in UFO research. She was, for many years, a historian for the Mutual UFO Research Network (MUFON) and mentor and research assistant to many investigators, including myself. Her massive contribution to research on both Mars and ufology was quiet, and without the recognition she never sought, but richly deserved. As well as lecturing at many venues, Rosemary contributed articles for a multitude of publications. She spoke at many international conferences on a variety of subjects including *'The Early UFO Era/Contactee Phase'* – Rosemary told me she 'already had a good beginning for that!'

In 1956 President Eisenhower established a Citizen Ambassador Program to promote international goodwill and exchange of knowledge across a broad spectrum of disciplines; Non-political, non-religious and inter-racial. In March 1995, the Program sent out its first UFO Delegation. This entailed Crop Circle Studies, Parapsychology, ESP, and included telepathy and other areas of research related to UFO phenomena. Rosemary was one of the 'Delegation' of eighteen experts who visited Britain and Ireland under the directorship of Dr. Leo Sprinkle. Besides being a friend of George Adamski, Rosemary was also well acquainted with Dan Fry, Wilbur Smith, George Hunt Williamson and many other well known researchers. She quietly supported them from the background, never seeking publicity herself.

Rosemary passed away in January 2009.

Contacts

I asked about earlier years, but Rosemary was more reticent. She would neither confirm nor deny earlier contacts of her own, but commented; "I am so grateful that my experiences did not include seeing any of those little robot-type extraterrestrials. They seem to be manufactured rather than actual people. No wonder folks get frightened."

Another time she mentioned a Visitor who left for 'Home' in 1960 – his last words to her and a friend were: "And do take care of your body." In 1995, in another correspondence to a colleague she wrote; "Don't recall if I told you that the friend and mentor from 'Upstairs' suggested to me (on the phone, shortly before he left) that I might want to write a book on the Mars-Earth connection someday. (That was over 30 years ago! Plainly my time scale and his were a bit different. No wonder he said: 'Try to cultivate patience,' to Millen and me, just as he was about to leave.)"

Comments such as this confirmed my suspicions that Rosemary and Millen were liaising with the Visitors. She once wrote: "My contacts were such fine ETs, and our close cousins genetically." As Rosemary was a friend and colleague of Dan Fry (who admitted providing false identity documents for Visitors), I wonder about Rosemary and Millen's involvement with helping the Space Brothers access human society.

Rosemary made some interesting observations about them; "There is an order in their authority structure. Many of us who experience both human-like types and the small, large-headed humanoids, consider that the human-like people, although seen less often, seem to be in charge of the operations. In describing the human-like types, one has to keep in mind that they are more advanced than Earth-humans. Telepathy and ESP abilities in general are fully natural to them, and there are some physiological differences. Obviously, there is some genetic connection with *homo sapiens*, which is apparently a hybrid race, as our Bible and other early sacred books inform us."

During her extensive research into ancient history, Rosemary liaised with Zechariah Sitchin on several occasions. Rosemary admired Sitchin's extensive research into the historical, archaeological and linguistic evidence for his thesis that today's human is a hybrid race, developed by a technologically and genetically advanced human race from beyond this planet.

Rosemary, in addition to historical research, devoted many years to the study of holograms, crop circles and Mars – her specialities.

Rosemary combined her research into holograms with investigations into the ever-increasing cases of crop circles, not only in British fields, but around the world. She was convinced they were actually 3-dimensional, with cryptic mathematical equations and instructions.

The Moon and Mars
For about five hundred years there have been lunar lights and transient phenomena reported. Rosemary liaised with a lot of astronomers, engineers and geologists, (many ex-NASA scientists), regarding the anomalies on the Moon and Mars, and the possibility they were intelligently constructed. Many started by working on their own projects, and later became a 'Team of Independent Mars Researchers'. In 1994 Rosemary helped organise a small local conference-networking weekend for some of them. One interesting facet of the research was their insistence that there was vegetation, albeit sparse, at certain times on our rocky companion. Their findings were dismissed at the time, however we now know that there **is** water on our Moon.

Rosemary also reported that, "most of the experts agreed that we needed to gain 'real space flight' – not the clumsy, expensive and excessively dangerous rocketry currently employed. Instead of fighting gravity, hopefully it can be harnessed, as electro-magnetism has begun to be."

Her research into the Mars connection spanned over forty years, and in 2004 she published her book '*35 Minutes to Mars*'. She told me a 'visitor' had suggested the title – and I wondered if that it was how long it took them to get there!! Her research had taken decades, and liaison with many astronomers and other respected experts. In the *'Foreword'* she acknowledged the assistance of Manly Hall (*'The Lost Keys of Freemasonary'*), Lowell Observatory, Dr E. Slipher,

Richard Hoagland and many other respected authorities. She also spoke of the lunar anomalies detailed by Patrick Moore and Percy Wilkin, and discussed man's connection to the Cosmos and Galactic Man.

Working with Contactees

Rosemary claimed the Visitors had given her the following advice in the early 1950s: "Be an observer". As a result, she worked quietly behind the scenes, often counselling people who had been traumatised by their experiences. She actually assisted me in my work with two, Jane and Elizabeth, (see *'The Alien Gene'*), and also shared some of the cases she had been involved with, especially where more than one generation of the same family was involved. She did not permit me to publish them at the time, but many years have now passed. Due to their positions in society, the strict confidentiality regarding some witnesses still has to be maintained.

When Adamski began making more and more outlandish claims, some of his acquaintances in the local community were having their own contacts, and wisely decided not to speak out. Maybe this was a good thing, because I have no doubt at least one government 'spook' would have infiltrated the gatherings, at a very early stage. Many experiencers were carefully surveying the situation first, then quietly confided in only a few people, like Rosemary, whom they felt they could trust.

In one account, like many, she said the details came from the witness's memory and not through hypnosis, so there were some 'gaps'. In 1988, a US university professor and his son were travelling along a highway at dusk. They were forced off the road by an 'unseen force' and encountered about nine small humanoid figures nearby – some were examining their vehicle. They were just over four feet tall, with thin bodies and limbs, but comparatively large heads and slanted eyes. There was also a taller 'normal' humanoid who took them through to a spacecraft in a secluded clearing in the nearby woods.

"They were all communicating with us telepathically," the professor said, "but my next memory was of being in a brightly lit room, where an implant was placed in my right nostril and beyond. There was also an injection near my thyroid area, and another near my thymus gland. The taller friendly man guided us back to our vehicle where we drove back to the highway and resumed our journey home."

While his son suffered no after-effects, the professor has noted that sometimes marks come and go at the sites of the two injections. Health-wise his immune system has improved, and many signs of 'male aging' seem to have been reversed. He also has developed some psychic abilities.

We were once discussing some personality clashes in one of the research groups, where some had wanted to debunk all the witnesses as being delusional. Rosemary was always exceptionally secretive about her own contacts, but at that time made the following observations: "I have no doubt that most of the larger organisations are, to some degree, infiltrated by official agencies, incognito. There is certainly a fear that the facts could become known. For this reason, I do not share either my own or others' greater knowledge with any of them. On the few occasions when recording specific instances, I withhold names and sometimes reverse sexes as well. I have urged several lecturers to be much more cautious than they tend to be. I am very glad you have learned caution.

"Some people lack discretion, and quite a large number are merely toying with the UFO field, enjoying the mystery, and would be disappointed or even paranoid if they perceived clearly. It is a pity that they have to be so petty – but par for humanoids on planet Earth. Doubly sad, because the main reason for all these recent visitations is the world crisis the Earth-human has been creating, endangering air, water, earth and a myriad of life-forms, not to mention human beings themselves. Co-operation and tolerance are crucially important, as you have observed and experienced all too often."

In 1991 I asked Rosemary her opinion about the humanoid-aliens presence among us? She considered for a moment: – "The 'Big Picture' of this visitation era? The questions and the answers are so many; so of course, no-one has THE answer. There is still so much even the most assiduous of us haven't learned, no matter how many years we've applied to the field. One factor does predominate and seems to be plain beyond all doubt. There is a tremendous, over-all effort on the part of beings from other places/other grades of substance to **shake Earth humanity awake** at this time of world crisis unprecedented in known history."

Rosemary often glossed over, or didn't discuss, the implications of reversed alien technology being used for the wrong purposes. In 1989, she shared the following thoughts with me: "Taking this 'reality' seriously implies the requirement to accept responsibility and therefore DO something to improve conditions. You and I, and many others, have widened horizons, and used our individual skills as best we know how. My work with learning-disabled children for the past twenty-seven years is the main thrust of my contribution. Others are engaged in ecological reform, animal protection, holistic healing, anthropology, education and many other fields."

Rosemary never sought publicity. Her main aim was to educate and assist. She told contactees, who were anxious to change the world, but did not know where to begin, that they should work within their own community. Actions were like pebbles in a pond – the ripples spread far and wide.

I often wondered if Rosemary was really 'of this Earth'. She certainly had a regular human family like the rest of us, but she was small, just like the other women I discussed in *'The Alien Gene'*. Her energy levels and intelligence were so exceptional, was there some genetic enhancement in her heritage? She had connected with, assisted and changed so many people from all walks of life. Rosemary also had a beautiful soul, so pure and loving. I could never bring myself to tell her that 'love and peace' would not always solve our problems. The global situation has only worsened in the years since; sometimes we have to fight the evil before it takes over the world.

I have been enriched in so many ways by knowing Rosemary; her life was more influential both locally and internationally, than we will ever know. She once wrote an analysis of her 'overview': "The UFO scenario unfolds in an orderly, phase-to-phase progression. Undoubtedly this unfolding will continue as long as there is hope Earth's humanity will get a glimmer of its cosmic heritage, and take the necessary steps upward on the long ladder to its Liberation – <u>while there is still time</u>."

Millen Le Poer Trench
Rosemary's friend and colleague, Millen, was an important and integral part of Rosemary's life and research. After Millen's death in 1995, Rosemary said, "Now I can include her contributions to the field, including the fact that she was also a contactee. I always respected her request for anonymity, contact-wise, and her very quiet way of working largely behind the scenes. I can be more open now she has 'moved on'. I nearly always leave out my own personal contacts – I always have. I must stress though, despite our close contact and

involvement with the Visitors, neither Millen nor I have ever been abducted or ab-doctored."

Millen was born Wilma Dorothy Millen Vermilyes in Portland in 1915. Her grandmother was Italian and her grandfather a French-Afghani, who migrated to the US. She lived with them until the age of 12, when she returned to her parents' home. Her other grandfather was also Italian, and between the two of them, Millen had a good education in ancient civilisations and literature. In her early years she studied music, languages, mathematics and architecture at college in San Francisco, and later in life spent two years there at the Tibetan Institute. Rosemary once let it slip that Millen's godfather was a Visitor, hence her enhanced abilities and knowledge.

As early as 1930, when she alluded to her first contact, Millen studied the folklore, and historic and religious records of peoples as diverse as the Sumerians, Egyptians, Tibetans and Amerindians. This brought her to the conclusion that Earth had been visited for millennia by advanced peoples from elsewhere, both extraterrestrials, and beings from other realms and dimensions. She possessed much esoteric knowledge, and besides her UFO writings had worked with Kahil Gibrau, a relative of the Dalai Lama, and many others. She was highly intelligent, and at the age of 18, not only gained her private pilot's licence, but also played violin in the Portland Philharmonic Orchestra.

Millen's first two marriages, ended in divorce, and she was left to raise two daughters, born in the early 1950s. She supported them by writing numerous magazine articles on a large variety of subjects.

Millen often commented that visitations had begun to recur on a much-accelerated scale within her lifetime, as Earth humanity approached a learning crisis that may entail a survival crisis as well. Millen and Rosemary had family connections, and as neighbours, were 'the dearest of pals' for over fifty years. It is apparent from Rosemary's comments that Millen also had contact or an association with another 'Visitor', whom they both referred to as 'D' in their correspondence.

It became obvious that 'D' was integrated into our society. He was also connected to both families, but not actually in the traditional way. 'D' had also met and interacted with a couple of young university students, who become influential world leaders later on. (In 1991 Rosemary forwarded some reports to me, indicating that another man in Alabama may also be an integrated Visitor.)

Millen always wrote in a cryptic way. One comment to me was: "In my book, life, as we understand it, is molecular, and DNA is by no means the First Chapter." In 1959, she wrote to Rosemary regarding their mutual contact, and the first piece of advice 'D' ever gave her: "Take the face value of any statement. If other values bubble up out of your accumulated data, claim them as your own creation. Puzzling over 'hidden meanings' in this universe has caused a lot of people to miss the bus."

Millen and Rosemary were part of a team researching Brinsley le Poer Trench's 1960 classic, *'The Sky People'*, which introduced our ancient civilisations/legends and the Mars-Earth connection to UFO literature. Brinsley was later to become the Earl of Clancarty, and a member of the House of Lords. Millen married Brinsley and collaborated with him in writing a further three books. I once asked her if she minded him getting full credit for her work. She looked rather pensive, and commented that she didn't mind him getting the accolades, but he had altered what she had said and written.

They later divorced, and I got to know her after she migrated to Australia in 1976 to live with her two daughters. She was reluctant to fully reveal her life history, especially her UFO connections, although her daughters recall several visits to a woman at Joshua Tree in the late 1950s, to 'watch UFOs over the desert'. Millen always avoided the limelight, preferring to quietly assist and counsel others. In fact, she was highly intelligent author, who usually used a pen-name.

Perhaps one of her most 'telling' articles was one she submitted to editor Ray Palmer. He published it in April 1947 – three months before the controversial flying saucer crash at Roswell, and five years before Adamski's meeting in the desert.

The original article did not attract much publicity, or a large readership, however, in later years she persuaded Gordon Creighton to republish it, in the 1958 edition of *'Flying Saucer Review'*, and Brinsley included it in one of his books. What it says could have been written by the Space Brothers themselves. Using the pseudonym 'Alexander Blade', was she writing under their guidance?

Son of the Sun
by
Alexander Blade

We are already here among you. Some of us have always been here, with you, yet apart from, watching and occasionally guiding you whenever the opportunity arose. Now, however, our numbers have been increased in preparation for a further step to the development of your planet: a step of which you are not yet aware, although it has been hinted at frequently enough in the parables of your prophets, who have garbled whatever inspiration they have been able to receive. Sometimes they were ignorant. Sometimes they were unable to translate clearly the concepts implanted in their minds. Sometimes they were cautious, and to insure the preservation of the information they wished to place upon the record in the world, they spoke in metaphors and symbols.

We have been confused with the gods of many world religions, although we are not gods, but your own fellow creatures, as you will learn directly before many more years have passed. You will find records of our presence in the mysterious symbols of ancient Egypt, where we made ourselves known in order to accomplish certain ends. Our principal symbol appears in the religious art of your present civilisation and occupies a position of importance upon the great seal of your country. It has been preserved in certain secret societies founded originally to keep alive the knowledge of our existence and our intentions toward mankind.

We have left you certain landmarks, placed carefully in different parts of the globe, but most prominently in Egypt where we established our headquarters upon the occasion of our last overt, or as you would say, public appearance. At that time the foundations of your present civilisation were 'laid in the earth', and the most ancient of your known landmarks established by means that would appear as miraculous to you now as they did to the pre-Egyptians, so many thousands of years ago. Since that time, the whole art of building in stone has become symbolic, to many of you, of the work in hand – the building of the human race towards its perfection.

Your ancestors knew us in those days as preceptors and as friends. Now, through your own efforts, you have almost reached, in your majority, a new step on the long ladder of your liberation. You have been constantly aided by our watchful 'inspiration', and hindered only by the difficulties natural to the processes of physical and moral development, for the so-called 'forces of evil and darkness' have always been recruited from among the ranks of your own humanity – a circumstance for which you would be exceedingly grateful if you possessed full knowledge of conditions in the universe.

You have lately achieved the means of destroying yourselves. Do not be hasty in your self-congratulation. Yours is not the first civilisation to have achieved – and used – such means. Yours will not be the first civilisation to be offered the means of preventing that destruction and proceeding, in the full glory of its accumulated knowledge, to establish an era of enlightenment upon the Earth.

However, if you do accept the means offered you, and if you do establish such a 'millenium' upon the basis of your present accomplishments, yours will be the first civilisation to do so. Always, before, the knowledge, the techniques, the instructions, have become the possessions of a chosen few: a few chose themselves by their own open-minded and clear-sighted realisation of the 'shapes of things to come'.

They endeavoured to pass on their knowledge in the best possible form, and by the most enduring means at their command. In a sense they succeeded, but in another sense their failure equalled their success. Human acceptance is, to a very large extent, measurable by human experience. Succeeding generations who never knew our actual presence, translated the teachings of their elders in the terms of their own experience. For instance, a cross-sectional drawing, much simplified and stylised by many copyings, of one of our travelling machines became the 'Eye of Horus', and then other eyes of other Gods. Finally, the ancient symbol that was once an accurate representation of an important mechanical device has been given connotations by the modern priesthood of psychology.

The important fact is, however, that we are here, among you, and that you, as a world-race will know it before much longer! The time is almost ripe but, as with ripening things, the process may not be hurried artificially without danger of damaging the fruit. There is a right time for every action, and the right time for our revelation of ourselves to your era is approaching.

Some of you have seen our 'advance guard' already. You have met us often in the streets of your cities, and you have not noticed us. But when we flash through your skies in the ancient traditional vehicles you are amazed, and those of you who open your mouths, and tell of what you have seen, are accounted dupes and fools. Actually, you are prophets, seers in the true sense of the word. You in Kansas and Oklahoma, you in Oregon and in California and Idaho, you know what you have seen. Do not be dismayed by meteorologists. Their business is the weather. One of you says; "I saw a torpedo-shaped object." Others report 'disc-like objects', some of you say 'spherical objects' or 'platter-like objects'. You are all reporting correctly and accurately what you saw, and in most cases you are describing the same sort of vehicle.

The 'golden-disc' – now confused with the solar disc and made part and parcel of religion – even in your own times. The 'discus' hurled sunward by the Grecian and your own athletes. The 'Eye of Horus' and the other eyes of symbology, alchemical and otherwise, these are our mechanical means of transport.

Now that the art of manufacturing plastic materials has reached a certain perfection among you, perhaps you can imagine a material, almost transparent to the rays of visible light, yet strong enough to endure the stresses of extremely rapid flight. Look again at the great nebulae, and think of the construction of your own galaxy, and behold the universal examples of what we have found to be the perfect shape for an object which is to travel through what you still fondly refer as 'empty' space.

In the centre of the discus, gyroscopically controlled within a central sphere of the same transparent material, our control rooms revolve freely, accommodating themselves and us to flat or edgewise flight. Both methods are suited to your atmosphere, and when we convert abruptly from one to the other, as we are sometimes obliged to do, and you are watching, our machines seem suddenly to appear or disappear. At our possible speeds your eyes, untrained and unprepared for the manoeuvre, do make mistakes – but not the mistakes your scientists so often accuse them of making.

We pass over your hilltops in horizontal flight. You see and report a torpedo shaped object. We pass over, in formation, flying vertically – 'edge-on' – and you report a series of 'disc-shaped', 'platter-like' objects, or perhaps a sphere. Or we go over at night, jet-slits glowing, and you see an orange disc. In any event you see us, and in any event we do not care. If we chose to remain invisible, we could do so, easily, and in fact we have done so, almost without exception, for hundreds of years. But you must become accustomed to our shapes in your skies, for one day they will become familiar, friendly and reassuring sights.

This time, it is to be hoped that the memory of them, passed on to your children, will be clear and precise. That you will not cause them to forget, as your ancestors forgot, the meaning of the diagrams and the instructions we will leave with you. If you do fail, as other civilisations have failed, we will see your descendants wearing wiring-diagrams for simple machines as amulets, expecting the diagrams to do what their forefathers were taught the completed article would accomplish. Then their children, forgetting even that much – or little – would preserve the amulet as a general protective device – or as an intellectual curiosity – or perhaps a religious symbol. Such is the cycle of forgetfulness!

Millen passed on so much knowledge to Brinsley le Poer Trench who died on May 18th 1995, just a couple of days before she also passed away. Gordon Creighton wrote a moving tribute to Brinsley and his contribution to UFO research, especially when he entered the House of Lords, establishing a House of Lords UFO Study Group, and placing the *'Flying Saucer Review'* into the parliamentary libraries. However, Gordon lamented that after he and Millen separated, Brinsley later subscribed to the 'Holes in the Poles' theory and supported the 'exploits of the ridiculous 'Tibetan Lama' Lobsang Rampa.'

It is only since their deaths I have realised how exceptionally knowledgeable Rosemary and Millen were, not only about benign human-type Visitors, but the more insidious Greys, other extraterrestrials, and their motives and agendas. They had both obviously worked quietly with some very influential people regarding the covert and undesirable activities of other entities, but never discussed that aspect with me. It was as if they interacted with each person on an individual 'need to know' basis.

Recently I have been asking myself just *how connected* both these friends of mine were to the Visitors? I have been able to learn that they had both had personal contacts before 1952. They had been in contact with Adamski and others since the 1940s, and also knew in advance of his meeting in the desert with Orthon, but chose to stay back at Mt.Palomar – why? Was Adamski the 'chosen one' to pass on messages?

I often wonder about what they knew, as both had extensive collections of early UFO material. After her death, Millen's material was passed on to Rosemary for safekeeping and further research. Rosemary told me that a considerable amount of Millen's writing remained unpublished, as she felt some of it was premature. We will never know their hidden secrets. A few years later, Rosemary's home burned down in California's forest fires, and everything was lost!

CHAPTER SIX

FRED and PHYLLIS DICKESON

Fred and Phyllis Dickeson, from New Zealand, spent many years investigating the UFO mystery. Fred's introduction to aircraft began at an early age. During the 1930s, his secondary school days, he attended Wellington College, and lived with his grandmother and uncle, Group Captain T.M. Wilkes, who was the Commanding Officer of the N.Z. Permanent Air Force. When the Air Board was formed, and the N.Z.P.A.F. became the Royal New Zealand Air Force, he was appointed to the position of Controller of Civil Aviation in New Zealand.

Fred and Phyllis Dickeson met and married when they were both photographers for the New Zealand Air Force during World War II. After the war, they continued working as professionals in the photography field.

The Dickesons always had an interest in ham radios. In fact they belonged to a local club, and were connected with other radio operators worldwide, long before their affiliation with George Adamski. Strangely enough, although there was a lot of correspondence between them regarding equipment and devising new gadgets, very little, if anything was mentioned regarding messages sent and received. I paid scant regard to this aspect of their lives until I read about the ham radio operators, around the world, communicating with their 'friends in space' in the 1950s. Certainly the Dickesons' correspondence and articles made no mention of this.

Perhaps part of the circumstances surrounding the Dickesons' interaction with George Adamski and Mr X can best be illustrated by a letter that they sent to a colleague several years later.

'Up to 1954 we knew nothing about flying saucers. We had never heard of them, but in June of that year we read a book – 'Flying Saucers Have Landed' – by Desmond Leslie and George Adamski. Fascinated by the possibility of being visited by people from space, and as we thought this to be the most momentous news in present day history, we wrote to Adamski for further information.

'Eventually we received a reply and statement that he had travelled into outer-space as far as our Moon. While on a space trip he claimed he had been informed by crewmen, (Venusians, Martians and Saturians) that there was air and water on the moon. There also supposedly existed, on the other side,

communities of people like us, forests, lakes and mountains covered with snow. At the time we and many others accepted his story as true – after all, he had been there – and who were we, to doubt his word?

'Over the following years to 1959, a correspondence was set up between us and tapes were exchanged. These were played to various meetings and groups throughout New Zealand and Australia. Later, we suggested to him that people could be chosen in countries throughout the world to help answer his mail more efficiently. He received hundreds of letters each month from people all over the earth wanting to know more about his exploits, and so the 'Adamski Correspondence Group' was born.

'In 1959, various groups sponsored Adamski on a world-wide lecture tour. The Henderson group, which had recently been formed, organised the North, and we the South. Adamski arrived – Auckland in January and Christchurch in February. After packed lectures throughout New Zealand, he left for Australia and Europe. Before leaving he promised to keep us posted with the latest news for our newsletters, but each month we received very little information from him. After he left, our Groups and Newsletters were renamed – 'The New Zealand Scientific Space Research Group'.

'We were not over-impressed with Adamski after personally meeting him. There were too many points we felt did not add up. There were too many questions left unanswered, yet strangely enough, when outsiders doubted him we would spring to his defence.

'Unfortunately, many groups have become deluded with their own interpretations, thus making a mockery of the subject. Others are static in-so-much that they are still trying to prove to everyone that these space craft exist. This is a waste of time! There is ample proof already available to accept the reality of their existence, without further questioning.

'The important point, so many overlook in this study is – THEY are HERE – but WHY? Are they here to warn us or help? Whatever it may be, then how can we, in our limited capacity, help them to carry out their mission?

'Incredible as it may seem, in September 1960, a local Timaru man was contacted personally by two Space Men. He was warned to 'tell no man' his name for his own protection – this has proved very wise in more ways than one! At this time we and our contactee were sceptical, someone could be hoaxing us.

They also conveyed to him information which was contrary to that given by Adamski over the previous years, especially when they said there was no air or water on the moon, and that the other side was little different from the side facing the earth. They also stated that they did not take earthlings for rides into the Creator's heavens.

'This was a bombshell! Who was telling the truth – Adamski or the 'Two Friends' as we now know them? With Adamski now being questioned we had the task of proving him correct, but alas, to our consternation, only the reverse was evident!

'After extensively analysing photographs reputedly taken by Adamski and published in his second book – 'Inside the Space Ships' – we were able to prove conclusively that certain photos were definite fakes. To analyse these, we used techniques we learnt in aerial survey work during World War II when with the RNZAF Photographic Section. The photos 'in space' of Adamski and crewman looking through the portholes of a 'small mothership' were calculated by us to have been taken by flashlight of a C124 Globemaster, by a third person, possibly standing on the wing, by a distance between 29ft. to 41ft., (depending on the Polaroid Camera model used at that time). Enquiries from the American manufacturers revealed only three models were made at that date.

'We openly challenged Adamski to refute our findings, and consequently became spurned by all the Adamski fans the world over. Our North Island counterpart at Henderson declared their allegiance and said they would continue to uphold Adamski in every way.

'In searching for the truth, we feel when discrepancies are found in this study, it is our duty to all researchers to reveal the true findings. Facts must be faced. To be scientific all the facts must be considered. One cannot pick and choose which fact he will accept and disregard others. This practice would be unscientific.

'Consequently we broke away and renamed our organisation 'The NZ Scientific Approach to Cosmic Understanding'. There is far more behind this story than we can reveal in the limited space available. Only a few of the many incidents can be given, but it will give the readers a small insight into what is now taking place.

'After Adamski's exposé we were completely on our own, a very lonely road, but as satellites eventually went around the moon and probed further into space, the advance information we had received through our contact was proving correct, not only space data but warnings on pending world crises have been foretold and eventually proved alarmingly accurate;-

'On August 20th 1961, we were warned about Atomic Bomb explosions. Much to the world's astonishment and dismay, twelve days later on September 1st 1961, Russia began detonating giant atomic weapons in the atmosphere. Newspapers and Nations everywhere expressed great surprise and alarm in their protests.

'Again, on May 23rd 1967, another warning was received wherein they stated that; 'Your world is on the brink of the most bloody and devastating war of all time,......etc. We immediately notified all overseas group leaders and correspondents by airmail, then on June 5th 1967, the Six Day war broke out between Israel and the Arabs. (Apparently this was only a 'curtain-raiser'). Later we learned that a spacecraft was photographed watching the battle. This was seen on T.V. but no comment was made at the time.

'The latest American success – landing and walking on the moon, proves a number of points. There is no air nor water on the moon! Adamski is wrong! Martians, Venusians and Saturnians don't exist! There is no one living on any of our neighbouring planets. In fact, it is as our Space Friends have told us – Earth is the only planet in our Solar System which supports life as we know it.

'Unfortunately there will be a number of die-hards still insisting that Mars and Venus are inhabited, but we would like to make it quite clear that our Space Friends are from outside our Solar System.

'Briefly, and according to what we have been told – including our fifteen years' study on the subject – our conclusions are that these beings are more likely to be the descendants of the 'Biblical Angels' who, in the past came in days of earthly tribulations to help. They are here today. If we could only heed their warnings, how different our world would be.

'If Damascus is destroyed, their prophecy will be fulfilled. Furthermore, if this does eventuate, then we can be rest assured that help shall come from them. Shortly, say our visitors, scientists will have all the proof they need that space craft exist.

'Would it not be more practicable and wiser for us to welcome these visitors as our guardians? Is it not what they are? Are Christians, in these days of degradation, truly heeding the signs which are before their eyes, or are they so blind that they cannot comprehend the truth when confronted by it?'

'F. Dickeson – P. Dickeson'

Over the following years their views altered and matured as they gained even more knowledge, and continued with serious scientific investigations. In the meantime, their son, my colleague Bryan Dickeson, who had only been a young lad when Adamski toured New Zealand, went on to gain a science degree during his university days. He supported and assisted his parents with their investigations and search for the truth. After moving to Australia in the 1980s, he later became an active member of *'The Independent Network of UFO Researchers'* and co-founded *'UFO Research NSW'*.

CHAPTER SEVEN

Mr. X

Up until his visit in 1959, the Dickesons and their group had faith in George Adamski, whose messages they passed on. Following their subsequent disillusionment, the Space Brothers' words and advice were no longer being publicised in the South Island of New Zealand. By 1964, the leaders of the Adamski Groups in South Africa, Switzerland, France and England would no longer act as his representatives. Perhaps the visitors needed new emissaries who would relay the exact information given, without colouring it with their own beliefs and ideas. 'Mr. X' is only one of several similar cases around the world.

In August 1960, a middle-aged colleague of Fred and Phyllis Dickeson saw a 'sparkling object' in the sky to the north of Timaru. Looking closer he noticed that 'sparks' were coming from a dark cylindrical object, which he observed for about five minutes before the sparks stopped, and the craft faded from view. He was initially a little sceptical regarding the existence of 'flying saucers and aliens', and told no-one except his wife about what he had seen.

Everything changed when, late at night, he received visits from two strangers– firstly a man and then, a few days later, a woman – both claimed to be extraterrestrial visitors.

One reason was that they needed to get the messages from a 'Higher Intelligence', out to the peoples of Earth. They said; "George Adamski is getting on in age, and we cannot expect him to stay with us forever."

They needed someone who understood, and was 'in tune' with nature and the world around them, to be able to communicate and take over the work which was needed to be done. Further, as witnessed by my colleagues Rosemary Decker and Millen le Poer Trench, they were not happy that George Adamski had been making false claims about going for rides in a spaceship to other planets in the Solar System. They said they don't take humans to Jupiter or Saturn, both of which are surrounded by poisonous gases.

They were not from our Solar System, and while they didn't specify how long they intended staying on Earth, they would be seen in greater numbers in the sky from the beginning of 1962 to the end of 1964.

He told the Dicksons about this visit, and how he would give them any information he received, however he needed anonymity, and wished to be known as 'Mr. X'.

(Perhaps George Adamski himself held part of the reason for the Space Brothers seeking out a new method and representative for their messages. Lou Zinsstag in Switzerland provided some of the answer when she wrote about how, in 1962, near the end of his life, she asked George about his space colleagues; *'I received a most disturbing answer to my question about 'the boys'. I asked George if they were still around and working with him. "Oh, no," he said. "There is now a new set of 'boys' here. They came to replace the others. I have been told, and I have not yet been informed what they are up to, but I shall certainly be, sooner or later."* It is obvious that they intended to proceed in an entirely different manner to their predecessors.)

On 19th September, there was a knock on Mr. X's door at 10.30pm. Outside were two well dressed strangers – one was about thirty years old and the other fifty or so. The older one did the talking.

He said "Good evening Mr........" and went on to say how pleased they were to have attracted his attention the other night. They had called to assure him that they would contact him later. They also said that they had tried to attract his attention several times before, but failed to do so.

As a joke, Mr. X said to them; "You wouldn't be Space People would you?"

There was no reply, but they smiled broadly at each other. Mr. X then asked them if they knew a certain Mr........, they answered they did, but that it was not necessary to see him because he did not need to be convinced. Mr. X then said; "You wouldn't be having me on, would you?" To this their expressions changed completely to ones of perplexity.

Mr. X then invited them inside. They refused, saying they had an important appointment to keep in a country district. They assured Mr. X that he would be hearing again from them shortly, said goodnight, and departed.

While they were with him he had no fear. They were ordinary well-spoken human beings – more like old friends. Later he became agitated, thinking he may have dreamt the whole meeting. He also wanted to know why they should pick on him, as he had always been a sceptic, and did not believe all he had read about UFOs. He said that he just would not accept it until he had further proof. Proof that he could touch or hold in his hands.

On 24th September, Mr. X found one note under his door, confirming their visit. It answered a number of questions which Mr. X had pondered over but had never spoken to a living soul. Mr. X was confused, and still not fully convinced. He showed the letter to the Dickesons, who photographed it. (Something they continued to do from then onwards.)

The September communication read as follows; *'Mr...... – We write this on material which is hurriedly available to us. It is because of your stand in not accepting every thought blown about by the winds of wishful thinking, that we have decided to treat you as trustworthy. To men in your own circle of friends you have been thought to be luke-warm in your belief re certain things.*

'You have not grabbed at every story concerning us. Indeed, it is because of this that we have approached you after a long period of observation. We now have every faith in your ability to use wisely these powers of discernment and discretion.

'We ask you not to become afraid because you suddenly find yourself in a position quite new to you. As promised, we shall see you again, and if further progress is made, your reward in this life will be made a real one in which very few have so far participated. In kindness to you, we have not told you who we are, because if we had, we would have broken your faith, since when things are a known certainty, there is no longer a need to have faith in them.

'We cannot openly reveal ourselves because of hostile surroundings, and we request that you do likewise, and that is why we say – "tell no man". Other things will be revealed to you according to your progress. Time is now fast running-out and our responsibilities become heavier as the focal point is reached.

'P.S. We leave the use of this epistle safely to your own discretion, and which we personally delivered at your address by a friend of ours. Lastly, it is not what you thought, but is the power of levitation, which is as old as time itself. This is your answer to the question which has bothered you for some time, and that distance and time have no relation to us.

'No. we caused it to miss by over 1,000 miles. It was from a Godless nation, and that ground is Holy. It is now in a part of space, where we can deal with it at our leisure. Yes, that nation will be supreme for a short time.'

This was the answer to a question about something Mr. X had often pondered over, but had never actually spoken of to any living soul. The Dickesons immediately relayed the contents of the letter to George Adamski, who did not seem very enthusiastic about the turn of events.

When he got up, on the morning of 8th October, Mr. X found a note he had written earlier on a notepad on the table. It was in his own handwriting, and not that of the letter under his door.

'Date; 8th October 1960 – Time; 4am woke – couldn't sleep – made a cup of tea then took a walk to the front gate – 4.45am The eastern sky was showing a little lightness – breaking day. On the one side of the street two men – same as before were waiting. We had no sooner seen one another when they greeted me with;

"Good morning Mr..........., we are sorry to have disturbed your early morning slumber, causing you to come out at such an early hour."

'They then came across to my side of the street, shook hands and said that it is most important for me to try harder to project my thoughts outward as it could save them personal contact with me, which takes up much time and is dangerous to them.

'They said that I was receiving them faintly, but that they were still unable to receive me at all. If I would cultivate the art of thought transference, they would be able to give me directions on important matters....

'That's all that happened. They again shook hands and departed, walking fairly briskly away.'

In November, the Dickesons agreed to publish the messages to their Group Leaders and Overseas Co-workers. Because they had always regarded Mr. X as a 'respected, level-headed, difficult to convince and very sceptical older man', they asked him to submit a covering, explanatory letter, which they included in their next Newsletter;

'6th November 1960

'I have certain friends here in N.Z. where I live, who have requested me to write about my attitude re space ships prior to recent happenings at my home.

'I have never fully believed in such things, but now I am not so sure. These friends know what happened because I told them everything. There is no need to relate it here. Sooner or later it will all be revealed, so until then I shall merely be known as 'Mr. X' for my own protection

'I shall go further and say that I am now fully convinced that I was visited by two people from outside this world of ours. The facts of the occurrence have been proved because of a letter I received from my two visitors. This was put under my door while I was away from home for about two hours, and which I found on my return.

'The letter is not the only occurrence – other things have happened which put it beyond all fiction. Ridicule is what I am afraid of. This is the last thing I want, so you can understand why I will not publicise my name. It matters little to me whether I am believed or not as I do not want publicity, but I shall continue to work quietly if such be my destiny.

'I now have perfect faith in the two friends who paid that visit. While in their company I felt at perfect peace and had a feeling of wonderful satisfaction. I have never had such a feeling like that before on meeting with strangers. This and other things which happened puts it beyond all doubt that I have had a privilege which makes me feel proud.

'I am not a man who can be bothered with fiction and do not read such stuff, so I can assure you that you can believe all I have said. I now admit that I feel most humble, and yet a little guilty because I previously did not believe in such things. I remain,

>   *'Yours in truth,'*
>   *'Mr. X'*

Mr. X retained his anonymity for the rest of his life, and only the Dickesons and a couple of close friends knew his real identity.

The Dickensons had already become cautiously enthusiastic, and wrote, in a private letter to one of their colleagues '...*Remember I endeavoured to stress to* *everyone present at the meeting that we must all realise the fact that the Space People **are** living among us!!! To see a flying saucer and to watch people coming out is not an indication that they are the only ones on Earth. NO – they **are** living among us. This is a most important point we must all accept.*

'In the past we have accepted George Adamski's word on this point, and some have doubted what he has said. It is therefore time we had some outsider in this, or other nations, to be visited and so confirm what Adamski has said. We need a lot more like him in the world. At this stage we are very pleased to say that this wish of many is now being realised.'

On 14th November, Mr. X rang the Dickensons to say the 'Brothers' had left another message in his mailbox. They said this would be the way they would be contacting him in the future. ...*'We will not mention you by name – this is for your own safety. Likely your first note from us is in trusty hands. Otherwise you would have a grave risk, and we do not wish to put you in such a position. We left that note to your own discretion, but we think that you can do more good in a quiet way.*

'We know you will receive this note safely from your own box. We have a reason for working in this way, so we thought that it would be better to advise you. Please tell your trustworthy friend to continue in his good work, and not to become too inpatient when things seem hopeless. There is much ahead still to be done, and you will have much to overcome, for many will not believe, even as in the days of old.' If their plans changed, or anything important came up, they would contact him personally.

Mr. X said there didn't seem to be much they didn't know about, including his own thoughts! They had told him to tell the Dickesons to carry on the good work, and there was also a secret code in the letters, so they would know that they were genuine.

On 8th December 1960, Mr. X received a letter from his 'two friends' wishing him a happy birthday. He was surprised as, until his wife reminded him, he had even forgotten it himself. The note not only gave his actual date of birth but included the comment – *'We knew then what is now your role. In between the beginning of the year 1962 and the end of 1964, we shall be seen in many parts by only those who are alert, and even they must be especially observant. Yes, we would land in numbers if that were possible.'*

By this time Mr. X and the Dickesons were convinced that these were Space Visitors, and it only stood to reason that there were probably many more living among us on Earth.

On 4th July 1961, this rather cryptic message was in the letter box; *'Mr. X (as you are at present known). You have wondered why we have not contacted you. We have been delayed by many things. But here is our most important message to you so far. Telepathy, or what we term 'an exchange of mental ideas', can be arranged quite simply by concerted effort. Where one individual fails, many can achieve sure results. So we give you fresh instructions, that you ask all groups throughout the world to make a definite time – GMT.*

'Let them be agreed on a definite time, and let them direct their thoughts to us, seeking advice at that hour. We shall be prepared and ready to answer all questions for the good of the world in general. Let all delegate one individual to receive our instructions and we shall give him our advice about which the leaders of all nations must be told.

'If our advice is ignored, then we can do no more than rescue all who are found worthy, and leave the others to the fate which they themselves have chosen. We are Your Two Friends'

Having some experience with telepathy, the Dickensons advised all their colleagues, both in New Zealand and overseas about this suggestion, and some agreed to participate in an experiment, using one only sane and sensible person in each group to act as a 'receiver' at twelve noon, Greenwich Meantime. There were to be no trances or controlled mediums involved. They felt this method of contact, if successful, would make the visitors' task less dangerous than delivering letters.

A few weeks later, on both 23rd July and just after midnight on 20th August, Mr. X received the same message. It is worth noting that, at about the same time, George Adamski claimed receiving a similar message.

'Since atoms are the material out of which the Creator builds all things, and that man should use this same thing to destroy his handiwork, thereby throwing back into the Creator's face this same material, then Nations found guilty of so doing shall surely perish by the same means.

Hold this message until we instruct you further. God bless you.'

Immediately after receipt of this message Russia resumed nuclear atmospheric testing. On the night of 5th September, Mrs. X found the following note in their letterbox.

'We know that the test has failed. And that no more can be done along those lines. For nations now know the consequence which they themselves have admitted. We can do no more! But we shall advise you of our plans from time to time.

'You must expect disbelief and opposition from those who have no faith. Wisdom may yet prevail among the nations. There is much sadness among us because the innocent will suffer along with the guilty, yet help shall come in an unexpected form if necessary – so fear not.

'Seven ships were met during the test, and departed on their various ways immediately after the test was over. It was the first meeting of its kind ever to take place. We cannot do the impossible and sweep away the Will of the Creator, being human, just like you are, but we can help those who are willing.

'You may publish or make known this message if you care, it matters little now.'

'We are your two friends'

The Dickesons began to regard the messages as authentic, and noted that the Space Brothers' warning on 20th August came ten days before the Russians commenced the greatest series of atmospheric testing the world had ever known.

Around this time, some self-appointed 'gurus' – dabbling in ufology – had been insisting that world affairs were linked to an alignment of the planets.

Another letter arrived on 7th December; *'Events in your world are in no way connected with the alignment of the planets, nor are they able to affect events in any way. We tell you this to stop any fears you may have.*

'Nothing will happen because of that, and there is no life on Jupiter or Saturn. Your Earth is the most favoured planet of them all. Perhaps when we have more time, we shall give you the reasons for this. Saturn is completely enveloped in dense clouds of gas from its many volcanoes. The red spot which is sometimes seen is the glow from some of these, which is so fierce that it can

be seen even through the clouds which surround it. Sometimes these volcanoes have less active periods when the red spot cannot be seen.

'Nothing can live there! We cannot even land there, we know from samples of material we have obtained by remote control. One breath of the atmosphere would kill any living thing. We are pleased that the truth is being made known.'

'God Bless you; - Your two friends'

This information was starting to contradict what George Adamski had been saying, and it was followed up a month later, on 9th January 1962, when a further note was received;

'Conditions on other planets are quite unsuitable to human life, and we now make this quite clear. On Pluto it is quite impossible. We have seen all your planets at close range and can assure you that what we have revealed to you is correct.

'Even to try and make Mars a habitation would be almost impossible as that planet is composed almost all of very hard red-tinted rock. Its water, from its snow caps at the poles, runs in streams across the surface, and cannot sink in. A little vegetation grows along these streams but soon withers as the water evaporates from the rock surfaces. It has a thinner atmosphere than your Earth, and cannot hold clouds like your atmosphere – so no rain falls except as a deposit of snow at its poles, which again completes the same cycle.

'We mentioned the red spot on Jupiter, but this is very spasmodic, depending on volcanic activity, and is unpredictable. We do not know all things, as you are apt to think, and we make mistakes, as do you. We die as you do, but our life-span is much longer.

'We are keeping our promise to you by revealing knowledge to you, a little at a time, as we are too busy except to snatch a few moments to give you this knowledge from time to time - Your two friends.'

The next message, received on 15th February 1962, was more to the point. Although it did not mention George Adamski, one can but wonder.

'We are watching events with considerable interest as earthlings put projectiles into space, and we keep a check on all, allowing some and stopping the effect of others.

'Many who started out well and worked according to our plan have fallen by the wayside. They have worked by their own plans and do no longer convey the truth to your world, but make fictions instead. It is for this reason that we turn to you, hoping that you will continue to proceed according to our plan, which we are sure that you will.

'You are extremely fortunate that your friend is in a position to make known our messages as you receive them. We too are fortunate that he is on the side of Truth. - Truth, in the past, has been tampered with to make it sound more mysterious. We again stress the point that we are not exhibitionists. We do not do or say many of the things which are said of us. Do not expect from us the impossible, because many statements of us are quite impossible, even for us to carry out. As we have said, we are just human like you.'

'God bless you - Your two friends'

In mid-1962, Mr. X, the Dickesons and their group began to understand, more fully, why their 'two friends' were so worried about our nuclear testing and the subsequent radio-active fallout.

The Americans said that the purpose of their proposed test was to determine the effects of a high altitude hydrogen bomb explosion on radio and radar communications. Scientists wanted to know if such a blast might furnish a defence screen against electronically guided intercontinental ballistic missiles.

On June 20th, the US attempted to test a high altitude bomb over Johnston Island, 4,000 miles to the north of New Zealand. It was not successful, as the Thor intermediate missile, used to rocket the nuclear package aloft, mysteriously failed.

In July they were successful. An 'aurora' started as an intense glow above the northern horizon and spread rapidly across the sky to the southern horizon. It was seen from all over the country. Severe distortions were recorded on both radio and TV.

Dr. Robertson from the Geophysics Division of the Department of Science said; "There's no doubt it was produced by the bomb. The aurora was very similar to that seen in Samoa in 1958, when similar tests were carried out."

No wonder the Space Brothers were concerned. Previously, a plan, in the 1950s, to detonate a nuclear bomb on the Moon, was thankfully never realised. It was top secret, and would never have been known, however Carl Sagan was part of the team researching the hypothetical explosion. He inadvertently presented some of the results when applying for an academic fellowship.

On 8th December 1962, Mr. X found the following note in his letterbox; *'We have not forgotten you. God bless you and all connected to you – not only today but every day. Your two friends.'*

A couple of weeks later, on 20th December, Mr. and Mrs. X were down at Caroline Bay, in Timaru, at about 3.30pm one afternoon. A very distinctive man approached and began talking to them. He looked to be about fifty years old, 5'8" tall and proportionately built. He had brown, brushed back hair, a high forehead and small moustache. He really stood out from the rest of the crowd, and was wearing sunglasses and a beautifully tailored green blazer.

His voice was low, quiet and cultured, and he started by commenting on how warm the water was, much better than Wainui Beach near Gisborne. When Mr. X asked the stranger if he came from Gisborne, he said no, he was only there for a short time.

Mr. X was going to do some reading while he sat on the shore, and was holding the book *'The Sky People'* by Brinsley le Poer Trench. The stranger asked if they were interested in the 'Sky People', and Mr. X handed him the book.

As he was talking to them the man kept running his fingers across the words on the bottom of the front cover – *'Visitors to this planet in Atlantean and Biblical times are with us today'*. He handed the book back and said; "I know all about it!"

During the conversation he said; "WE are very concerned about the world situation, they speak of the atomic threat in the abstract, as though it is a thing which is bound to happen."

Mr. X commented that it was just a matter of mankind pressing the button and bringing on his own destruction. Really, psychologically speaking, the world was mentally sick.

"You are quite right," the stranger agreed. He murmured something else in a foreign language, which almost sounded like symbols. He then spoke up in English, as if translating it. The original sentence was not any recognisable language to Mr. X, so he muttered a short reply in Esperanto. They all laughed, and the stranger departed.

During their conversation the couple asked him if he would be staying in Timaru, and he said not. When queried about belonging to any particular organisation, the stranger said he had no headquarters but 'travelled extensively'.

Mr. and Mrs. X were almost sure he was a 'spaceman'. Mr. X said, that although a different 'person', he had the same look about him as the 'friends' he had met before. Further conversation between them clearly indicated that he was no ordinary visitor to the Bay.

On 17th February 1963, the note they received was more disturbing. (I wonder if it related to the less than pleasant aliens, of different appearance, who later abducted and mistreated innocent victims? Were they referring to the 'Greys', or CTRs which the 'Amicizia' spoke about?)

'We are sorely troubled at the trend of events in our sphere of influence. Rebellion has been threatening among certain cosmic entities which are even now moving in the direction of your location. We are doing our best to divert their direction of travel. If they come too close to your place in space, their influence will be tragic for your present uneasy peace, as past wars will be nothing to what this will cause if they succeed.

'We have been too busy with this cosmic trouble to communicate with you, but give this as a kindly warning that trouble may come your way. We hope to be strong enough to stop it. May the good Lord help us.'

'God bless you and all who look for truth.'

'Your two friends'

At one stage, his two friends promised to appear in the sky overhead to prove their presence. On the night of 27th November, 1963, Mr. X found the following letter under his front door;

'Sorry our display was not a full success. It is the first time we have made a display by arrangement. Regret that you yourself did not see it and glad that others did. The weather was against it. So again, we did not fail you as others saw it, which carries more weight than if you alone saw it.

'More and more will follow you when they see that you cannot know these things before-hand without our help. We expected to be called from duty with you long ago, but we are still with you and seems that may be for a long time yet. We are not the force of evil, as some would brand us – nor do we have wings on our backs or fly like fowls of the air – but we know the ways of men, and must expect opposition.

'You have noticed how everything has dropped into place for you since you have known us – and so it will be for your world if it will look our way. Our display was not intended for you in particular, but to convince the doubters. You need no convincing – you have met us – know us – spoken with us! We have already dispelled your doubts. Do not weaken! Be strong. Be steadfast. Be not led astray by would-be or seemingly scientific writings!'

'God bless you and all who are with us'
'Your two friends.'

In 1964, Fred Stone, a well respected Australian researcher, visited New Zealand. He himself also had contact with the Space Brothers, something very few people were aware of, and felt that the 'Mr. X' story tallied with his own. He needed to know if Mr. X was genuine, and after they had met on a couple of occasions, he wrote the following;

'When in New Zealand I was continually asked if I thought Mr. X was genuine. Previous to my visit I had received, from Fred Dickeson, several tapes and letters telling me all about Mr. X, much of which seemed to me to be very co-related to messages received by my own workers and myself here in Australia. Hence I felt his case to be genuine, but preferred to meet him face-to-face, and by personal contact make a better assessment.

'At last, when I arrived in Timaru, the opportunity came and I met Mr. X and his wife several times under the hospitality of the Dickesons, very happy occasions indeed. These meetings with Mr X were indeed wonderful experiences, and in my earlier Editorials this year, I spoke of and related some *of the very deep and happy events which took place on these occasions. After this I said openly that I felt that his case was indeed very genuine.*

'Much of what was revealed to him was in concord with that which we ourselves had received, and also from many other places overseas, all of which had no connection with each other. It was only right that I should say his case was genuine in that it showed no contradictory statements to that which we already knew.

'The more we met together, the greater affinity we found with each other, and it seemed that this was to be blessed by an unction. Before we parted, we met together with others at his home.

'Mr. X is a great musician and composer. He claimed the 'Space People' had inspired many of his compositions. Half way during the evening he said he felt moved to improve a piece of music – a simple composition which had just come floating through his mind. He went to the piano and began playing. Suddenly I felt myself also being moved, and as each note was played, I knew what was coming and began to hum the tune as though I had known it all the while. At the end I asked Mr. X if he knew the name of the tune, and he replied that - no he didn't know – what was it?

'Without thinking I said 'Dedication'- there are verses to it. Play it again.' He returned to the piano, and as he replayed the theme, the verses came into the mind telepathically from the Space Brothers, who were unseen, yet present. This was witnessed by everyone present at the time.

'Surely this was evidence that we two men were being moved together in unison to be instruments of service. Maybe you may not be impressed by this account, or feel it was a proof of the genuineness of either party, but one had to be present to know what was felt and transpired in that room. We were not being moved by our own powers, but from those of a much higher source.'

Mr. X's 'music' has intrigued me. Perhaps he was unwittingly channelling it and passing on more information and inspirational contact from his two friends. Our bodies and cells react to sound – their vibrations and frequencies. Perhaps there were more messages being secretly transmitted within the pulse and harmonics of the notes.

George van Tassel and his family also sang popular songs, and sometimes hymns to their guests under the Giant Rock. A couple who were visiting commented; "On one occasion they sang a certain song which Van had obtained directly from one of his space contacts. To us the music was very unusual, and the words were both simple and beautiful."

As an investigator, I have always found the claims of self-professed 'contactee', Howard Menger, to be very dubious. It is, however, interesting that he also claimed that although he could not play the piano, he was able to play music that the Space Brothers had taught him.

They explained that every note had a specific density and frequency which causes a sympathetic vibration when created at the correct frequency and in certain combinations. People hearing the themes would react in their conscious state with increased understanding and brotherly love toward one another.

In *'The Alien Gene'* I discuss the events on Waiheke Island, which is just off the coast of New Zealand. In the 1970s they witnessed many visitations by, and had contact with, humanoid aliens who were working with scientists on a secret project. Patty said that sometimes the 'visitors' would walk around, unrecognised, in the town. The project closed down later, and when the children reached adulthood, many left the island.

In 1999 Patty and Mark went back to visit her father, and they met up with all their childhood friends in the local pub, where Mark and Patty were singing in a band.

Their friend Gillian reminisced; "It was so strange, a lot of others were there, people we had gone to school with. It was like something had simultaneously drawn us all to come back at the same time. Many of our contemporaries were very musical, it was something in the notes and rhythm, and we all felt this tremendous bond and connection with each other."

Throughout history we have been aware of the hidden elements in sound and music. Acoustic phenomena – sound, pitch, rhythm, frequency, vibration, resonance – have all been known to produce an amazing effect and outcomes in unimaginable ways. In fact, these subliminal forces are far more powerful than most people realise.

The Egyptians, Greeks and Romans all incorporated music in their sacred rituals and ceremonies, as did the Sumerians before them. The Gregorian Chants of the Catholic Church were believed to impart spiritual blessings when sung in harmony during religious masses. The Tibetans use sound and vibration in their religious practices, including the art of levitation.

Two modern 'New Age' composers, Steve Halpern and Medwyn Goodall, both credit their music to 'higher sources'.

Steve Halpern said; "As my life and career have unfolded, I've had a number of experiences that suggest some of the insights I've received in vision, meditation and dreams had an extraterrestrial dimension."

Medwyn Goodall was also forthcoming; "I have four guides who assist me with my music. They act as a single entity. They do not communicate with me verbally, and there is nothing written down, we communicate through music.

"Today, I have a clearer picture of the guides. There are four entities who appear to be humanoid males. They pool their talents together and act as one. They have a spokesperson who I now know by name. He has long white hair, blue eyes and a youthful appearance.

"I have now come to understand that their work with me is to inter-weave light and high vibrational frequency into the very fabric of my music. The albums are light encoded and have the divine capacity to spiritually awaken people, to heal, to trigger dormant artistic talents and to ground light into Mother Earth.

"I have come to understand that other guides assist on a program which is very specific. If I wanted to produce a very ethnic album, a guide who has experience of that culture would join in the influencing of the music."

On 25th June 1964, Mr. X received another letter; *'We have been long in writing to you, but we have been fighting a terrible battle, only partly successful. Many evil ones have broken through and are now at work on your Earth. We cannot foretell the result as we ourselves do not know yet. But you may expect trouble at any time. If so, we shall be seen in your skies in greater numbers as we shall be there to help. If the following sign is seen it will be the warning of trouble. Watch your skies for this 'Z' and know that we are not far away. These evil ones have already influenced one we trusted. They will spoil those in higher places. - Your Two Friends'*

Fred and Phyllis Dickeson wrote the following report about the next incident:

'On the evening of January 13th, 1965, we called on Mr. and Mrs. X at their home, and after a very enjoyable evening watching TV, the conversation eventually turned to the two Space Friends and the fact that it had been a very long time since we had heard anything from them.

'After we had left for home Mr. X took his milk bottles out to the gate, and while there, for some unknown reason, he checked his letter box. To his surprise, he found a note inside from the Two Friends. He went back into the house, and once he and his wife read the note, he immediately began calling our telephone number.

'When we reached home, some fifteen minutes later, we could hear the phone ringing, and as is always the case, it stopped when we were about to pick it up. However, a few minutes later Mr. X called again. The note he had received read as follows:

'*Take up your pen and write, for we shall guide you each time you do this. We shall not allow you to make a mistake in the knowledge given to you. We can give you more this way. When you feel the urge to write – write! We shall guide you in each word! There is much to tell that this world should know. We will have a strong knowledge of what is not truth, and we shall know all that you write. This is all part of our promise to you. You may think it to be your own work, but it will not be so, so as with your music, which was never your own work.*'

'Your two friends.'

'You can imagine how dumbfounded Mr. X was after he read the note out to us.

'He said, "What do they expect me to do? It's a pretty tall order!"

'As usual, after a discussion we came to the conclusion that none of us could do anything. We just had to wait and see what happened next.

'It was not long, however, before Mr. X was sitting down at his typewriter. Amazingly enough he just began typing with no thought of whatever or what was coming next. He said that he just doesn't have to think – he just writes! He can get up and leave it for a spell, then come back, read the last sentence, and then he is off again.

'Just what people will think about the information contained in these writings is hard to imagine. We think a great many will not, or could not, possibly believe what has been written, and yet there will be some who will know, deep down, somewhere in the subconscious that it is true.

'We must admit that we too had great difficulty in digesting and absorbing the information given. However, we have our part to do, and so we print the writings and leave it to the reader to either accept or reject, depending on whatever degree of understanding they have reached.

'If these are really truth, then we have no hesitation in eventually believing that they will prove correct as time goes on....With no further comment, we leave you, the reader. To evaluate the information contained herein as you see fit. We feel it just cannot be read through, it must be studied and reasoned out.'

One night, when Mr. X received the note in his mail box, a Qantas airliner had visual and radar sightings of seven UFOs over the Tasman Sea, and in the days to follow the daily papers carried many stories of other sightings throughout the country, which were being investigated by both the RNZAF and the RAAF.

Mr. X also automatically typed another message; *'This work is not telepathic to you, as this method of communication is prone to error. We use the method of inspiring you to write, just as we have always done for you when we gave you all your musical inspirations. All good literary work is inspired.'*

It was after this that Mr. X composed the following poem.

> How long must men turn their heads away
> From the things that really matter?
> How long will the needy grow poorer
> While the rich grow richer and fatter?
> How long. Oh Lord, how long?
>
> How long must men not understand,
> That they can only profit at the expense of others?
> When will pink men ever learn the truth

Of their same origin as their darker brothers?
How long, Oh Lord, how long?

How long must men not realise
That they cannot move a finger far
Without somewhere in the universe
They disturb a distant star?
Teach them Lord, Oh teach them.

The unborn do not, yeas cannot ask
For entry to this crazy earth,
Yet they are forced by circumstance
To a future of darkness and dearth.
How long, Oh Lord, how long?

How long must man waste time and money
On edifices of cold dead stones,
Wherein they give lip service
In whispers and undertones?
How long, Oh Lord, how long?

How long must men talk peace around tables
Yet continue to prepare for war?
Will men never learn more wisdom
Than in the days of yore?
How long, Oh Lord, how long?

How long will men continue to ask their God
To "Lead us not into temptation"?
Do they seriously believe that He would
Since sin is of their own creation?
How long, Oh Lord, how long?

If men could only realise
How stupid they can be,
I'm sure they'd take another look
At grim reality.
Teach them Lord, Oh teach them.

Fred Stone, in Australia, was not happy about the recent turn of events, and at the end of 1965 commented that *'in contra to the methods used by the Brothers in leaving messages for Mr. X, he had suddenly been 'moved' to write it out himself. – In having some experience with others using this method, I am well aware this is open to many kinds of traps for the unwary. Unless a very distinct method of discernment regarding where, what, and how the origination of the message is clearly made, one can be open to all sorts of mental 'take-over' which can lead to contradictions and errors'*

After this Fred Stone, and others who also had strong religious beliefs of their own, would not endorse Mr. X's messages. Further, Fred Stone felt that Mr. X was not taking sufficient measures to protect himself against influence by 'lower entities'.

At the end of 1965, Mr. X left his Timaru flat of twenty-six years, moved to a house further out of town, and wondered if his 'two friends' would find him.

Early in 1967, the Dickesons had lost their eldest son, Ian, in a tragic accident. Three days later Mr. X received a note from the 'Two Friends' - the first in two years. Part of it was personal to the family regarding their loss – it ended saying – *'Yes, things are happening as we promised they would. We have been too busy to give you any messages of late, but you can already see the results, and more profound changes are to follow. We will not forget you. Sorry we have been so long in silence.'*

On 29th May, 1967, Mr. X was in his sitting room, and at about 3pm he saw, through the window, a yellow coloured car drive off from his gateway. He went down to his letterbox, thinking it was probably stuffed with pamphlets, to find another note from his 'Two Friends'. It read; *'Your world is on the brink of the most bloody and devastating war of all time. We have done our best but have failed to prevent it. We shall give help where we can. Please make this widely known. Watch for us in your darkest hour of despair. We shall not make ourselves too conspicuous, but we shall be with you all the same. It will happen at any moment, but cannot go beyond your year 1970.'*

Later, on 8th June, another letter arrived; *'We are making further attempts to rectify the world trouble. We believe we have made some headway, but we cannot do the impossible. Israel is on the side of justice, for she has a destiny to fulfil. We shall watch her with much interest. That is where our sympathies are. Her part is all-important to us and the whole world. In our prophecies of long ago, we told of her rise to great things. Justice is on her side. We believe we can soften the blow. There is now vileness in the highest of places and men are afraid of the things that are on Earth. They know not where to look for help. We know, and you know. We thank you for your help. Your Two Friends.'*

In 1969 the Dickesons commented to a colleague that no-one knew the answers. They had lived with the fascinating 'X-Case' for nine years, and so far had not been able to fault him or the messages. At the time some things appeared to be 'way out', but were later proved correct.

On the 26th March of that year, Mr. X received another brief note in his letter-box: *'We give you the following sign to watch for; When the city of Damascus becomes a heap of ruins, you will know that the real trouble has started. We may be able to delay it. Watch for it. - Your Two Friends.'*

On 27th, 28th and 29th July 1971, several witnesses had reported a large golden glow shining very brightly in the sky. It moved slowly and silently, later appearing to land in the distant foothills. On 29th July, Mr. X received another visit from two Space Friends.

At 7.30pm there was a knock on the door, and Mr. and Mrs. X immediately asked them in. Mr. X recognised his visitors as the same two men that he had met all those years ago. He shook their hands and said; "I know you!'

One replied; "You ought to – we met you early one morning, years ago."

This was the first time Mrs. X had seen them, and was impressed with the two well dressed men in neat suits, (no hats), with eye-catching shoes – an indistinguishable red-grey colour with a metal clasp up the centre. The older man was taller, and did most of the talking. The younger man was shorter, and had a somewhat round face. Their visitors politely declined to come in, and said they would be in contact within a few days.

The Dickesons had noted it was only on rare occasions, since 1960, that they had appeared in person. During the ensuing years they had usually kept contact with him and the Dickesons through notes being left either under the door or in his letterbox. One of the notes had mentioned that if they had anything of an urgent nature, they would contact him personally.

Communicating in this manner may have seemed strange to some, but had proven more accurate in conveying the message. Word of mouth could result in important points being forgotten, confused, coloured by retelling or interpretation and generally unwittingly distorted. Further, Mr. X and the Dickesons had photographed each note after it was received.

A few days later, on 3rd August, 1971, Mr. X found the following handwritten note in his letterbox.

'This is bad news, but we will be compelled to abandon all our attempts to help earthlings to a better way of life. Even our own brothers are not safe amongst you. One of our most trusted and loved Brothers has been murdered by earthlings while doing his duties. We have been recalled to our own sphere, and given instructions to break-off all contacts in the meantime.

'All the good we have done has been set-back to nothing in almost every case. No sooner than we put something right, then it is immediately put to nought by vested interests. We can almost smell the stench of your society, your political jostling for high places, your corrupt monetary system, your badness morally.

'Political untruths flow with the greatness of ease from the tongues of rulers throughout your world, and even your League of Nations is powerless to prevent iniquity in your world. It is powerless because it is composed of these very same elements of which we speak.

'We saw and spoke with you a few nights ago, yet there may still be the chance that we shall have need of your kind help, but how long it will be we cannot even guess at the moment. And now you understand why we made this last personal visit to you, and this last time so that your wife could be present.'

'We shall watch over you'
'Your two friends'

It was at this time that the Dickesons received word from their colleagues in Holland and Brazil that whilst UFOs were withdrawing their people off Earth, some would still remain.

In 1972 the Dickesons visited Mr. X, who was getting frailer, but still composed and recorded his music. Then, on 12th August, he was surprised to receive another note; *'Pick up your pen and write, and we shall guide you in all you reveal. We have much to tell you. Please reveal it faithfully. We are sorry that we made a mistake in our prophecy regarding the Far East War. But your world is still in for the greatest financial smash it has ever known. On the 25th September we shall be over your city at twelve midnight. Please watch for us. – Your Two Friends.'*

Unfortunately, someone in the group, having heard about the message, told the local media. As a result, many people were out watching the skies. Considering that the authorities would also have been aware of the message, it is understandable that very little was seen.

Another note arrived unexpectedly on 6th March 1973. *'Some time ago we warned you about your world-wide financial crash. This you now are in the commencement of. If wisdom prevails your world may weather the storm. But we cannot see an international agreement coming out of it. We have our own monetary system, which cannot be impregnated with self gains. There are many who stand to gain from a recession in trading. They will never find a place with us. We shall try to contact you in about three months - Your Two Friends.'*

In August 1973, Mr. X was distressed when he received the following note; *'We are sorry, but we must find someone else who is prepared to write – Your Two Friends.'*

He rang the Dickesons, who had also received a similar note under their own door, with a postscript asking them not to tell Mr. X – they would do that themselves. Whilst the Dickesons realised that Mr. and Mrs. X were very frail both mentally and physically, they commented that – 'it was such a cold dismissal – very strange!'

In 1975 the Dickesons reflected upon the entire Mr. X saga. The situation was not unique - there had been other 'X Cases' around the world, and two more of the 'overseas leaders' had confirmed that 'space people' were being taken off the earth.

They well understood that some researchers will reject a particular event because it does not fit with their personal belief in how the UFO phenomena should be. They believed that any theory or belief should be examined to the extent both its strengths and weaknesses became apparent.

Some colleagues had become quite hostile, saying George Adamski was genuine and Mr. X was not. There were even differences of opinion in the Dickesons' own group and family.

'We, on the other-hand, felt as unbiased investigators, we had to look at all angles, and disclose the truth as we found it, regardless of anything else. We are seeking the truth – that has always been our policy.

'There are at least four 'X notes' not published at all. Two referred to personal matters involving the Xs or ourselves, and were of little use to those not directly concerned.... Some we could not cope with in a public context at all....

'Besides the Two Friends' notes, there were also the 'X Writings'- three very long and involved, apparently inspired pieces. We published very limited copies of these under separate cover. The few which we did produce deeply disturbed some of our older members, and our credibility in some quarters. There was nothing about the 'guiding angels from God leading us out of sin, or the usual spiritual fringes to the messages received from George Adamski and others.'

Mr. X's 'Writings' can be found in Annex B. They are very different in content and nature to much of the information promoted by George Adamski, who in 1963, admitted to Lou Zinnstag that he hadn't seen Orthon in a long time. His Space Brother companions were obviously a different, replacement group of visitors, who had an entirely different approach and message to give Mr. X and others like him.

In 1976 Mr. X was devastated when his wife broke her hip, was hospitalised, and died soon after. He lost all interest in UFOs and the Space Brothers. By 1982 his own health had deteriorated to the extent that he lived in a nursing home, close to his two married children.

It seems the Space Brothers had one more message for their friends in New Zealand, but with Mr. X out of the picture, had to find another recipient. One of his friends - 'V' – who, rather sceptically, had followed Adamski's telepathy practices seemed to be the ideal conduit.

On 5th March 1978, 'V' was painting his basement, not thinking of anything in particular, when a voice in his head suddenly startled him. It was a message like none other before, and he raced for a pen and paper.

'We have tried to reach many souls by means of miracles and the like for many centuries, and many have suffered for their beliefs at the hands of men who refused to understand God's laws.

'In modern times, the UFO, as you call it, has been used to get people whose minds will respond to certain forms of external stimulation, through what might be called a part of their inward imaginative 'scene'.

'The Space Brothers have thus been called to assist in a manner whereby direct or indirect contacts are made with Earth beings which will lead their souls into an inquiring state of mind. This state will eventually lead to spiritual truths, provided that the free-will of the individual concerned will allow him or her to do.

'We cannot offer direct 'en-masse' contact, for as you know, there are all levels of developing souls on your planet, and as such some could accept, and some would not. We offer, therefore, the stimulation in the hope that all who have earned the right of this influence, will follow their curiosity such an event arouses, and thereby walk onto the spiritual path of New Awareness. The many sightings, and indeed contacts being made these days, show the new levels of awareness man is reaching out towards. We cannot force the individuals involved, only indirectly stimulate their consciousness towards the overall plan.'

'V's mind was racing with many questions, and after a couple of hours of quiet meditation, received the following; *'It is pointless to explain where we come from. The point is we are! Many have seen our craft, and some have seen our Brothers who pilot them. To tell Earthmen that we come from one part of the galaxy or another is futile, for he will spend much time in arguing why there can or cannot be life in this particular part or state of the Universe, instead of getting on with what must be done at this immediate time..... Putting himself in order, firstly on an individual basis, then as a whole. Man must realise that he and his brothers are all individual parts of an overall whole, and until some unison can be brought to play in his society, then chaos will continue to reign.*

'Why do you spend so much time in idle pursuit for new fields of mental endeavour, beyond that which your planet affords you? All secrets of the Universe are locked within your own planet, and indeed your own minds. Just as the recently discovered secrets of the DNA spiral has shown you that each cell of your bodies contains all the information to re-create an exact duplicate, under certain conditions so does your planet hold the keys to the entire Universe.

'Nobody has said it will be easy, for all must show a willingness and effort to work for the good of the whole, either as a group or individually before such knowledge can be revealed. In the wrong hands, such knowledge, in past years, has proved disastrous. So be patient and strive for personal perfection, and though it may take many years, take note of the little things that are learned as you walk your paths. These are the things that matter. The inner expression of yourself, which is the Higher Being you call God, will be brought further and further to the surface, and then can the Universe truly be yours.'

Two days later, 'V' received one final message; *'It is now 1978 – not 1958 – and if you on Earth are not already aware that your individual consciousness, each in its own manner, has vastly expanded over these past years, then these messages may not serve to help at this time. Hold them in mind, for in due time they will. All the secrets of anything you have ever desired are within these, provided the motive is correct. You must make what you will of them, and if in doubt, search within for that own inner voice that will verify for you that which is said.'*

CHAPTER EIGHT

THE RADIO CONTACTS

Perhaps it only seems logical that, before making their physical presence known, extraterrestrials would first try a less dangerous means of contact. Our early ventures into radio and other transmissions could certainly facilitate safer communication.

In September 1931, Bishop Barnes told the audience at the Congress of the British Association for the Advancement of Science that we may well be the recipients of signals from other worlds; *"There are many other inhabited worlds.....and on some of them, beings exist who are immeasurably beyond our mental level. We would be rash to deny that they can use radiation so penetrating as to convey messages to Earth. Probably, such messages come now. When these are first made intelligible, a new era in the history of humanity will dawn.*

'At the beginning of the new era, the opposition between those who welcome the new knowledge, and those who deem it dangerously subversive, may lead to a world war.....But I should like to be living then. When we begin this new era, we might get a true understanding of the beginning of the universe.'

Bishop Barnes died in 1954. I wonder if he got the answer to any of his questions.

Whilst the majority of astronomers believed that strange noises and 'signals' from space were mainly a natural phenomena, the prospect of radio communications from space people was not a new one. In 1896 British scientist Sir Francis Gaulton believed we were receiving signals from the planet Mars. Four years later, Nikola Tesla also reported receiving similar signals, and in 1937 he claimed that communications between Earth and other planets would be possible in the foreseeable future.

In 1921 Gugliemo Marconi believed that he had intercepted a signal from Mars, and astronomer Percival Lowell, whilst conceding that the code could not be translated, supported his claim.

In 1956 the U.S. Navy reported two separate unusual transmissions had been received, on shortwave radio, from most probably Mars and Venus. That same year, Dr John Kraus and other scientists reported 'interesting radio signals'.

The earlier reports always assumed that messages were being sent from neighbouring planets. In 1950, two years before the initial 'Adamski incident', Canadian, A. Matthews suggested that these transmissions may be coming from 'a Venusian spaceship'.

'Le Courier Interplanetaire' published an extract from Matthew's report; *'On September 26th 1950, while experimenting with my Tesla ultra-short-wave set, I heard a voice which called my name....'Matthews – Matthews – attention! – attention!' This was repeated for thirty minutes, after which I heard the following; 'Keep tuned in to this wave length, for this message will not be repeated. We are the group which has been landing on your planet for several centuries. This message is reaching you because of your belief in Tesla, which enables you to construct the only machine by which we can contact you.*

'We wish to know if you have been able to carry out the project which Tesla entrusted to you in 1935. No doubt you are wondering who we are? We are speaking in your own language, which we have learned in the course of previous visits to your planet.'

Matthews report then described a strange voice speaking about the general problems Earth seemed to be experiencing, including political unrest and wars. The unknown speaker then stated that spacecraft from their home world, Venus, had attempted to land on Earth on several occasions, but had been met with gunfire.

The message ended with; *'We still have the intention of visiting you. We shall come again.'*

In 1954, George Hunt Williamson wrote the book *'The Saucers Speak',* and followed up with a revised version in 1963, where he spoke of radio messages from space and revealed the identity of some of his witnesses.

George Hunt Williamson was an anthropologist with a particular interest in South America and ancient cultures. He was a colourful character, and he and some colleagues had been communicating, telepathically and by other various dubious means, with space beings for some time. When they were having some difficulty with the messages, they were told time was of the utmost importance.

On 17th August 1952, they received a message telling them to attempt radio contact. Williamson was to immediately go to Arizona and contact Lyman Streeter in Winslow, Arizona. Williamson complied, and after that many messages were sent and received. I consider that this whole series of events was instrumental in the witnessed meeting between Adamski and Orthon in the desert in 1952.

Lyman Streeter was a licensed commercial and amateur ham radio operator, and worked as a radio operator for the Sante Fe Railroad. He also had a radio shack in the backyard of his home in Winslow, Arizona.

On 22nd August 1952, Lyman and other witnesses saw what appeared to be a meteorite display over Winslow, followed by a bright light travelling high in the sky overhead. Suddenly, Lyman and others in the area, could hear strange coded signals which were not connected with their radio equipment, and seemed to be in the air around them.

Two days later the same phenomenon occurred, and resembled two people communicating with each other in an unfamiliar code. This time it was coming over Lyman's receiver in loud clear tones. His boss at work told him about previous instances of this happening, and thought they were from space intelligences, as the Arizona Lowell Observatory had reported, earlier on 22nd August, that they were planning to focus their large telescope over Winslow that evening. They hadn't given any reason.

Later, whilst out in the field, on duty for the Santa Fe Railroad, Lyman noticed a heavily guarded, fenced off area near the observatory. People who looked like Navy personnel were moving new electronic equipment in and out of a little building. Several years later, it was said this was equipment to track artificial satellites.

At first, although Lyman had no interest in UFOs, he had an episode, two years earlier, where he suffered amnesia for an eight day period. Later he recalled a spiritual type experience where he met with people who told him he must work rapidly to complete his task on planet Earth. His wife said that during that eight days he behaved very strangely, but afterwards spent long hours studying electronics and generally perfecting his skills.

After Williamson arrived, the messages came thick and fast, and on 30th August many witnesses were crowded into the radio shack. Lyman had used certain secret devious methods to see if this was all a hoax, and had satisfied himself that this was indeed genuine.

Although, right throughout this scenario, a lot of the information was, in my opinion, a lot of 'mumbo-jumbo', some communications were more meaningful;- *'Your Government contacted us a few years ago. They would like to know our secrets, but never will, no matter how hard they try. As time goes by our way will be made harder – harder to make contact with us for evil will be pushed closer and closer.'*

One message, which really caught my attention was; - *'We walk the streets, but cannot come to visit you in your home just yet.'*

In September messages began to arrive which suggested a landing place and meeting were needed in the near future. Time was short, and they couldn't wait much longer.

One rendezvous proved unsuccessful, and soon after Williamson left Winslow, and joined the Baileys in Prescott, Arizona. They received more messages, and I believe these led to the Williamsons and Baileys meeting Adamski near Palomar Gardens on 20th November 1952. Some of those present during the trip into the desert have claimed that it was Williamson who gave Adamski the directions of where to go.

Michel Zirger published an interesting article which commented on George Hunt Williamson's further interest in radio communications. In 1955 he created a non-profit organisation, 'Telonic Research Centre', which published a journal, but only for just over twelve months. Its aims were to spread information on UFOs, and structure a network of interested radio amateurs. By using specialised equipment enthusiasts were encouraged to contact the visitors and transmit and receive messages.

(George Hunt Williamson, whilst he maintained contact with Adamski, was essentially an archaeologist and explorer, especially in South America. He believed that ancient ruins and extraterrestrials were intimately intertwined, and often held public lectures to raise money for his next expedition. Witnesses claimed that on several occasions saucers appeared over his meeting venues. He later wrote several books, but his beliefs did not always agree with those of the Space Brothers. He died in his fifties in 1986, and many of his writing projects were never finished nor published.)

In October 1952, a light plane crashed at Winslow, and a few days later a man claiming to be from the Civil Aeronautics Authority called in on Lyman. He said he had just finished his investigation into the crash, and being a ham radio operator himself decided to drop by.

When the visitor sat down, he asked; "Do you believe in flying saucers?"

After Lyman said he thought they came from outer space, the stranger replied; "You've had contact with them, haven't you?"

Further discussion revealed that this man was obviously from the government, and his agency had been monitoring all the transmissions made by Lyman and fifteen other radio operators. The other operators had already agreed to co-operate with him and the government, and Lyman was to say nothing to anyone about the matter or he would lose his license and his job.

The visitor urged Lyman to dissuade George Hunt Williamson from publishing his book, *'The Saucers Speak',* that he was currently writing on the subject. When Lyman suggested that they contact Williamson themselves, the stranger said that this would indicate to him that his information was authentic. They did not want the public to know that extraterrestrials were visiting Earth.

Lyman had no option but to co-operate. They wanted him to continue with his transmissions, and sent him more powerful equipment to operate with, but from then onwards he received no more transmissions from space. Obviously the "Brothers' were aware of what was happening.

In early 1955, Dave Middleton, a senior member of the Institute of Radio Engineers, talked to a very scared Lyman. Middleton believed him, as he had received several reports of UFO radio contacts in Canada. On the 9th April, Middleton wrote a letter to Washington, hoping to learn more about the matter. Two weeks later, on 23rd April 1955, a relatively young Lyman Streeter suddenly died.

Author and researcher, John Keel, spoke about Wilbur Wilkinson, who held a responsible position with Hoffman Radio Corporation in Los Angeles. His wife said that he had tape recordings of conversations with men from other planets who had landed here in saucers. His basement was full of photographs and weird symbols and formulae, supposedly passed on by his friends from space.

Wilkinson's friend and partner claimed to have information about where the saucers had landed, and persuaded him to rent a plane to go and meet them. They took off from Gardena Airport, California, with a three hour supply of fuel, and neither they, nor their plane, were ever seen or heard from again.

One witness told UFO Research Qld. how her father had been a communications expert during World War II. He also had a keen interest in UFOs and collected magazines which he hid in his shed, along with his amateur radio, which he had built himself, and which he would sit at for hours. She wondered if he was listening for signals of an unknown origin, as he would he would create written records of what she described as 'Morse Code' transmissions.

One night she heard the dogs barking, and when she went outside, felt a buzzing sensation in her head. She looked towards her father's shed, and screamed when saw a strange figure in the shadows. When she fell into the back door of the house, her father seemed to already know what had frightened her.

After her father died, a man, who claimed to be from some private electronics sector, came to the house, and demanded the radio, which her mother gave him. He also took most of the books in which her father had recorded the Morse Code messages.

An interesting article was written by Edward Ruppelt, who had headed the US Government's sceptical Project Blue Book from 1951 to 1953. In August 1953, he left the Air Force because of the limitations placed on his work by the CIA.

In 1955 he attended a 'Giant Rock Convention' in California. He obviously still had an interest in the subject, but once people realised who he was, most of them ostracised him.

He later wrote; *'I had gone to the Convention feeling like an infidel trying to sneak into the Mohammadans' forbidden city of Medina.*

'While I was in the Air Force, I had made public and official statements about most of the speakers, and I had been base enough to say that their stories contained absolutely no basis in fact. If I were recognised, I halfway expected to have my eyeballs gouged out or to be spread-eagles on the sun-blistered side of 'The Rock', and have them throw spaceship-shaped darts at my poor racked body.

'Before long I could see people looking and pointing. I felt like a man in a B.O. ad. I even had an offer to speak, but since I've never even seen a flying saucer, I would have felt horribly inadequate. With the cat out of the bag, I felt a definite chill every time I approached a little group of eager listeners, so I went back to my car to listen to the speeches.

'Personally, I guess I'm like the people who laughed at the Wright Brothers and tapped their heads when they saw the German rocket people at work.'

Two speakers, Williams and Miller, who were not seeking the 'publicity bandwagon', interested Ruppelt. They spoke about contacting extraterrestrials by ham radio and other equipment.

He was sure he had heard similar stories when he was in the Air Force. Another friend, who was a ham radio operator, had told him that he had listened to two other radio operators discussing this 'interplanetary radio business', and later, another colleague, from the Military Amateur Radio System had recounted a similar story, saying he was very impressed by what he had overheard.

These two men, at Giant Rock, represented a nationwide net of 'hams'. They talked about making several dozen contacts with spacecraft. On occasions they had even contacted other planets. A group in Michigan had made twelve contacts since September 1954.

One of these was made with a new type of equipment that transmits messages on a pulsating infrared beam. The design for this new equipment had been given to them all by an electronics specialist from a flying saucer. Communicating with flying saucers, by radio or light beams, was something Ruppelt had never considered before, and it aroused his interest.

Before he left the Convention, Ruppelt met privately with the two men, Williams and Miller. He considered their story quite believable. They told of how, in 1952, a few ham radio operators got together in Arizona. They were playing around with the radio receiver when they picked up a strange signal. It was international code coming in at a fantastically fast and powerful rate from a spaceship hovering over the Earth.

Over a period of time, half a dozen hams were eventually able to set up voice contact, and started receiving snippets of technical and philosophical advice. On a couple of occasions they had seen a saucer over their radio shack, but at that stage, afraid of ridicule, they had told no-one else.

In 1953 the 'saucer people' urged them to spread the word to all the other ham operators, and if considered 'fit', they also would be contacted. This is when connected groups, around the world, were secretly making contact.

In 1954 Miller was alone in the radio shack when he received a message to go to a certain point near Detroit – 'Contact Imperative'. He couldn't notify his colleagues, so he scribbled an explanation, and went alone to the designated place, where he found a landed craft.

He got on board, and the saucer rose from the ground, not leaving the Earth's atmosphere. He talked to the crew about their technology, and the world situation in general. Before they returned him to the landing spot, they let him speak to his colleagues from the spacecraft's equipment, so they could verify his experience and where he was.

A year later Ruppelt wrote the book *'The Report on Unidentified Flying Objects'*, which he revised in 1959, still proclaiming there was no evidence to suggest UFOs were extraterrestrial. Was Ruppelt having second thoughts about the extraterrestrial scenario? We will never know, in 1960 he suddenly died of a heart attack, only thirty-seven years old!

In August 1956, a United States radio ham, Dick Miller, told an audience at Caxton Hall, London, that a craft would hover over Los Angeles at 10.30pm on 7th November. Miller played a tape of the radio transmission that he claimed to have received, and it requested that at the designated time, US radio stations would interrupt their regular broadcasts to receive a message for Earthmen.

On 11th November, the *'Empire News'* suggested it may have been a hoax, because despite intense interest, with many radio receivers strategically placed, no message was received. However, in a later article they reported that radar had plotted a speeding UFO over Los Angeles that night.

On 3rd August 1958, ham radio operators from Florida to Kentucky heard the voice of a man on the 75 metre international band. He claimed to be broadcasting from a spaceship fifty thousand miles away from Earth. Some radio operators, and the Federal Communications Commission made tapes of the transmission.

The message was for the Americans, who must stop hydrogen and atom bomb tests, otherwise they will eventually cause the entire Solar System to blow up. He spoke in English, German, Norwegian and a musical gibberish he said was the language of his home planet. The broadcast, which lasted two-and-a-half hours, was very strong, causing much speculation as to its origin, especially since the authorities were unable to trace it. Many considered it to be the work of the Soviets, but the whole episode was kept quiet, and the authorities knew more than they were prepared to say.

In the 1950s the American Radio Relay League and International Amateur Radio Union were holding conferences where contact with extraterrestrials was never publically mentioned. Behind the scenes were furtive meetings where equipment and frequencies were discussed. Most ham radio operators usually worked in secret from 'radio shacks' in their backyards. One participant claimed contact since 1932, and said that many of the transmissions came from a mobile station on a spaceship just outside Earth's atmosphere.

In 1959, the *'Flying Saucer Review'* also mentioned radio communications with the space people, specifically mentioning 'light beam' radio equipment, which had been developed for secret communications during the war. The article gave instructions, and said that the equipment had been reported successful in the USA.

One report to come out of the 1950s was the testimony of sisters Helen and Betty Mitchell who claimed to have met two 'Space Brothers' in a St. Louis coffee shop. Their detailed, adventurous story, published much later, may well be true, however there appears to be no independent witnesses or investigation to verify their accounts.

There were just a couple of paragraphs, from 1957, which grabbed my attention; *'When we entered the door, we again saw one of the Space Brothers, and he gave us instructions, at that time, for building a device whereby we could contact the Space People. His instructions were explicit and precise, for he warned us that unless we placed every piece of the device in the proper place we would not be able to contact them with it. We were not allowed to take the drawn diagram of the device with us, but we had to remember it as it was explained to us.*

'When we obtained the proper pieces for the device, we constructed it when we returned home, and were happy to find the results were satisfactory. We were amazed when we tuned in on the mother craft and spoke with the same person we had earlier seen. We were also allowed to speak with the commander of the craft.....In the following six months we spoke many times with the space people

through the device, and received much information about their homes, science and craft.'

During the 1950s ham radio operators in Australia and New Zealand were also communicating and co-operating with each other. I have copies of many of their private letters. They contain extensive directions for modifying their apparatus and antennae, but carefully never once mention in their correspondence whom they intend to contact with their enhanced gear.

Given the understandable government and intelligence interest in these clandestine activities, it is not surprising that, in 1979, one ham operator complained that, after some unwanted publicity in the local press, his colleague had been visited by three men supposedly from the South Australian Police. They had confiscated the group's 'specially wired transceiver', and they were 'cut off from the transmissions', which apparently were from the 'space people'.

During October 1958, the tracking facility at Cape Canaveral began picking up unusual radio signals. Other stations were alerted and also monitored the frequency. Technicians, using Doppler and radio direction finding equipment, tried to locate the source of the anomalous transmissions. The object sending the signals was three thousand miles from Earth and moving at nine thousand miles per hour toward the Moon. Moments later, it altered course and headed into deep space. It was never identified.

Certainly in the late 1960s ham radio operators, all over the world, were tuning into, and taping all transmissions from the Moon Missions and landings, including the parts which had been deleted by NASA. One ham operator, in the US, Carl Horton, had apparently got his first crystal radio in 1920, and had later joined a 'Radio Club' where he met Tesla, and later learned of the special equipment required to monitor our space missions.

Some radio operators claimed that they had their own equipment which by-passed NASA broadcast outlets. Despite NASA denying that they ever censored transmissions, they claimed that there was a portion of the earth-moon dialog that was quickly cut off by the NASA monitoring staff.

Researcher William Moore reported that the eavesdropping on some of our space missions was a much simpler affair. NASA's Goddard Space Centre in Maryland, had an Amateur Radio Club which picked up the 'Discovery' to

Houston transmissions directly from the satellite downlink and rebroadcast them over a ham radio frequency for the benefit of radio amateurs around the world. NASA tried to claim it was a hoax, but a later independent analysis identified the voice of Dr. Bagian, the mission medical specialist, who being neither a pilot nor military officer was least familiar with various communication channels and procedures.

In 1973, the Russian newsagency *'Tass'* reported that their scientists had picked up alien signals from other intelligent beings in space. They were unsure where they had emanated from, but insisted they did not originate from any satellites launched from Earth. They said that when the signals were picked up again, other radio telescopes, at four different parts of the Soviet Union, were locked in to confirm that genuine intelligent messages were being beamed toward Earth. Some western scientists suggested that there may be a robotic probe in our Solar System, and others lamented the fact that they did not have the funding to purchase the same advanced equipment as the Russians.

Perhaps these reports of extraterrestrial radio contact are not so doubtful as one may think. In 1979, Science Correspondence for *'The Observer'* made the following report; *'Intelligent beings elsewhere in the universe, who are trying to get in touch with us, face a disappointment this week in Geneva.*

'Attempts by American scientists to persuade the World Administrative Radio Conference, which opens tomorrow, to allocate a special frequency band, on which they could listen for alien intelligences, has been cold shouldered..... This conference is likely to be more acrimonious than any previous gathering called by the International Telecommunications Union which organises the conference. It happens only once every twenty years, and, as in the past, is likely to be in charge, with the strongest arguments being a gentlemanly affair, run by technical experts.

'This time the politicians are centring on conserving the shortwave high-frequency band of the spectrum. These are the wavelengths which offer really long-range communication, without the use of satellites, and provide the cheapest way for a developing country to establish its internal communications.' These countries wanted to be allocated their frequencies ahead of time, something the Americans opposed in their bid to achieve their own special 'ET' frequency!

In some instances, we will never know whether radio transmissions were genuine, or just a hoax. In 1993, Swiss astronomer, Dr. Alain Kiefer, claimed to have received a garbled message from an extraterrestrial base on the Moon. A meteor had cracked the protective shell of their base, thus compromising the artificial atmosphere.

The Americans confirmed that Dr. Kiefer had immediately contacted them, but refused to say what, if anything they planned to do. There was a lot of controversy among the scientists as to whether the message had originated on Earth. Dr Kiefer disputed this, saying if it was a prankster, he must have been a genius. The message was sent in a mathematical code which took a pair of computers two weeks to decipher.

In 2001, an Australian researcher, who had obviously only just learned about these secret communications, wrote to another ham radio ufologist, specifically requesting details of the technology required to contact 'ETs'. No information was forthcoming. By that time, our own intelligence agencies would have been able to monitor any covert activity.

CHAPTER NINE

CONTACTS and DEBATE in LATER YEARS

As time went on, and our own technology improved, not only were the visitors in greater danger of being discovered, we cannot be sure that some encounters were actually with humans on advanced terrestrial craft. I suspect that many, (certainly not all), of the strange craft, seen over the last century, were in fact experimental prototypes being tested by one or more of our own foremost nations. Often, years later, when reviewing earlier sightings, they can be explained as products of our own secret research and development. Perhaps, in order to preserve the secrecy of our new prototypes, our governments deliberately let witnesses think they were extraterrestrials.

When considering this possibility, I am only referring to the more primitive type of small saucers, and not the sophisticated, technologically advanced larger craft reported by most witnesses.

Following the seizure of wartime technology and scientists from Nazi Germany, much of the covert experimental work was relegated to secret bases and establishments including in the remote Canadian areas of Alberta and British Columbia.

In November 2000, *'Popular Mechanics'* Magazine published recently declassified information regarding our own research and prototypes during the mid-twentieth century. Initial projects, in the 1950s, were 'Silver Bug', which concentrated on vertical take-off and landing, and 'Pye Wacket', which created small discs for use as air-to-air missiles. These craft were anything from 25 feet to 125 feet in diameter, and were unstable and frequently crashed.

One crash, which may or may not have been extraterrestrial, was recounted by retired Lt. Col. William Anderson. In 1952 he was piloting a F-94 out of Andrews AFB, when he was asked to divert over a remote Virginia tidewater swamp region, and check on a crash report.

He reported seeing a saucer-shaped craft, burrowed into a mud flat, and then returned to base. The radio operator had said that the area was being sealed off, and helicopters with teams were on the way. He was later told that when the choppers arrived they found that its crew had been retrieved by an identical saucer, seen on radar at the crash site before anyone else arrived.

The wreckage was brought back to a guarded hanger at Andrews, and Anderson discovered that it was a perfect saucer, thirty feet in diameter, with a raised cockpit in the centre. The wreckage was so battered that, although involving familiar materials, the entire propulsion system, and most of the instrumentation was totally destroyed. Nobody involved thought that it was a craft from outer space.

There were also the alleged AVRO VZ-9 experiments, apparently unsuccessful, but a convenient 'smoke-screen' for the genuine UFOs being seen in increasing numbers. (In his book *'Earth- An Alien Enterprise'*, Timothy Good describes some later proto-types called ARVs (Alien Reproduction Vehicles), reported in 1988.)

Then our own 40-ft nuclear 'flying saucer' arrived – the Lenticular Re-entry Vehicle (LRV) – which could hold a crew of four. It was suggested that debris found in 1975, on an Australian farm, south of Brisbane, may have come from a LRV. The British also had shared military ventures with the Australians, and it would be logical to assume that in any joint projects involving secret craft, they would find the vast outback of Australia an ideal area and quite useful.

Several cases, which I discussed in *'Contact Down Under'*, occurred during the early 1950s, in the Western NSW towns of Broken Hill and Wilcannia. In each instance the RAAF were quick to confiscate the witness's photographs.

One local resident, the famous Australian artist, Pro Hart, had served in the army, and along with friends and colleagues, was witness to more than one sighting. He was convinced that these objects were secret government test craft.

Perhaps he was right. Many years later the ABC's morning radio show, had a segment on UFO sightings. One man rang in and said during the 1950s he held a senior position with BP Australia, and spoke of a colleague who was involved with vertical flight experiments at the Air Defence Base in Adelaide. Apparently this involved a 'round object' under the cover of a high hanger. Whilst undergoing tests, the object lifted up to the ceiling whilst a technician was hanging onto the rim. He had to keep hanging on until someone figured out how to get him down safely.

It must be remembered that, after World War II, the Russians also commandeered many of the German scientists and technicians. They have been busy developing new technology and 'flying machines' as well.

It wasn't just western ufologists, but also the military, who were considering this possibility. In 1954, *'Contact'*, the New Zealand National Journal of the Air Force Association published an article titled *'Are Flying Saucers of Russian Origin?'* by Ronald Hamilton.

He referred to a claim by K.F. Feldman, that was published earlier in the year by the *'Auckland Star'*. Feldman said there was strong evidence that Russia had jet disc factories, near the Aral Sea, in the Kazakh province of Russia. He said that the machine being developed could be operated either as a guided missile, or with a crew of four. Hamilton noted the lack of hard evidence, and asked if this was another piece of Russian propaganda, designed to intimidate the West, or was it a revelation of extreme importance?

In 1957 Russian Professor S. Zonshain published an article in the science monthly *'Knowledge is Strength'*. Along with a sketch, he described a flying saucer with a *'TU 104 and a four-engine turbo jet Ukrania'*. He said that these fast flying saucers, with no wings, had nothing in common with aeroplanes.

Later reports, indicating that the Soviets also knew many UFOs were not of Earthly origin, were published in a 1991 edition of *'Rabochaya Tribuna'*. Professor V. Burdakov said that Sergei Korolyev, a leading rocket scientist in 1947, had been summoned to the Ministry of State Security in Moscow.

They had numerous foreign documents that dealt with flying saucers, including the Roswell incident. After they were translated into Russian, he had three days to prepare an opinion for Stalin. When he met the leader, he said that he did not consider the saucers were weapons manufactured by the Americans. While the phenomenon was real, it did not appear to pose a threat. Stalin agreed with his conclusion, which was shared by other scientists he had consulted with.

Regardless of whether any discs seen were extraterrestrial or our own prototypes, the Russians were determined to keep all sightings and incidents top secret.

On 16th June 1948, Soviet Air Force pilot Arkadii Apraksin was testing a new jet aircraft near his home base at Kapustin Yar, Basunchak. He spotted a 'cucumber-shaped' UFO, and once it was confirmed on radar, his base commander ordered him to pursue the object, and order it to land – by use of force if necessary.

As he approached the intruder, it projected an en3ormous light beam which engulfed his aircraft, rendering him temporarily blind in the process. All his electrical systems suddenly failed, but luckily he was able to glide his plane down to a safe landing.

Despite the fact he was a highly decorated Soviet pilot, he was subjected to intense questioning by intelligence agents, and then posted to far-flung bases across the country. On 6th May 1949, after reporting another chance encounter with a UFO, he was confined to a mental hospital. Following six months of shock treatment and psychotherapy, he was discharged from the military as being 'Group One Disabled'.

Even in the 1950s, UFO reports from behind the Iron Curtain were few and far between, however Ronald Hamilton discussed one from 1953; *'Towards the end of July last year, the inhabitants of a number of Baltic villages near the Polish-German border, were amazed to see flights of strange saucer-like objects travelling across the sky at great speed. They were in formations varying from two to six in number. These flights continued for seven days and were usually seen about the time of sunrise and sunset.*

'For the first two days the police and military displayed exceptional interest in collating the reports which were coming in from a large area. Suddenly their attitude changed. They denied that anything unusual was happening in the heavens, and said that people who sent in further reports would be prosecuted as imperialistic war-mongers. This threat was enough to silence the reports, but it did not stop the people talking amongst themselves - nor did it stop the objects flying. After a full week of activity there came a lull of a few days, and then, on 29th July, further flights were observed. On the last day of the month one of the machines landed near a village called Walin.

'A group of Poles and two Germans were labouring in a field when their attention was drawn to an object which they saw descending almost vertically and at high speed. When it was near the ground it slowed down, almost to a hover, and then made a gentle landing.

'The group of workers made their way to the scene and stared at the object. A few minutes later, a Polish policeman arrived, took one look at the circular machine, uttered the Polish equivalent of "Crikey" and dashed off to make a report.

It was estimated that the diameter of the machine was between forty and sixty feet. It had a spherical metal centre, which was entirely closed. On the outside was a large flat circle bearing wide exhaust pipes, similar to those of jet engines. The outer circle was also of metal. The machine appeared to have no crew'

Several parts of the machine had some indecipherable inscriptions, which the witnesses assumed must be Russian. During the excitement, one of the Germans used the opportunity to escape to the West. The rest of the group remained until the policeman arrived with reinforcements. Shortly after, a Russian helicopter arrived with several MVD men who immediately cordoned off the area.

Nothing further was heard from the witnesses, and the Russians tried, unsuccessfully, to trace the German worker who had escaped.

The Soviets appeared to be having their fair share of inexplicable incidents. In 1961, the Moscow Aviation Institute was unable to explain a strange event which occurred near Sverdlovsk.

An Antonov An-2P mail plane, with seven people on board, was about one hundred and fifty kilometres out of Sverdlovsk, bound for Kurgan, when it suddenly disappeared from the radar screen. At the same time, an unidentified object was tracked on radar, accompanied by unusual radio signals.

Following a large air and ground search, the aircraft was found, perfectly intact, in the middle of a dense forest. There was no way the plane could have landed there, unless it had been gently lowered from above. The mail was intact, but there was no sign of the passengers and crew.

About one hundred metres from the aircraft, they found a well defined thirty metre circle of scorched grass and depressed earth.

In 1981, Dr Felix Zigel, a leading Russian ufologist said that there were some fifty thousand UFO reports on file, comprising eight volumes. Only one volume had been published, because they did not want to cause 'fear and unrest' among the population.

'We have seen those UFOs over the USSR, craft of every possible shape: small, big, flattened, spherical. They are able to remain stationary in the atmosphere, or to shoot along at ten thousand kilometres per hour.

'They move without producing the slightest sound, by creating around themselves a pneumatic vacuum that protects them from the hazard of burning up in our atmosphere. So refined a technology can only be the fruit of an intelligence that is indeed far superior to man.'

Throughout the decades, successive Russian presidents have always had an interest in this subject. In 1990 Mikhail Gorbachev said; *'The phenomenon of UFOs is real, and we should approach it seriously and study it. I know that there are scientific organisations which study this problem.'*

Although we know they must share the West's intense interest, the Chinese have always remained silent about UFOs and extraterrestrials. In 1995, Teresa Poole wrote an enlightening piece for the *'Independent'* newspaper. Three years earlier, she had interviewed Wang Changtin, and didn't really believe his claim that the 'China UFO Research Association' was an 'independent, unofficial, civil, academic body'.

'The organisation was housed at the 'Military Weapons Industry Academic Department' of the state 'China North Industries Group' in western Beijing. Changtin said that they had collected over five thousand reports in Chinese airspace, and added an intriguing postscript;

'We also study the application of UFO phenomena to the national economy, such as new materials and new technologies.'

Had they also embarked on a programme of 'back-engineering' alien technologies to further advance their own? Perhaps, they also had more 'contact' than they would ever admit?

Sometimes it is difficult to ascertain whether strange craft are from Earth or elsewhere. One interesting case from South Africa, in 1961, was reported by Juan Benitez and translated by Gordon Creighton. The witness, Englishman 'HM', was an engineer working on aircraft automated pilot systems for a Spanish company. 'HM' was travelling twenty miles out of Cape Town when a man, who looked about forty, asked for help to get some water. After taking him to a mountain stream, 'HM' gave him a lift back to a rock face about one hundred meters off the road.
There was a strange object, about four metres high and ten to fifteen metres in diameter, with steps leading up to an opening in the craft. 'HM' was invited up

to the entrance, but not allowed beyond the doorway. Inside he could see a circular room with square windows, beneath which there was a couch going all the way around. There seemed to be a white light, 'coming from everywhere', and in the centre were two rows of levers, set in a rectangle. On the other side of the room there appeared to be an instrument panel.

There were four other men inside. Three of them were attending the fourth, who appeared to have been burned in an accident, and was lying down. They looked completely normal, dressed in beige laboratory-type overalls, about five feet, to five feet three inches tall, of slim build with chestnut-coloured, short hair. 'HM' asked the man he brought back if they needed a doctor. He was told 'No', but asked if 'HM' had any questions? He spoke English, but with a strange, unidentifiable accent, and said his colleague had been injured as they were entering our atmosphere.

'HM' asked how their craft worked and was told that they nullified gravity using a heavy fluid, which circulated in a tube at infinite speed, and created a magnetic field. (This propulsion system, whilst unknown to us, is similar to that described by other witnesses.) When asked where they came from, the man pointed to the sky without any further detail; shortly afterwards he firmly invited 'HM' to leave.

In 1964, New Zealand's *'Spaceview'* discussed a number of sightings of the same craft, which only occurred in the week commencing the 23rd April before abruptly ceasing. The various locations were all in a three hundred mile narrow strip in New Mexico. It was suggested that this was an experimental craft of revolutionary design, which had to remain in close proximity to one of the nearby bases.

On 28th December 1968, a forty-five year old carpenter, hunting foxes near the Australian town of Goulburn, encountered a strange saucer-shaped craft, resting on the ground. It was about forty feet in diameter, and ten feet high.

As he approached the object, a 'being' walked around from the other side. It was about 5ft 6in tall, with human characteristics, youngish features and long hair. The 'being' spoke in English to the hunter for about three minutes, but seemed in a hurry to get away. He asked the being where it had come from, and only got 'Saturn' as a reply.

He got back into the saucer, which rose about fifteen feet off the ground, hovered, and then moved away and disappeared over a hill. The witness, who had an automatic camera with him, took four photos as the craft departed. The grass was scorched around the area where the saucer had landed, with an eighteen inch deep hole right in the centre.

Australia's vast outback is often reputed as being an ideal place to secretly test the latest military prototypes. Sometimes the pilots stray off course. Was this the case in this encounter, or was our visitor truly extraterrestrial?

Mervyn Dykes reported an incident in 1972, at Lower Hutt in New Zealand. A woman heard a humming noise, and noticed an unusual blue light outside her open bedroom window. She got up and looked out.

About sixteen feet away was a classic UFO. It was like two saucers which had been fitted together- rim to rim. Around the outer edge were alternating red and yellow lights, spinning around as though they were rotating. On the top was a transparent dome, and she could see two men inside.

She could see them 'from just below the shoulders – up', and they were dressed in blue 'satiny' suits with no helmets; "They looked just like us, and I saw one turn, throw his hands up, and laugh."

The craft hovered for two or three minutes, and then just shot straight up and arced away in a south westerly direction over the hill. The witness, scared that the object might come back, scrambled back into bed and pulled the blankets over her head. It was many years later before she told anyone about the incident.

The island of Puerto Rica hosts the American Radio Observatory, where since the 1960s they have conducted a search for extraterrestrial life. At about eleven o'clock one night, in 1981, Puerto Rican housewife, Gertrudis Mendoza, along with her small daughters, was driving to pick up her husband from work.

Travelling up a hill, about a kilometre from her home, she saw a brilliant object on the left hand side of the road. She pulled over, and looked through some bordering railings, to see, about twenty feet away, three 'people' who had their backs to Gertrudis. They appeared to be examining an object which was glowing brightly and hanging, suspended, about three feet above the ground. It was a large round craft, grey metallic in colour, with a cupola on top, and a series of bright lights around it.

One of the beings was small, maybe only three feet tall, with a large head, no hair, and a slim build. His skin looked a greyish colour, and he was wearing some kind of a greenish grey close-fitting garb. The other two were much taller, and looked perfectly human. They also had tight-fitting clothing, but of a silvery-grey colour.

Gertrudis, anxious to get a better look, got out of the car, intending to climb over the railings. Her younger daughter was frightened, and started to cry. Knowing this would attract the attention of these strange people, she jumped back into the car and drove away as fast as she could.

When she returned with her husband, the craft and beings had gone. She said he was angry with her for having endangered herself and the children; "They could have carried us off, and he would have never known what happened to us."

On May 9th 1985, Douglas Oliver was on his motorbike, and travelling along the British A580 East Lancashire Road between Liverpool and Oldham. At 4.30am he pulled over to have a cigarette, and could hear a humming noise coming from a nearby field. Curious, he walked about thirty feet into the field, and could see a silvery-white glow about one hundred feet further on.

Two figures, each about five feet tall approached him, and when they paused about eight feet away, he could see them quite clearly. It was a man and a woman, and both had short blond hair, and looked like 'perfect human beings'. They were wearing lurex-type ski-suits, which seemed to sparkle from the lights of the craft and his motorbike. Around their waists they had a wide belt, with a 'egg-shaped canister thing' on the right hand side.

Douglas backed away a little, and asked the woman where had they come from? She told him that they were from another Solar System, and he shouldn't be afraid. They had just stopped to make some minor adjustments to their ship, which she explained was powered by magnetic fields and gravitational pull. They walked back to their craft, the humming noise increased, and a silvery, cigar-shaped object took off at tremendous speed on a 45 degree angle.

Later, Douglas made the mistake of ringing Manchester Airport to ask if any aircraft had been around at that time, but none had.

On 13th July, Douglas, who had told nobody of the incident, was home alone. Just after 11am, there was a knock on the door. Two men were there, both in their early forties, and except for their white shirts, dressed in black including their shoes and hats. Their car, parked outside, was also black.

They told him that they knew of his encounter and his call to the airport. For his own safety, he should 'say nothing to anybody'. Douglas became angry, asked why they were threatening him, and told them to "**** off". Some days later, he received a visit from an Air Force officer who gave him some similar advice.

It was after this that Douglas, who had no previous knowledge of UFOs, heard about BUFORA, and told Norman Oliver about the incidents.

If these people were from our own military or space corporations, why, after all these years, has there not been a whistleblower, or at least somebody involved speaking out?

The British Government and Aristocracy

After World War II, and the wartime reports of Foo Fighters and other strange craft, many of Britain's aristocracy had more than a passing interest in UFOs, some privately, and others such as Desmond Leslie, Lord Dowding, Lord Hill Norton, and Brinsley le Poer Trench, (the Earl of Clancarty), more openly.

Desmond Leslie was the son of Sir Shane Leslie, and in 1954, following the publication of *'Flying Saucers Have Landed'*, he started questioning some of his father's colleagues.

There had been a case of a UFO, travelling at about eight hundred miles per hour, which had also been tracked on radar. When the matter was raised in parliament, Lord Ward, the newly appointed Minister for Air, dismissed it as being a 'weather balloon.'

Desmond Leslie later wrote; *'I could not let this go unchallenged, so I phoned the Minister, and politely hinted he was a fibber. He laughed and said; "What am I to say. I know it wasn't a balloon. You know it wasn't a balloon – but until I've got a saucer on the ground in Hyde Park and can charge the public 6d a go to enter, it must be balloons. Otherwise the government would fall, and I'd lose my job."*

'He went on to explain the difficult position he found himself in along with other members of the government. If he admitted to flying saucers without evidence that the general public could actually touch, they would consider the Government had gone barmy and lose their faith in them.

'I also challenged him at the time of the Flight Lieutenant Saladin Case. (Saladin almost flew smack into a saucer near the Thames Estuary), when the aerodrome responsible had its switchboard blocked with enquiries. I asked why the Air Minister had issued an order forbidding pilots to report such happenings to the public or the press.

'He replied; "Look, I'm trying to run an Air Force. When a story like this breaks, the poor C.O. is driven frantic. His telephone is jammed with calls, and he is unable to get on with the business of running an efficient airfield."

'He was rather apologetic, but I sympathised with him....I think he was politically right. If he believed that to go into the House and admit the truth about flying saucers, without being able to show a landed saucer to an all-party select committee, it would court laughter and cries of 'resign'. His party loyalties come first – as a politician that is.'

On 11th July 1954, Lord Dowding, who was at one time, Air Chief Marshall, published a very controversial article on the subject. He claimed; *'More than 10,000 sightings have been reported, the majority of which cannot be accounted for by any 'scientific' explanation, eg. that they are hallucinations, the effects of light refraction, meteors, wheels falling off aeroplanes, and the like....They have been tracked on radar screens...and the observed speeds have been as great as 9,000 miles per hour......I am convinced that these objects do exist and that they are not manufactured by any nation on earth. I can therefore see no alternative to accepting the theory that they came from an extraterrestrial source..'*

Earl Mountbatten, had a distinguished military career, and was Chief of Defence Staff from 1958 to 1965. His interest in the subject was heightened by an incident which occurred on his Broadlands estate in Hampshire in 1955.

Employee Frederick Briggs was cycling to work at about 8.30am, on 23rd February, when he saw an object hovering, about sixty feet away, over a nearby field. It was about twenty-five feet in diameter, and shaped like a child's humming-top. He dismounted from his bike, and watched as a 'column' descended from the centre of the saucer down to the ground. Standing on it was a 'man', dressed in a 'dark suit of overalls', and wearing some form of close fitting hat or helmet.

A bluish coloured beam of light appeared in one of the craft's portholes, and Briggs and his bike toppled over. He lay there, unable to move, as the object rose vertically into the air and disappeared at an unbelievable speed.

He was still shaken and dazed by the experience when he made his way to the estate house and reported the event. Lord Mountbatten arranged for Briggs to make a written statement, and independently wrote up the details of his own investigation of the incident.

In 1960, Sir John Langford-Holt MP asked about the implications of UFOs to air-defence, and suggested more thorough investigations. Prime Minister Harold Wilson refused to alter the existing procedures and made the familiar references to weather balloons and natural phenomena.

The same year, Canadian Wilbur Smith pointed out that politicians have two main priorities – to win the next election and represent their constituents. They are naturally sensitive to public reaction, especially when such a controversial subject is raised. The *'Flying Saucer Review'* published a verbatim review of a US Congressional debate 'Pressing for Flying Saucer Inquiry' held on July 15th 1959. One Congressman later said; "We are told one thing in closed door sessions, and the public is told something entirely different."

Of course, members of the British House of Lords are by right of birth and inheritance, members for life. They could not be so easily silenced or dismissed. Brinsley le Poer Trench, the Earl of Clancarty, convinced the British Government was involved in a 'cover-up', formed a House of Lords All-Party UFO Study Group in the late 1970s. It did not last for many years, but during its existence held monthly meetings where various researchers and experts gave presentations.

Earl Kimberley, a former Liberal spokesman on aerospace said; *'I think the general public should be encouraged to come forward with evidence. Many do not, for fear of being ridiculed. Let them be open, let them be honest, let them badger their Member of Parliament and the Government to be open with them and to cease what I am convinced is a cover-up here.'*

Lord Rankeillour also had something to say; '...*those who report seeing UFOs are taken to be misinformed, misguided, and rather below par in intelligence. If Technology? Why should this Ministry waste its time gathering false information?*

'*Of course, it is not false information: it is data reported by civil and air force pilots, policemen, sailors and members of the general public who have all had a personal experience which has intrigued and/or frightened them. I suspect that the British Government do have a Department studying UFO sightings, for why else should they bother to publicly debunk reported ones if they are of no interest to them? Quite apart from the fact that the Government have not admitted to the existence of UFOs, these machines are potentially dangerous.*'

Years earlier, in 1963, Harold Watkinson, who had been Britain's Minister of Defence from 1959 to 1962, was asked, at a public meeting, why the Government was trying to 'hush-up the sightings of flying saucers'.

He replied; '*Before I left the Ministry I had to sign a large number of papers promising never to reveal certain facts I had learned as Minister of Defence. The subject of flying saucers may be included.*'

In 1980 the Group was addressed by retired Danish Air Force Major Hans Petersen. At first he talked about instances which occurred during his military service; '*I have had more than fifty experiences with UFOs on the physical level myself. I have seen how they reacted in order to avoid the result of my instructions to intercepting pilots. I have had them holding in the approach lights. I have had a touch-down at the end of the runway. I have had a huge ship holding right in front of my villa, and I have had them pass my car at close quarters, and I have seen one land.*

... '*My personal view is that UFOs are physical spaceships from other planets, and that they and their crews, of highly advanced human beings of flesh and blood, have visited us from as far back as this planet has benefit to live in.*'

He went on to talk about historical and Biblical references of 'Gods' who came from the skies; '*One thing is proven through all the many available reports on space activity in our atmosphere from the oldest reports from ancient times to the first reports in our time, and that is that – the visitors were and are human beings able to live among us – without recognition if they prefer.*'

He did not consider the more recent 'abduction' reports, where people reported 'missing time', were in any way connected to the 'Space Brothers'; *'Soon they get nervous, and finally they end up with a psychiatrist, who via hypnosis, reveals that these people have been abducted, and that they have experienced this and that.....Please remember that this is all new – it did not happen before – say – 1960, which points in the direction of something man made.'*

He spoke at length about how these cases, involving 'reptilian', and possibly the taller 'greys' and other definitely 'non-human' beings, which he considered to be paranormal, could be created in order to cause confusion. However, he felt that some alien creatures reported, were genuine physical beings – namely advanced biological robots – the little 'workers'.

'And talking about small crew-members, it is my firm belief that they are robots. In our world today we have created various robot types to different tasks. Our visitors, who are thousands of years ahead of us in evolution, also create robots, but, of course, these robots are advanced to suit the purposes of these people's high state of development. So these robots are created as close to the real humans as possible. They are creatures of living substance, but without a brain of their own and without a soul. They are artificially created and are nothing but robots.

'It is often reported by contactees that they have seen such small creatures in the bigger spaceships, apparently serving as crew members. That is, of course, the explanation for the many different shapes of robots, and this again is the explanation for many of the reported strange crew members of landed spaceships. They are robots executing special tasks.'

Either he was not aware of the Amicizia reports of the rebellious CTRs, or he chose not to mention them.

Hans Petersen had been an enthusiastic follower of George Adamski since the early 1950s, and in 1958 had already established twenty-three groups in Denmark. He also helped sponsor and organise Adamski's overseas tour in 1959.

In an earlier interview he had stated that he believed that people from other worlds are visiting our planet, and were in contact with certain political and scientific circles in the East and the West. Further, people from all over the world, in all walks of life have been contacted, but so far, most of these contacts have been kept secret. He finalised by saying that the message promoted by George Adamski was non-political, non-religious and non-sectarian.

It was this same message he advocated to the UFO Study Group; *'This group should work freely, independently and openly, receiving reports and other information from equally qualified national groups throughout the world.*

'The purpose for this should be;
1. To try to establish contact with the visitors.
2. To inform the United Nations and all member states of the information gained through these efforts.
3. To get the world to understand that a new way of life is necessary to avoid destruction through wars, starvation, illness, pollution, drugs and crime.
4. To start a new education system...starting in kindergarten, to teach people to live for the positive things in life.

His hope of attracting the official interest of the United Nations was not to be realised at that time. Years before, Dr. Gairy, the former president of Granada, had endeavoured to involve the United Nations in the subject of UFOs. His efforts were delayed by Dr. Hynek and the USA, and a coup removed him from his position as President before his plans could be realised.

Dag Hammarskjold, who was the United Nations Secretary in 1961, also promised he would speak about UFOs when he returned from the Congo. His plane subsequently crashed, and we will never know what he was going to say.

In March and April 1982, during House of Lords debates, the Earl of Clancarty, Lord Hill Norton, the Earl of Cork and Orrery, and the Earl of Kimberley all pressed Viscount Long for answers on the number of UFO sightings reported in the country.

His answers were sometimes flippant, and always vague and uninformative. He admitted that although all reports from 1967 onwards had been preserved, most from before 1962 were generally destroyed.

In late December 1980, an unknown object landed in Rendlesham Forest, in the vicinity of Woodbridge and Bentwaters Air Force Bases. Lord Norton-Hill, formerly the UK's Chief of Defence Staff, took particular interest in the case, and several years later, when more information became available, he started asking questions the establishment would rather not answer.

Did the US have a large 'nuclear arms dump', stored at the time, at RAF Bases Woodbridge and Bentwaters? (Both Bases are now closed). Lord Hill-Norton's letter, sent to a UK Defence Minister, seems to indicate that this may have been so. He also shared a copy of part of this letter with investigator Leslie Kean, (author of the book - *'UFOs'*).

"My position, both privately and publicly, expressed over the last dozen of years or more, is that there are only two possibilities, either

- a) *An intrusion into our Air Space and a landing by unidentified craft took place at Rendelsham, as described. Or;*
- b) *The Deputy Commander of an operational, nuclear armed, U.S. Air Force Base in England, and a large number of his enlisted men, were either hallucinating or lying.*
- c) *Either of these simply must be 'of interest to the Ministry of Defence', which has been repeatedly denied, in precisely those terms."*

Lord Hill-Norton was not about to let the matter rest there. He had been interviewed by David Jack of the *'Sunday People'* in December 1994, who attributed following comment to the retired Chief of Defence Staff: *"A series of chilling encounters with alien spacecraft have been covered up"*.

The newspaper reporter then went on to elaborate on the 'Rendlesham Forest' incident: *'On December 27th 1980, radar operators at RAF Watton, near Norwich, picked up an unusual 'blip'. As RAF Phantom jets closed in on the object, pilots reported seeing intense bright lights in the sky.'*

'Former radar operator Mal Scurrah said: "As the Phantoms got close, the hovering object shot upwards at phenomenal speed – monitored at more than 1,000 mph."

Three years later Lord Hill-Norton raised the issues in parliament. The answers he received were totally inadequate, and only fuelled speculation that there was one massive 'cover-up' of the entire incident.

He obviously had support amongst some of his colleagues. In 1982, Lady Falkender wrote the *'Foreward'* to Timothy Good's book *'George Adamski-The Untold Story,'* where she said, in part; *'The authors realise the scepticism they have to confront from all those who do not approach this highly sensitive but fascinating subject with an open mind.'*

By 1996 most reports being made were of the iniquitous 'Greys' and Lord Hill-Norton initiated a Memorandum - *'UFO Concern'* - offering to establish an informal, but influential group to study both the objective and subjective facets of the UFO phenomenon.

He wrote, in part; *'Objectively, the available evidence indicates that alien, non-human intelligences and influences are operating increasingly amongst mankind, frequently in a manner which should cause real concern, not only from a national security standpoint, but also because (whatever they are) these 'UFOs' actually appear in a physical, material sense. Reported contacts with them have seldom been beneficial, even if sometimes they have appeared to be so....It is my present view that the first – and perhaps the most difficult – task will be to persuade the public that there really is a problem, and a serious one at that.'*

In 1994, after three years of preparation, a committee formed by several members of the European Parliament, proposed the establishment of a European UFO Observation Centre. The motion was defeated, and not even debated, mainly because of the ridicule it had received from several British MEPs!

Perhaps it was not because of the genuine UFOs. Even in a unified Europe, most member countries would not want anyone else knowing about their own prototypes being tested over home soil.

In the years following the heady 1950s to 1970s, many of the Adamski and other 'believer' groups had fallen by the wayside, and been replaced by more scientific based organisations.

In the United States, one investigator surprisingly emerged. Astronomer Professor Allen Hynek, previously consultant to the sceptical 'Blue Book' project had established 'The Centre for UFO Studies', and made some interesting comments, stating that he now believed UFOs to be real, and not figments of the imagination or misinterpretations of natural phenomena. During his time with the Air Force, well over six hundred cases were 'inexplicable', many displaying the characteristics attributed to 'flying saucers'.

Earlier, in 1966, he attempted to redeem himself when he said that the question as to whether UFOs are extraterrestrial must obviously remain open; "I have in my files hundreds of 'brain-teasers'. The truly puzzling reports come from reliable, stable, educated people who generally consider such reports bunk until shaken by their own experiences. Very few are from cranks or low IQ people.

"In the last two years, UFO sightings have reached a new high. Each wave of sightings adds to the accumulation of reports which defy analysis by present methods of attack. No true scientific investigation of the UFO phenomena has ever been undertaken, despite the great volume of hard data."

In 1973, he visited Australia, and paid his own expenses. Most of his time was spent interviewing witnesses, and of the few lectures he delivered, some were about UFOs but many were on astronomy and science.

CHAPTER TEN

ALIENS AMONG US – Part One

There are multiple claims of humanoid aliens, living among us in our society. Most serious investigators, myself included, start out by being very uncertain regarding these statements, but soon change their minds. Some researchers rely upon the more sane and believable reports, others are fortunate enough to meet a 'space person' themselves.

Over the last few decades our entertainment industry has produced many movies and television series which some believe are designed to familiarise the general public with the concept of extraterrestrials. It was what my colleague, Rosemary Decker, called 'Cosmic Education'.

Gene Roddenberry, the genius who brought decades of *'Star Trek'* into our lounge rooms, concentrated on all kinds of wild and wonderful adventures in outer space in centuries to come. Roddenberry was extremely well informed as to future technology, much of which I suspect had alien origins.

Very few productions featured aliens living among us on Earth. Was this a 'no-no' as far as the authorities were concerned? One exception was an interesting television series, *'The Event'*, which was pulled after nine of its first 21-episode season. This was a fictional tale of human-looking aliens – some in 'detention' and some living secretly in society after their spacecraft crashed.

There were some thought-provoking aspects to this series before it was brought to a sudden halt. The aliens, although they aged more slowly, were genetically compatible with us, and had married and produced children with our normal population. Although some wanted to get the chance to return to their own planet, others had been sufficiently integrated to want to remain here.

A few years ago, French researcher, Leo Noury, shared his thoughts about extraterrestrials in our midst; *'However, the more I read contactee claims, the more I continued hearing about aliens living among us. The sources were very varied: from controversial people like George Adamski to irreproachable researchers like Timothy Good in his superb book 'Alien Base'.*

'With time, as I continued my own research, I began to meet contactees, who were more often than not extremely credible, intelligent and sane people. What

was so extraordinary was that an important percentage of them spoke of meeting aliens in everyday situations! These beings were actually living amongst us in major European cities.'

The humanoid aliens have always been careful to keep a very low profile, and usually make contact in secret. They are careful with whom they communicate, and refuse to have their photograph taken, for fear of being recognised whilst mingling with human populations.

Timothy Beckley wrote about several cases from the 1960s and 1970s where normal people had chance meetings with these undercover aliens. In 1967, Michael Montecalvo, a young student at Maryland University, came across a thirty-feet diameter disc, landed across a highway as he travelled south toward Washington D.C. Two young men were standing in front of it, and one, dressed in a light blue coverall, who had short light brown hair and blue eyes, approached him. During their fifteen minute conversation the man told him his name was 'Vadig' and he was from another planet, outside of our Solar System. He was leaving, but would be seeing him again 'in time'.

In 1968 Michael was working nights in a restaurant, when Vadig came in, sat down and smiled at him. He was wearing conventional clothes, and could was indistinguishable from anyone else in the cafe. The following week Vadig came in again at about 8.30p.m., and said if Michael wished he and his associates would pick him up after he left work.

Michael later joined Vadig in his old sedan car. There was another man in the front seat, "who looked just as normal as anyone I was used to waiting on." Michael said they looked so human, the only thing that convinced him they weren't a couple of hoaxers, was when they took him for a ride in a UFO that was identical to the one that he had seen landed on the road.

Not all our assimilated visitors are young, fair haired, blue eyed men. They tend to resemble our neighbours, or other people in our community. In *'The Alien Gene'* I reported contactee Leesa's reaction to unexpectedly meeting one of them.

"His appearance rather threw me. He was middle-aged, Caucasian, of solid build, about five feet eight inches tall, with sandy, slightly greying hair pulled back in a short ponytail. Whilst my conscious mind warned me this might be some 'psycho' my subconscious instantly recognised the strong electric-type vibes that emanate from these beings. He was not one of us, and yet here he was in broad daylight in the middle of the shopping centre's newsagent. I thought perhaps they come to our normal environment so as not to frighten us.

"As he stood by my side a silent dialogue commenced between our minds. 'Are you?' I queried. 'Yes, I am who you think. It's been a long time, I said we would return.' I was freaked out - in a state of shock, confusion, and panic, but tried not to show it. This guy was talking to me telepathically."

In the 1950s, then celebrated contactee, Howard Menger, made many dubious claims, which were discredited by mainstream researchers. In later years, some of what he insists he was told does make sense. He said that some visitors were coming to trace and make contact with their own distant relatives who were descendants of an ancient race which did not originate on Earth.

Of even more interest is an alleged quote from one of the visitors; *'A lot of our people are amongst you, mingling with your kind, observing and helping where they can. They are in all walks of life – working in factories, offices, banks. Some of them hold responsible positions in communities, in government. Some may be the cleaning lady or even garbage collectors.'*

Many decades ago, mathematician and physicist, James McCampbell, who was highly respected and Chairman of the Northern California American Nuclear Society, did a study of Dr. Jaques Vallee's computerised findings into the various groups of aliens reported by witnesses. Out of just over two hundred cases, eighty five resembled normal humans. He classified these visitors as being; - 'handsome or youthful, with typically long blond hair, a high forehead and usually Caucasian of varying skin tones.'

Of these eighty five he said; *'It is suspected that UFO entities of average height would have little difficulty in infiltrating modern society. They are obviously capable of breathing Earth's atmosphere, and they could not be distinguished in a crowd by their appearance. Of course, they would benefit by being fluent in an appropriate language, and they would require common styles of clothing.*

'In a well planned mission, one or several of them could be landed in the middle of the night, not too far from a populated area, walk into town and blend completely with the population on the sidewalks. Provided with adequate funds,

they could establish residences, take jobs, and become an undifferentiated element of the society.'

This isn't just a situation existing in western countries. Rosanne Lin, of the *'Shanghai Star'*, was reported as saying, in 2005, that Professor Sun Shili, a retired government official, and president of Beijing's UFO Research Society, believes that extraterrestrials are living among us. He does not rule out the possibility of aliens living and working in Chinese society, as China's extraordinary development could be attracting the attention of the visitors. Certainly, a few contactees have noted the 'Asian' appearance of some of the beings.

George Adamski was not the first person of his era to experience contact with visiting extraterrestrials.

Dan Fry
In 1949, Dr. Dan Fry, was an engineering executive, with over thirty years' experience working in Aeronautics and Rocketry Science. Born in 1908, he was in his early thirties when World War II broke out, and spent the duration working for the California Institute of Technology, testing the double base propellent missile which was being developed for use by the armed forces. After the war, from 1949 to 1955, he was employed by the Aerojet General Corporation as an electronics engineer/rocket motor technician.

He claimed an unusual and enlightening experience on 4th July 1949, while stationed at the White Sands Missile Proving Ground in New Mexico. Everyone on the base had gone into a nearby town, to celebrate Independence Day, but Dan had, unfortunately, missed the last bus. It was an uncomfortable, hot night, and the air-conditioning unit in his quarters had broken down.

He decided to go for a walk - a walk which would cause a radical effect on his personality and thinking. When he was some distance from his quarters, he noticed a dark shape was blocking out the stars overhead. He was even more startled when a thirty feet wide object landed near him in the desert. It was about sixteen feet high, spherical, flat top and bottom, and the colour of silver polished metal. As Dan inched closer he noticed it had no visible seams, doors, or windows.

A voice, with a strong American accent, came from the craft, telling him this was a remotely controlled sampling craft, and the 'man' was speaking to him through a communications system from a mother ship, some nine hundred miles above. He apologised and advised that they had superimposed their will upon Dan to lead him to the landing site, something they rarely did unless warranted.

The voice, who said his earthly name was 'Alan', over time imparted the following information: A research ship, from a Galactic Federation, had been monitoring Earth more closely once we invented aeroplanes and flight. They wanted chart our progress to the next step – Space.

Alan told Dan that other civilizations in the galaxy find us of great interest. Firstly, they believe we were genetically engineered much earlier by another advanced intelligent race, which used the Earth as a testing ground for a diversity of life forms. Secondly, our humanoid race is in so many different stages of development at the same time, from stone-age cultures through to modern nuclear-powered communities.

The problem on Earth is that we lack spiritual basis, and cannot control our increasing inventions and technological growth. In fact, they control us. (This was articulated in 1949. Our development of 'doomsday' weapons, and recent dependence on digital technology, confirms this early prediction.)

Some of their people have been sent here to help and advise us, as we need assistance to progress and achieve lasting peace. Without this, we cannot attain the understanding needed for our advancement and continued existence. Alan said he was part of this continuing mission, but he needed Dan's help for his forthcoming assignment. He and his people had advanced technology, which let them live on self-supporting space ships. He was neither American nor from Earth, and his current assignment required him to infiltrate our society as both.

While his people, who had been coming here for centuries, were biologically and physically similar to us, it would take him four to five years to become accustomed to our different atmosphere and stronger gravity, and learn to speak our language fluently. Also, the sampling craft was checking our atmosphere for micro-organisms to identify any immunity he might require.

After Dan agreed to help, he was allowed to enter the craft for a thirty minute 'joy flight', during which time he noticed that the ship rotated, and reached an altitude of about thirty-five miles. As he travelled, Alan explained the physics, gravity and propulsion of the vessel. (This later proved invaluable to Dan in his own work in aeronautics.) Alan also advised that we all possess mental telepathy, an ability we rarely use, and they had recorded Dan's 'frequency pattern' for future use.

This encounter had a radical effect on Dan's personality and thinking. A few months later a small glowing ball appeared, giving him instructions to leave textbooks and newspapers etc. for Alan to study. These were collected by a sampling device and then returned. Fry then helped Alan and his colleague, Vera, with birth certificates, passports, bank accounts and professions. While Dan, and others who arranged false identifications were possibly involved in espionage activities, I don't think anyone was ever charged. Perhaps the government and military didn't need the publicity!

Dan Fry had other meetings with Alan, and in 1954 was told to write his experiences and pass the message on to others, because our social and spiritual values do not equal our material science, a fatal flaw in previous civilisations which were annihilated. Efforts to change must come from humans themselves. Dan felt it would be futile, the media would distort the message, and he would be ridiculed. Alan agreed but encouraged him saying: "Ridicule is the barrier which the ignorant erect between themselves and any truth which frightens or disturbs them."

In 1955, Dan founded a group called '*Understanding*', and published a regular newsletter. In the 1960s he went on several lecture tours to promote his book, '*The White Sands Incident*', and stressed that his audiences needed scientific explanations when asking questions about this subject. While he never brought religion or politics into his assertions, he did stress that; 'We are all one', hence his support for understanding and unity amongst mankind. This was the key to world peace and happiness.

He rarely, if ever, promoted or entered into any religious debate or beliefs. He did, however, say; "The followers of each religion are required to accept all of the dogma of that religion, and are denied the right to consider the merits of the others. And so, however much good the present religions of Earth may accomplish, they must fail as a unifying force."

Dan suggested that Alan and his colleagues were here more as 'missionaries', in the service of humanity, to offer us such portion of their culture and knowledge which may be useful and accepted by us.

They likened their interaction with Earth to our own experiences when coming in contact with remote indigenous tribes; *'If the missionaries wished to avoid being cooked in the village stew-pots, or becoming burnt offerings to the village gods, they would have to proceed very slowly and very carefully.*

'If an advanced race upon another planet decided to send missionaries to planet Earth, they would be well advised to proceed in the same way. In fact, the perusal of the front page of any metropolitan newspaper should be enough to cause them to give up the whole project as a hopeless undertaking, and to leave for home at once.'

Dan kept in covert contact with Alan who told him that there were other alien races here, with different agendas. Another meaningful disclosure was that they can tune into our individual frequencies, and if necessary probe our minds or superimpose their will on us. This certainly explains some of the experiences reported by contactees and abductees.

Was Dan being misled? Other White Sands employees certainly saw UFOs, and believed in them. Alan told Fry that they had chosen him because of his open mind about scientific concepts, and details of advanced physics, which Alan imparted to him, were also proven in later years. Dan also commented that some information had been exceedingly useful to him in his own work. There was no way it could have all originated in his own mind.

In 1981, some of the *'Understanding'* groups had fallen by the wayside, but many had emerged as independent 'study groups'. Dan said that he occasionally received a phone call from Alan, who had now relocated here on Earth, and was operating an import-export business in Cairo, Egypt.

In 1989, realising he was aging, Dan wrote a letter titled *'The Sad Time of Parting'*, to his friends. He mentioned two books he was writing, and hoped to finish. The most important, *'When in Cairo'*, would "deal with the problems and concerns of Alan in his struggle to keep the world at peace. It is about 70% true and 30% fiction, which is necessary to avoid disclosure of the true names of some of the characters, who still need security. Those of you who have read *'To Men of Earth'* will find little difficulty determining who the characters actually are."

Dan Fry died in 1992, and I am not sure if he ever completed or published his second planned book, *'The Tachyon Drive'*; 'an educational science book about an astronaut who starts out for one place and winds up somewhere else, due to the tricks of an automatic launching system.'

(I had US colleagues, personal friends, who were Dan Fry's contemporaries. They knew him well and believed him. Desmond Leslie also met Dan Fry, and had this to say; "Fry struck me as an intelligent and matter-of-fact kind of man; neither the type to suffer from delusions nor the type to invent fairy tales.")

Astronaut Gordon Cooper knew Dan when he was in charge of instruments for missile control and guidance at White Sands. He said "I have seen my share of wide-eyed UFO fanatics and lunatics – Fry was not in that category. I found him totally credible."

In later life Dan Fry was quoted as saying; "My most significant experience that I had is probably finding out the major purpose for this invasion, so to speak, was to keep this planet alive. The ETs went on to say; *'When those among you, responsible for your scientific achievements, realise the significance of the destructive forces you are creating, only then will you understand that you are destroying your living planet which is responsible for your very existence.*

'We are here to advise, guide and encourage you to turn your eyes towards the creation of a planet of peace and understanding, where your invention and universal ability co-exist with the creative force of the cosmos. We are your brothers of the Galactic Federation who wish only to have you by our side. We cannot join you until your thoughts turn from self-destruction to the eternal law of universal knowledge."

George Adamski also described how easy it was in the 1950s to arrange false ID materials for aliens to 'set themselves up', if required.

He wrote; *'Let us remember that travelling in space is not new to our neighbours. They have been coming our way for centuries, so family ties and friendships are well established throughout the world. Records are kept of those living on Earth, and when a newcomer arrives, a meeting is arranged. Remember too, that the necessity for personal identification papers is a comparatively recent requirement, particularly in the USA. You will find many people who do not have a birth certificate, for not too many years ago, registration of a birth was left to the discretion of the attending physician.*

'Others have lost their records through fires, storms or similar disasters which destroyed official records. It has only been in later years that some States have required children entering school to show a birth certificate. Before then it was not considered necessary for a person to prove by a piece of paper that he had been born.

'As for obtaining a Social Security number in this country, so far as I know it is not necessary to produce a birth certificate or any other record. The driver's license, one of our accepted methods of identification, can be obtained by anyone with good eyesight and the ability to drive a car. While it is true that birth certificates and other means of identification are a requisite to obtain work in certain industries, by far the greater number of companies never ask for these records. We have made much ado about personal identification papers, but actually, most of these are not too difficult to secure.'

Those living in our society had many problems to overcome. Not only did they need to assume false identities and avoid detection, the need for money necessitated them to fund and support themselves by various ingenious means. The Ummites supposedly used 'off planet' diamonds as a major source of income. Adamski said that, in order to generate funds, the space people had once been involved in the British shipping industry, and implied that they had moved on to other money-earning ventures in America. I have heard several reports of the Visitors running cafes and restaurants, where their colleagues could meet, and if necessary take refuge.

In 1960, Hans Petersen, a Danish Air Force officer and UFO researcher, disclosed that he was aware of two Scandinavian cases of contact with space people living amongst us. At the time of his writing to a colleague about the reports, investigations into a Norwegian case were not yet complete.

In Denmark, the visitor who had been present during the 1950s, had since departed, with a replacement yet to appear. He contacted a forty year-old engineer, and asked him to liaise with, and pass information to other people in the country with whom they could not establish direct contact.

Many senior military officers retired after World War II, and returned to civilian life. Some developed more than a passing interest in the UFO phenomenon. Hans Petersen also received a letter from a former American Brigadier-General, regarding incidents in the late 1950s and early 1960s. Hans allowed Fred Stone to reprint it, without divulging the source, in 1971.

'Now, in regard to the Space Ships and their crews, so-called 'Flying Saucers'. What I am about to impart to you, I am asking you as a fellow veteran not to divulge the source of – you are free to repeat it, but not the source.

'Now, do I have an explanation to your good wife's question. And not a theory, but facts from my own personal experiences and contacts. Let me first state that through no effort or expectation on my part, I was contacted late one night, eleven years ago, while working late in my shop to finish a printing job.

'True, like most intelligent beings, I was interested and curious, but had no expectations of contact. They came to my shop door, insisted on my opening it, came in, looked around a bit, spoke no word, and motioned me to come outside. As I did so I became aware of a large object, a few feet overhead. I was taken aboard, and had my first experience of positive telepathy, a very informative few minutes. They left saying they would return soon. They kept their word and they returned. I think I can honestly say a few hundred times since, in the past eleven years.

'They have requested that I act as their physical earth-man contact with quite a number of our national and religious leaders, and my identity and nationality must remain a strict secret, except with their permission as in your case. You can understand, that if my identity and work were to become known, I would never have a moment's rest, and would soon become worthless to both them and the problems I attempt to handle.

'Now to the ability to speak perfect English.......Among their own people they use thought only, but we of Earth, because of our habit, they have learned our language so perfectly that if one of them was to stop up and speak to you in your place of business or your home or on the street, you would not recognise him from one of your own people, and in appearance probably the greatest difference you would note would be his handsome features and perfect proportions physically.'

The letter went on to say that that the Brigadier-General's humanoid contacts had initiated several of our modern technological discoveries. They also claimed to come from Venus, and that different alien races lived on other planets in the Solar System. I honestly believe that our 'Space Brothers' deliberately lied about their place of origin. Perhaps this was for their own protection, or alternatively maybe they considered that we were not yet able to comprehend space travel light years across the galaxy. It is always possible they merely have bases within our Solar System. One assertion I do believe, is that there are other alien races also visiting our planet.

In his book, *'Earth; An Alien Enterprise'*, Timothy Good quotes several sources who state that what we have been told about Venus is wrong. Whilst I am always open, given the evidence, to change my mind, I prefer to stay with the scientific and astronomical data currently available.

The Brigadier-General finalised his letter by saying;.... *'I think you can see why I have had to ask you to withhold the information source. You now have some information that so far as I am aware, not a dozen earth men have as yet, and you would not have that without, as we call them, "The Boys Upstairs' permission to do so.'*

It is interesting that the Brigadier-General was 'allowed' to share this information with Hans Petersen and Fred Stone, because both of these ufologists had claimed to have met the Space Brothers themselves.

At the other end of the globe, in South Africa, the Space Brothers were also intermingling with human society. The Durban Branch of 'Contact South Africa' investigated, at some length, the following incidents. (Pseudonyms have been used.)

Edwin, who was born in Transvaal, and later raised in Durban, had known about UFOs and 'visitors' from his father, who possibly had contacts with them. He died when Edwin was in his teens, but the boy already had some knowledge about these matters.

Shortly after, in 1960, when Edwin was eighteen, he was working for a company who advertised for a radio technician. They employed George, one of the applicants, who started work in the same departmental section as Edwin. They got to know each other, and soon became friends. George, who said he was from Johannesburg, was staying at a hotel. Edwin, who lived further out of town, would stop by every morning, on his motorbike, and give George a lift to work.

As their friendship developed, they would go out together on weekends, and often went fishing; *"It was then he really started to work on me. One night, when we were on Patterson's Groyne, we saw a light in the sky. I mentioned to George that I wondered if it was a Sputnik or a UFO. He then asked for my opinion on UFOs, people from other worlds, and so on."*

Once Edwin had confirmed that he believed there must be life somewhere 'out there', George initiated many conversations about life in space, and often referred to our own historical references.

Edwin said; *"I suppose it took him about eight months to really convince me, and then one day he said that he was going to give me absolute proof that the lights in the sky aren't all Sputniks. We made arrangements to go fishing again, at the same spot, on a Saturday night."*

George always used to borrow Edwin's fishing rod, but that night Edwin noticed George had a leather bag with him, and thought it must contain something to eat later.

When they reached Patterson's Groyne, there were quite a few people about, but by 2am only a couple were left. It was then George said he wanted to prove something, and opened the leather bag. Inside was a type of instrument. Later George told him that it was a device which could amplify telepathic messages, and they used it to communicate with each other. George pulled out a type of antenna which was attached to the gadget, and then started to talk in a strange language which Edwin had never heard before.

After thirty minutes had passed, a light came in from the sea, moved along the shore, and hovered above the two men. The object was emitting a constant blue-white light, and then performed a couple of aerial manoeuvres. George said that it was responding to a homing device which he had already placed nearby.

George spoke into his instrument again, and Edwin was surprised when a voice replied. It was speaking in English, and addressing Edwin.

"The voice said that he was the commander of the spacecraft above us. He described the manoeuvres he had just performed, and gave the altitude. The Commander then said he was going to show me what happens when a spacecraft leaves at maximum acceleration, and to listen carefully.

"Before he left, he told me who George was, and he had come specially to find someone suitable who was willing to start a group so that interested people could join. George would tell me exactly what his mission was, and what my mission was to be, if I was willing to accept. The craft then moved off, making a sonic boom as it streaked away."

George stayed for two years, and Edwin helped him research all the information he could gain from libraries, museums and churches. They attended every religious service in the area, as George wanted to know what the ministers were preaching. He was dismayed at the amount of drunks, brawls and general lawlessness in the community.

In 1962, it was time for George to depart, but before he left, he taught Edwin how to communicate with him telepathically. Edwin claims that he was able to keep contact with him over the following years.

At Easter, 1962, Edwin took George fishing to Richards Bay. They waited for nightfall, and went to the beach where he had to be at 10pm. George was now wearing his blue uniform, which looked like a tight-fitting track suit. He said it was made of a special material which gave him protection against certain radiations. He also had two suitcases and his leather bag, and spoke into the gadget inside.

A light approached from the sea, and George said as Edwin had no radiation protection, he must move back as far as possible next to the sand dunes. They shook hands, and said their farewells. George said that he would be away for a while, but they would meet again.

It was low tide, and the large disc-shaped craft was able to land on the beach. It was about 160 feet in diameter, with a dome on the top. There were large observation windows, with a figure standing at one of them, and bright white light shining through.

A column, like a lift shaft, extended from the bottom of the craft, and after George entered it retracted back inside. The disc took to the air, moved over the sea, and climbed rapidly out of sight.

In keeping with George's request, Edwin and his wife organised a group of interested people. In 1963, they formed their first 'Q-Base', where a handful of enthusiasts received messages via a 'radio tuner/transmitter'. It seems that George had advised him of the technological specifics to make this possible.

Some communication was apparently established, but not as much as some people claimed. In later years, possibly in 1974, the group was disbanded. It had become disorganised, perhaps due to the members' personal egos and conflicting claims. Whilst Edwin had always proved trustworthy, the reports from others during this time were somewhat suspect.

There are some interesting parallels between this and the 'Mr X' case in New Zealand. Firstly; that for some time the space beings had a base not far from Durban, and communicated by 'talking' and delivering notes to Edwin's post box at night. (Although, unlike the 'Mr X' case, Edwin does not seem to have made the correspondence available for verification.)

Secondly; the use of music; although apparently not of their composition, the visitors had used tunes of earthly origin as signature identification for their transmissions.

In 1998, prominent South African researcher, Cynthia Hind published a 'follow-up' report on Edwin's case. One night, at about 10.30pm, there was a knock on his door in Pinetown. Three men in civilian clothing, produced police badges and came in. They said that they wanted to see the radio he used to receive alien messages.

They took Edwin and his radio to a building, and into what was supposedly their office. It was small, but looked genuine enough, with filing cabinets, and a woman typing at a desk. They sat him down, and questioned him for nearly three hours, and then warned him not to receive nor send messages to 'alien' countries as he was not a licensed radio ham.

Ten days later, Edwin went to the nearby police station, and asked for his radio back, however they denied any knowledge of the matter. He took a friend over to the old building, and the 'office' where the three men had interviewed him. It was locked and empty, except for a few papers strewn on the floor.

Cynthia said Edwin's radio was eventually returned in mysterious, and possibly anonymous circumstances. When I heard about this, I began to understand why the similarly affiliated radio hams in Australia, New Zealand and the USA exchanged a flurry of correspondence about specialised equipment, but never once mentioned why they needed it and with whom they were communicating.

The night sky over Patterson's Groyne, at North Beach Durban, seemed to be a favourite spot for our space visitors. In March 1961, Fred White and his friend Henry O'Dank were fishing alone at about 3am, when they saw a light, high in the eastern sky. It was travelling south, and then changed course and headed towards the two men, coming to a halt over the sea, about seventy-five feet away. It was only about one hundred feet above the water, from where Fred and Henry got a clear view of the amazing craft.

It was large and circular, over one hundred feet in diameter, with a distinct dome and large portholes at regular intervals. It was lit with a greenish glow, and silently hovered at a slight angle for about five minutes. Afterwards, it levelled off and with a slight whining noise, followed the coast for about half a mile, circled a few times, and rapidly climbed away.

The two friends agreed not to tell anyone about it, but at Easter, the following year, Fred went fishing with another friend, Michael, to Richard's Bay, about 150 miles north of Durban.

On the Saturday night they returned to their campsite, about a mile out of the village, to have some supper. When they tried to listen to the radio, they only got static, despite having an excellent reception earlier. Michael decided to have an early night, and Fred went for a walk.

He stopped to have a cigarette, and sat down on the side of a steep sand dune going down to the beach. Everything around was peaceful and deserted. He suddenly heard a high pitched whine and saw a bright light, as big as the moon, travelling from the east, low over the sea. It had been moving south, but changed course and headed to where Fred was resting.

It was only about one hundred feet above the shore, and when it started to descend, Fred panicked and started trying to climb away up the steep sand dune where he had been sitting. The more he struggled to get away, the more he became stuck in the loose sand. Eventually, almost paralysed with fear, he sat back down, fearing the worst.

By that time, the craft was only yards away, and as the whining sound stopped, and it appeared to hover just over the beach. He could feel a strong down-draft which scattered the sand around him.

It was similar to the disc he and Henry had seen the previous year, but this time from a closer vantage point. It had the same green glow, and was metallic, at least one hundred feet in diameter and seventy-five feet high. This time he could see through the large port-holes. The interior of the craft was brilliantly lit, with what looked like a circular control panel running along the outer wall.

He then noticed a man staring at him from the nearest porthole. He could only see him from the waist up, but he had a muscular build and fair complexion. He was wearing a shining metallic helmet which seemed to merge with a high collared blue material tunic. When he raised his hands, he appeared to have shiny mesh gloves.

For about six minutes he and this strange man stared at each other, then there was a hum which increased to a distinct whine. The craft slowly rose from the sand, and at a height of about two hundred feet, paused, then moved out to sea and disappeared at an incredible speed.

Fred rushed back to camp, but Michael was asleep. By morning, he thought better about saying anything. The radio was working again, the tide had come in over the landing spot, and there was no evidence of what had happened the previous night.

It was several years before he confided in one of the researchers at the Durban branch of Contact South Africa, which he had quietly joined after his experience. Fred, like many others around the world, had secretly built himself a powerful radio receiver, and was picking up strange signals.

In September 1966, Fred was rushed to hospital with a collapsed lung, which had a large hole in it. The next morning, during visiting hour, a strange man sat down next to his bedside. He was of medium height and build, with fair hair, glowing Caucasian skin, and blue eyes which Fred felt were probing his very soul. He spoke with a slight foreign accent, and seemed to be uncomfortable and fidgety in the tailored suit he was wearing.

The stranger, who did not identify himself, called Fred by name, as if he knew him well. At first Fred did not recognise him, but was convinced, later, that it was the same man he had seen through the porthole of the spaceship over four years earlier.

After inquiring about Fred's medical condition, his visitor quickly changed the conversation to his radio receiver, and the 'dead-end' Fred had been encountering. Fred was flabbergasted, as he thought no-one else knew about it.

"Never mind," said his visitor. "You will meet a certain man, who will help you along. Be prepared for great changes, and there will be more contacts."

After the man left, Fred realised all the pain had gone and there was no more rattle in his chest. That afternoon, the doctors were astounded at the improvement in his health. X-rays showed his lung was fully inflated, and the hole had healed without even a sign of a scar.

CHAPTER ELEVEN

ALIENS AMONG US – Part Two

THE 'AMICIZIA'
There were many incidents in Italy in late 1962, early 1963, and the following years. The 'Amicizia', (Friendship), was the name used for a very secretive forty year interaction between normal citizens and humanoid and other friendly aliens. To the best of investigators' knowledge, it began in 1956, however it might have been occurring much earlier. There is evidence of similar groups in Switzerland and other neighbouring areas, where the same terminology was used; 'Amitie' in France and 'Freundschaft' in Germany and Austria.

In Australia, we have many migrants from Europe, who arrived in the decades after World War II. Colleagues and acquaintances who came from Northern Italy, Switzerland, Austria, Germany, France and Northern Siberia told me of some of their older relatives who had been involved with the 'Friendship Groups'.

(Given the still centralised area of these particular groups I have wondered how long they were actually there, and about any possible connection, good or bad, with the Third Reich who were the occupying force, during World War II.)

The visitors had their bases in a variety of hidden subterranean locations, some under mountains, others below existing buildings, or even under the sea.

Anthony Huneeus, a leading researcher in Chile, claimed that at one time, the Amicizia had established a base on an island off the county's south coast. This was divulged to the public during a TV program, when a well-known radio broadcaster claimed the aliens on the island had healed him of a terminal illness.

Naturally, the military sat up and took notice. There were hundreds of small islands off the coast, and the Chilean Navy's investigations led them to a small island where a mysterious ship, the *'Mytilus'*, which was not registered in accordance with Chilean law, used to ferry people back and forth. Of course, by the time the Navy got there, they found no evidence of a base.

South American researchers, Liliana Flotta and Eduardo Grosso, of the ONIFE group, wrote a fascinating article about, Orlando Ferraudi who is now over eighty years old.

In 1956, Orlando, then only eighteen, was fishing at a remote spot on the northern shore of Buenos Aires in Argentina. A strange man came up and took him by the arm, mentally asking him to come with him. Orlando 'lost his will', and couldn't refuse this 'person's' commands.

The man was over six feet tall, with an athletic build, white skin, blond cropped hair and amber eyes. He was wearing a yellow/orange one piece suit which gave off small 'sparks', and Orlando realised that this fellow was not terrestrial.

He was 'receiving' assurances to stay calm, they were going on a journey, and no harm would befall him. Orlando saw a huge dark shadow coming from the river, and an object, about seventy metres in diameter, and shaped like a soup bowl, was close to the bank. A ramp appeared, and his companion and another being helped him to walk across and into the craft.

He entered a small domed room, where there was a young Argentinean girl, Elena, who had also been taken from her home. A tall blond woman, obviously also an extraterrestrial, gave Orlando a change of clothes, and performed some decontamination processes.

All communication was still telepathic. He and Elena were told that they were going into space, but to avoid detection would go underwater to the Bay of San Borombon, to the coast of Uruguay, and finally cross over to Africa from where they would leave our atmosphere.

Orlando gave investigators a detailed description of the disc's interior, and controls, which needed to be manned by a minimum of nine beings. He also explained some of the alien technology, which I am sure would have been of great interest to our own military and scientists.

He watched as they passed the Earth and Moon, and soon their captors told them they would be returning, at an incredible speed. This time they plunged into the Caribbean, and soon saw a transparent underwater structure, which must have covered five or six hectares of the ocean floor. They also spotted several other craft, and were told it was a 'maintenance station'.

They entered the facility via a 'sort of tunnel', and once there, subjected to medical examinations. Later they were given back their clothes, and told that 'work' had been done on their pineal glands. This would enable the beings to more easily telepathically contact them in the future.

Orlando was full of questions, many of which they answered. They also explained the need for secrecy regarding their base; "We must take these precautions so that we can avoid being regarded as invaders or conquerors. We want your people to get used to us slowly, to see us just like anybody else, because we are not strangers in this part of the Universe."

They also demonstrated a fearful weapon. A small hand-held device, which when activated totally disintegrated the target. He was given a stern warning for humans of Earth; "We want you to know that this power will be brought to bear against you, much to our regret, if you jeopardise interstellar harmony."

He didn't know how, but next the thing he remembered was waking up at sunrise from the same place he had been taken. Six hours were missing from his life, but the complex technology he could describe added credence to his report.

Another similar, but slightly more dubious report was documented by researcher Warren Aston, who considered the account of the witness, Enrique Rincon, whilst initially straight forward and believable, later spiralled down into a 'more quasi religious morass of vague and ludicrous prophecies.' However, this has been a pattern with some contactees, and perhaps, if they divulged too much, it was an effort by the visitors to discredit them.

Basically, Enrique met a 'Swiss' man in Caracas, Venezuela in 1969. They became friends and socialised until the man was transferred elsewhere. In later years, Enrique made physical contact with a large spacecraft only to discover his 'friend' was one of the crew.

What followed were several purported trips in the craft, including one to a secret base, high in the Andes, and another to an underwater alien base.

There are many reports of secret alien bases on Earth. Gordon Creighton wrote of a Swedish account from August 1960.

Olaf Nielsen, an agricultural student, was walking along a lonely Halmstad spot, between a wood and some fields, when he suddenly felt dizzy and was inexplicably being sucked up into the air. When he was about twenty metres off the ground, he realised he was being drawn straight up into a flying saucer.

He lost consciousness, and when he recovered, he was lying on a soft couch inside a small cabin. A door opened, and a man came in. He looked totally human, and was wearing a pair of overalls.

Olaf said; "He approached, smiled at me, and in my own language, begged my pardon for the way in which I had been carried off."

The craft moved rapidly, and landed in a 'subterranean base', which looked like a huge, brightly-lit cavern. His guide explained that these bases had existed on Earth for many years. Some were on the high plateau of the Pamirs, and others in Africa and South America, where the space visitors had adapted pre-Incan cities for their own purposes.

Before he left, he was shown a subterranean hangar, where several saucers were kept. Apparently there was a protective magnetic curtain defending the entrance. This was not directed against the people of Earth. The visitors main concern were bellicose space-beings they called the 'Dark Ones'.

It was suggested that after the US rejected their offer for help in 1954, these aliens, (who were in opposition to another more hostile race – the *'contrari'* or 'CTR' – who were also visiting Earth), decided to convey their message of peace and morality to the general public.

Umberto Visani documented this situation, saying it did not just involve a small group of individuals, but specifically chosen people of varying walks in life, from professionals to students and housewives. Politicians, university professors, engineers and journalists were all reputed to be incorporated in this clandestine interaction. Further, there was ample evidence at the time, including recordings, photos and videos. The level of contact went from one time encounters to deep participation lasting over forty years.

In 2009 Professor Stefano Breccia, who was apparently involved, wrote a book *'Mass Contacts'* which details the accounts of Bruno Sammaciccia, the leader of the Italian group. Sammaciccia was a prominent Italian theologian and psychologist, and he entrusted his notes to Breccia, to be published after his death in 2003. Other books and articles have also surfaced, but usually after the supposed 'departure' of the visitors and the demise of the witnesses.

One observation, which sounded familiar to me, was that Breccia claimed that one of the Visitors told him, in 1967, that there was another star, as yet undiscovered, fairly close to our Solar System. (It reminded me of what the 'Khan' had told Ruth, and the multiple reports over the last few years, that there was a large body near the Solar System which some considered may be a brown dwarf binary companion to our Sun – detailed in *'UFOs Now and Then'*)

Breccia said that they had nicknamed the 'Amicizia' visitors the 'W56' due to their first contact in 1956. Some of these beings were much shorter or taller than their human counterparts, and far different in physical appearance. Others were essentially the same as us. Together, they comprised a 'joint task force', collectively known as the 'Akrij'.

Bruno described the visitors, who looked human, as having either blond or black hair, with greyish-blue or black eyes. They had slim, but strong bodies, and often sported a beard. Unlike some of their colleagues, it was relatively easy for them to integrate and live incognito in society. It seems that they had been here for a long time, and a few are still among us. He claimed that they are so closely related to us genetically that they can, and probably have interbred.

Bruno made mention of radio contacts with the 'W56', who were able to 'hide their radio signals and transmit their own messages'. This supports the evidence of other ham radio operators, around the globe, surreptitiously communicating with the 'space people'.

Most of the craft seen in the skies were primarily used for observation, rather than transportation. The 'Akrij' who mingled in society adopted assumed identities and used normal earth vehicles such as cars, trucks and sometimes small planes. They were often so imbedded in everyday life, they engaged in worldly professions. Stefano Breccia mentioned how one was a university researcher, another a textile company manager, and a third a senior manager of a large German telecommunications corporation. Their true identities were strictly secret, and never divulged.

Why were they here? Australian ufologist, Warren Aston, Timothy Good and other investigators have researched the Amicizia. Warren published the following letter, written in 1967, by Franco Saiji, a magistrate from Turin, Italy, to Count Gian Luigi Zoccoli of Bologna, where he described his experiences with his Akrij friends;

'We are dwarfs with respect to their values! We cannot hope to receive easily from them what we are meant to achieve, day after day, as centuries go by...We have to dig our own road. This is the purpose of life and human evolution. Man has a divine destiny!

'Only one thing is possible to those who have confronted this new reality...to witness that elsewhere the purpose of life and the Universe has been understood. The dreadful questions that have always tormented us about existence have been answered. But the right road is different from the one we are now on, and we must change now, before it is too late.'

Warren wrote a very persuasive comment regarding this letter; *'The pathos in Saiji's letter is an eloquent commentary on humanity's common destiny. It echoes the underlying conclusion of all the genuine contactees: we are meant for much more, a future in a universe of limitless possibilities.'*

Timothy Good also reported that in 1978 the CTRs attacked and destroyed most of the W56 bases, including ones under the Adriatic. The largest, which was the scene of a heated battle, was at a depth of twelve miles from the surface, and extended from the centre of the Adriatic to the centre of Italy.

The references to the CTRs also became much more meaningful in later years, when hapless victims reported unpleasant abductions by the 'greys' with skinny bodies, large heads, black wrap-around eyes, and no visible reproductive organs. One of the W56 told Stefano that; "The CTRs are the result of a W56 experiment that has run out of control. They are robots, in the full sense of the word, even if centuries ago they began as a biological reproduction with no soul or emotions."

He added that it would be difficult for us to discriminate between a natural being and a biological robot, and these entities are trying to understand how to bridge the difference between themselves and us. This certainly would explain the behaviour of the 'greys', and makes sense of their interest in genetics, and human and animal reproductive and biological material.

While most of the Akrij departed Earth by 1986, they promised that they would return. Some have remained integrated in our society, and maintain smaller bases elsewhere on the planet. Since then, reports of flying saucers with beautiful blond haired emissaries have been almost non-existent.

British author and investigator, Timothy Good, wrote of the testimony of respected Italian science journalist, Bruno Ghibaudi, who said that he, along with other witnesses, met with several of the W56 aliens; *'They explained that although nuclear weapons remained one of their principal reasons for their increased presence, there were other reasons he was forbidden from disclosing,* (The alleged conflict with the CTRs undoubtedly being one, I would assume).

The Space Brothers were also present in the United States, and indeed around the world. Lucius Farrish reported on a radio discussion on the Armed Forces Radio from Bad Kissingen in Germany.

'On March 9th 1960, a small, wingless, circular plane landed on top of a large mesa in the State of Nevada. The occupants consisted of two men of average size. They appeared to be quite friendly, and spoke the English language well.

'They approached a small ranch dwelling owned by an Edwin Connell, making him an offer. In exchange for room and board, they would take him on one trip in their plane. The destination was not given. Though frightened by the appearance of the strange plane, he later agreed. He was a bachelor, and the visitors stayed with him for thirteen months, making frequent trips by train and bus to New York and other major cities, including Little Rock, Arkansas.

Connell described the plane as being saucer shaped and it made a large hum when departing. Though offered a considerable amount of money, Connell would give no information concerning the ship's interior, the contents, the trip he had supposedly taken or the 'visitors' mission. The rancher would only state; "All mankind shall benefit within a few years."

'The reality of the plane, and its outward appearance was verified by three local residents who visited the scene. Quoting one spectator; "It appeared to be about fifty feet across and round – almost flat – standing only about seven feet tall. It rested flat upon the ground. There were no visible signs of doors, windows or opening of any type. The edge was quite sharp to the touch, and the metal seemed to be highly polished aluminium."

'The plane vanished within a few days, reappearing in the early part of April 1961. On April 16th, the visitors entered the craft, and within moments were gone. The final departure was verified by a sixteen year old youth who stated;

"I visited the object several times when it was first here. Later, after it disappeared, I would walk over occasionally. That day, I saw it again. It was at the edge of the mesa, and being alone, I was afraid to go to near. It was then I saw Mr. Connell and two men walking toward the plane. About twenty-five to thirty yards from the plane they stopped and talked for a few minutes. They shook hands, and the two men continued toward the ship. As they drew near, a small, narrow door began to open from the bottom upward. The men went inside and the door shut. There was a loud, high pitched 'hum', and the craft began vibrating. I blinked my eyes, and it was gone."

Lucius also said the broadcast mentioned other 'visitors', both male and female, living among us – sometimes permanently. Their normal length of stay was supposed to be one year before a replacement was sent, but some chose to stay longer. Their reason for being here was – *'helping mankind mechanically and preventing total destruction should war occur.'*

If aliens were already present on Earth, then there would be no way to know of their hidden locations or possible secret bases.

When George Adamski was on the Asian leg of his world tour in 1959, he spoke of dining with some businessmen in India, who also reported the secretive presence of aliens.

Five years later, in 1964, German businessman, Ludwig Pallman, was travelling on a train from Bombay to Madras. He began talking to a fellow passenger in his compartment. He had light brown skin, small mouth and huge dark eyes, not uncommon in the sub-continent. Pallman also noticed his unusual chin line, something often reported by contactees.

During their conversation, the stranger said that his name was Satu Ra, and he came from a place called Cotosoti, another world far out in space. He said that he and his colleagues were explorers who had discovered Earth and its abundance of plant life, in 1946. His people had established several plantations in South America, where they collected, researched and hybridised diverse plant species for their diet.

Pallman became friends with Satu and some of his alien companions. In about 1967, while working in Peru, he was taken on board one of their ships and spent some time with them at their jungle base. He learned that they administered medicine to the local people whenever they could be of help. When Pallman himself became ill with kidney disease, and was cured with medicine given to him by Satu's sister.

Timothy Good wrote about one witness, Joelle, whom he knew well. She claimed contact with two Visitors, Mark and Val, who she had met in 1963, when their craft landed in the Derbyshire Peak District. For well over a year she maintained contact with them at several places in England, and entertained them in her flat on at least two occasions.

Joelle claimed they were physical beings who looked totally human and fair-skinned, with perfect teeth, although she noticed that there was a dark-skinned man who was part of the group. They spoke their own language together, but could also use mental communication between minds, and advised they usually employed telepathy to influence people, and on odd occasions interfered directly. They told her they came from a similar planet in another Solar System, and admitted that on two occasions in the past, their people had genetically interfered with us. While they did not discuss their reasons for coming, they did suggest that we need to evolve psychologically and spiritually, and remarked: "What a beautiful planet. Such a pity you're destroying it." They also referred to other extraterrestrials also coming here, who were 'not so well disposed towards us'.

They had told her that their 'people' had facilities in several countries including South America, Australia and the Soviet Union. She also claimed they said they had been liaising in secret with a team of scientists from several nations, and some of them had worked at their bases. She once asked about George Adamski, and they confirmed being connected to the same group he was involved with. They said that once he started revealing sensitive details they started feeding him disinformation.

In 1967, three years after her last contact with Mark and Val, Joelle received a visit from two people from the Home Office in London. They were enquiring about the disappearance of some scientists who were mutual acquaintances.

They seemed reasonably knowledgeable about everything, but actually seemed pleased when she refused to answer certain questions.

During their discussions, Mark had mentioned that to Joelle they had bases on two unspecified moons around Jupiter. (Upon reflection, this made me consider there may be other similar bases 'out there'. Since we are on an outer arm of the Milky Way, perhaps our Solar System has some significance – a military outpost in the Galaxy? Is there more than one extraterrestrial race anxious to have a presence? No wonder the aliens were getting fidgety about our own ventures into space!)

I had always assumed that aliens integrated into our society would either be lone individuals or couples, adept at making a quick escape if discovered. I had never considered that complete families would have infiltrated, until a colleague told me of an unusual happening – not decades ago, but now in the twenty-first century.

He was walking along the street when he saw a man and a woman with three children coming towards him. They seemed to be flawless examples of mankind, almost angelic with blond hair, fair skin and perfect features. He looked at the little boy, and thought to himself 'what a beautiful child'. The youngster turned and silently stared back at him. "Thank you!" said a voice in his head!

I realised that there were a couple of other instances which suggested that perhaps there were some extraterrestrial families here on Earth.

In his book *'Earth – an Alien Enterprise'*, Timothy Good tells of a case related to him by Carl Anderson; *'He recounts how a trusted friend of his, a native American chief, who lived in east Los Angeles, was camping one night in 1965 at Salton Sea, (a National Wildlife lake recreation area where he owned quite a lot of land), when he and his wife witnessed at close proximity the landing of an alien vehicle. The people came over and conversed with him in his own tongue – an Indian language.*

'They told him they were coming here to study the ways of our people. They wanted him to find them a place to live, because they wanted to mingle among us and associate with the people of Earth, to try and find out what made us do

the things we do; why we have wars, why we kill one another, and why don't we have any brotherly love.'

The group consisted of a man, woman and three children, who were all clothed in white, and had noticeable red hair. He put them up in a motel, and took them out to buy suitable clothing and a change of hair colour.

'They are now living in a town in the east Los Angeles area. My son-in-law was driving a bakery cart, and he delivered bakery goods to them. The three children are going to school in the Los Angeles County School System, and they get coached, almost daily, by their parents to make boo-boos – to actually make mistakes on purpose so that they won't be recognised as being out of the ordinary. Those children are such geniuses that they are almost incapable of making any mistakes. As far as I know, they still live in the area. The man works putting vegetables on the counters of a large supermarket....'

Some cases leave us wondering and undecided. US investigator John Schroeder interviewed five independent witnesses to an unusual case in St. Louis USA in May 1970. At about 10.30p.m., a family of four people arrived at the front desk of a high-rise motel. They appeared to be a husband and wife, no taller than four feet with two children, only a little shorter. At first the night clerk thought they may be dwarfs, but their features and bodily proportions were that of almost perfect human specimens, and they looked very similar: "they could have been cast from the same mould." He then wondered if they could be indigenous Mexicans or South Americans, some of whom are very short.

The man, and his son had shiny black hair, and youthful unlined faces. His wife and daughter had long bright blond hair. The father and son both wore dark, tailored expensive suits, and the mother and daughter twin dresses in pastel peach. With pale skin, their eyes were large, dark and slightly slanted 'like those of Orientals', and their lips and noses smaller than average. The staff said they could have been wearing wigs, they weren't sure. When they spoke, their voices were strange: "somewhat like that of a ventriloquist".

The man's voice was slightly falsetto and he wanted "a room to stay". He seemed confused when given details, eventually placing a large roll of currency on the desk. The wife said nothing. The night clerk requested his name for the register and the husband said, "A. Bell". When asked where they were from the man pointed his arm skyward and said: "We come from up there...up there." His wife pulled his arm down and said in an unusual voice: "from Hammond, Indiana." The staff did a quick identity check. Although their names and addresses were false, with no identifiable car parked outside, the transaction was allowed. They had, after all, paid in cash.

While the bell hop took their bags to the room, the dining room waitress said their behaviour and eating habits were strange. She had to confirm for them that 'milk was from a cow' and the vegetables were grown on a farm. They required their food be cut into small pieces, which they sucked rather than chewed.

They did not seem to know how the elevator worked, and when the bell hop tried to turn on the television the man got angry saying it would hurt the children's eyes. The staff were so perplexed they decided to follow this strange family when they checked out, to see where they went. All the entrances had security alarms, and the only exit was past the desk via the front door.

At 7.30am., when they had not come down, the bell hop went to the room, and found it empty, the television unplugged and the keys on the desk. No other exit had been opened and the door alarms were still operative. Who were these strangers, and where had they really come from? Was it just a family holiday to planet Earth?

Another unusual case was reported by MUFON in 2010. A veteran flight attendant spoke of an unusual incident which occurred in the late 1980s on a flight from Palm Springs, California to Portland, Oregon.

She noted three unusual passengers, who had no luggage. One was a middle-aged man, and accompanying him an eight year old boy and a younger man, about thirty years old with 'piercing eyes'. During the entire trip, only the younger man spoke. He asked the mass and velocity of the plane, and didn't seem to understand the names of the food and drinks.

During the flight, he started asking another passenger some very unusual questions, and repeated everything to his two companions. The flight attendant sat next to someone she didn't like, just so she could overhear the conversation.

Later in the flight she asked the man his age, and he replied that he was 'light years old', and added that he had been to other planets. When they arrived at Portland, he asked her why she had sat next to someone she didn't like, as if he was able to read her mind. The last she saw of her three mysterious passengers was when they drove away in a darkened limousine.

Dan Wright, a MUFON Michigan investigator, presented a 1967 case from Albion, which demonstrates that our space visitors can be present, without our knowledge, within our community. When their identity is discovered, often human colleagues will keep silent, in order to protect them.

In late August, 1967, Charles Smith was driving along a deserted road near his home, when the engine in his pickup truck suddenly stalled. A large domed saucer was hovering overhead, and he got a telepathic message to tell his local priest, Father Gerald Boyer, of their presence.

The craft moved away, and Smith drove home. Minutes after he arrived, he and his wife saw two orange/red balls of light, each about fifteen feet across, come over their barn, pass slowly and silently over their house, then descend and 'wink out' over nearby swampy woods. He was hesitant about approaching his priest, but in November, another smaller fireball momentarily hovered over their home, then accelerated away, out of sight.

He went to see Father Boyer, and nervously told him of the sightings and related the message he had been instructed to convey. Instead of disbelief, the priest not only believed him, he told Smith that he was actually one of the extraterrestrials, here in human form.

From then onwards, Father Boyer was a frequent visitor to Smith's home, and Dan Wright said that 'they were not disappointed'. On March 14th 1968, Father Boyer, along with Smith, his wife and eight other witnesses saw three fireballs close by in the sky. Four of the witnesses were nuns, who fled in terror.

On May 7th 1968, Father Boyer, Smith and one other witness, saw a huge craft in the sky. It seemed to be ejecting a number of glowing discs, one of which later landed. Several short beings descended from a ramp. They were wearing silver suits, and telepathically tried to persuade Smith to 'go for a ride'. He was too scared, but they said he would receive future telepathic messages for his priest.

Obviously, the authorities had heard about the unusual events. Soon after, a helicopter landed on his farm, and the crew told him to 'get out' of his own field. Shortly after, a man wearing civilian clothes arrived at his door. He identified himself as 'Major Holmes' and asked questions about the encounters. Smith didn't trust the government, and keeping his priest's secret, told him nothing.

After the heady days of the 1950s and 1960s, there were very few reports of humanoid type visitors and their spaceships landing on Earth. Were they indeed more covert, and had resorted to 'living among' us? Australian colleague, John Pinkney, reported the following case.

Darren, from Victoria, claimed to have rented a room to an alien for three months. He said that in 1979 he advertised a furnished room to rent. A potential tenant soon turned up, and moved in immediately. All he had was a bag and a small trunk.

One night, at about 2am., Darren was woken by strange noises coming from another room. They sounded like they were coming from a radio receiver. He got out of bed and quietly went out, sneaking a look through his lodger's door.

The trunk was open, and inside were a 'chasm of lights'. Darren said; "The bloke was talking directly into the trunk, squeaking and gibbering in an extraordinary way. When he realised I'd caught him, he took me into his confidence.

"He said he was just one of a vast number of aliens living on Earth, disguised as humans. He said he knew of thirteen universes – ranging from the homes of microscopic civilisations to mega-galaxies where giants lived. In some universes time elapsed in different ways."

He then told Darren that extraterrestrials from several different civilisations were visiting Earth, not just as observers, but also to ensure that humans never went beyond the Solar System. We were regarded as a violent race which couldn't be trusted.

Dan Fry, in his June 1973 issue of *'Understanding'*, told of a letter written to the local evening paper, *'El Mundo'*, by Madrid physician Dr. Guillermo. He spoke of visiting Dr. Antonio Arocha, at his country house at the town of San Juan de los Morros, nearly one hundred miles east of Caracas.

At about 6pm, he along with Dr. Arocha and his family, saw a brand new vermillion Mustang vehicle, which caught their attention as it pulled up just down the road. Two gentlemen dressed in black, with red ties and dark glasses, alighted. They appeared to be quietly talking to each other, and after about five minutes they fastened orange coloured belts around their waists, which seemed strange.

Suddenly, a brilliant object appeared in the sky. It quickly descended until it was nearly touching the ground. It had rapidly changed colour, from light orange to blue and then white. It was bell shaped at the bottom, with a 'tower' on the upper part. As it became stationary, it gyrated nearly 180 degrees, and a tiny 'parabolloid' ladder was lowered from the base.

The two men calmly went on board, after which the ladder was withdrawn. The craft inclined slightly, and seemed to float upwards on this trajectory before silently shooting into the sky at an impressive speed.

The Visitors have still made their presence known in more recent years, usually carefully selecting with whom they make contact.

Dr Leopoldo Diaz reported this incident during a 1978 interview on Radio WOAI in San Antonio, Texas. In 1976, when Diaz was head of surgery in a major hospital in Guadalajara, Mexico, a normal looking man came in and requested an examination because he had been travelling extensively. The doctor soon realised he was quite healthy, but not 'human'. His patient advised that he was alien and Diaz said that he showed great wisdom and knowledge.

He told the doctor that humans are about to destroy themselves because of divisions and separations which lead to selfishness, envy and deceit, resulting in war and death. He said how many people from his planet were living undetected among us, trying to help us avert catastrophe. He and the doctor had a long discussion about the Earth's future, religion, and other matters.

They had a second meeting, when the visitor said he had come because he wanted someone respected and influential to pass on a message. After he left, the doctor was so impressed, and concerned about our future, he flew to New York in an unsuccessful attempt to have a United Nations delegation initiate an investigation.

In 1993, British researcher, Alan Hilton, reported an unusual event which occurred at his home in South-East England.

Two strangers, who introduced themselves as 'Peter' and 'Neil' knocked on his door, and told him that his home was on a leyline, which was of considerable importance to them. They explained how leylines carry much of the Earth's natural energies, and how they were building a series of beacons to energise the grid, and enhance this natural power.

"One leyline runs under your house and crosses with another not far from your house," they said. "This grid will be weakened if the new road is built across it. Therefore we plan to move the grid and put it under your house."

They asked him to keep the house, as they also planned to put one of their beacons underneath. They said they came from another star system, and Alan believed them, as they knew so many unknown things about him. They said would return for further meetings, but Hilton has remained silent about this.

The presence of these humanoid visitors is not a new event. History has recorded such incidents over thousands of years. There have been several reports in the early twentieth century, long before we embarked on our first tentative trips into space.

In 1962, South Australian researcher, Fred Stone, reported on the unusual case related by Nursing Sister Ruth Heathcock.

In 1941 she was on duty in the Northern Territory, near the Gulf of Carpentaria. In those days Australia was at war, and the Flying Doctor Service was unable to land anywhere near the injured patient, Horace Foster, who lived in rough, inaccessible terrain. They gave Ruth a full medical kit, and left her, with two native guides, to make a three day, dangerous sixty mile canoe trip back to Horace.

After a nerve racking and exhausting trip, Ruth reached her patient. She was horrified to see he was feverish and suffering a gunshot wound with a compound fracture to his leg, and an injured thigh which was swollen and festering. She cleaned his wounds, but despite praying that she could help this man, realised that competent treatment was beyond her capabilities.

Suddenly two men appeared, the elder about thirty-five, and the other a few years younger. They wore white operating theatre type gowns, and stared intently at the wounds. The older man stretched out his hand 'instructively', and Ruth placed the artery clip she was holding into his hand.

"He deftly worked, aided by his assistant, while I passed the required articles and dressings."

The strangers had done a perfect job, splinting the leg and dressing and draining the wound. When Ruth raised her head to thank them, and ask who they were and how they got there, they had 'vanished'. At first she wondered if the arduous trip had caused her to hallucinate, but the aboriginals had seen the 'two fellow good doctor bin give missus hand.'

Unfortunately, Horace didn't make it, and died a few days later, from tetanus, before medics could give him a life saving injection.

Have you ever wondered what happens when our 'visitors' tour of duty ends, and they return to their home planet?

One such report came from Arlington in the USA. A college student, working in a paint shop, said that one peculiar client had claimed alien encounters on several occasions. They became friends, and the customer told him about these beings from other planets, who'd shown him their spaceships and advanced technology.

The man told him that he had no family, and intended leaving this Earth to live on another planet. Before he departed, and knowing the student was struggling to support a young family, he wished to deed his house and land to him. The student didn't believe a word of it, but agreed to the older man's request. A few days later he transferred his house, land and all his assets to the young man, who then received a call to go to a certain field on the property that evening. The painter said he was leaving Earth with the spacemen, and would never return.

The student drove up to the property, parked his car, and walked over to the field. He could see a strange mist-like green light ahead, and a saucer-shaped craft hovering a couple of feet above the ground. His friend was there, and after giving a wave, entered through an opening which appeared on the saucer. In a matter of seconds the craft shot up into the sky and disappeared from view. Once he realised his benefactor really wasn't coming back, he moved his wife and children into the house, but didn't stay long. He told the researcher that many strange, eerie things happened there, but added that some of the advanced technology, which the painter had told him about, and seemed so far-fetched at the time, exists in today's world.

One would think that the Earth's intelligence agencies would be extremely concerned about alien visitors walking around, incognito and undetected in our community. Indeed they were, and in the 1970s the US Air Force Office of Special Investigations set up 'Operation TANGO-SIERRA' to track down and capture one or more of these intruders. The entire operation was compartmentalised and top secret, and some researchers have suggested that this report is a hoax.

It only stands to reason that the government would keep this in their 'need to know' files. If the general public were to know that we had extraterrestrials incognito in our midst, it wouldn't be long before every 'nut job' in our community would be accusing their neighbours, or others, of being 'aliens' and taking the law into their own hands!

We may never know the truth or results of any investigation, however it only stands to reason that there must be other intelligence projects still being conducted today.

CHAPTER TWELVE

TELEPATHY

When George Adamski taught telepathy, he was insistent that it can be very powerful, and must be between two conscious minds. It did not involve any 'trance-like' state.

In the late 1950s, a Florida woman had read George Adamski's book, and many others, on flying saucers. She wanted nothing more than to contact these visitors from outer space herself. For weeks she put out a mental and emotional call to them. She, and other people in the town, had seen UFOs, which only strengthened her resolve to make contact.

One night, during an exceptional heavy downpour of rain, there was a knock on the door. She opened it, and there stood a handsome man in an unfamiliar uniform. Strangely enough, his clothes and shoes were quite dry. He asked if he could come in for a minute. There was an aura of well-being and positive assurance about him, and even though she did not know him, and she lived alone, she invited him into her home.

He started to speak to her, and she was astounded that he knew details of her earlier life. Some of the events she had actually forgotten, and were only known to her.

"We have been aware of your interest in us, and appreciate it very much," he said in excellent English. "But you must be warned, in all seriousness, that not all 'Visitors' in your skies are of goodwill. If you persist in sending out this indiscriminate call you may find yourself in serious trouble. Continue your studies of ESP, but until you gain more understanding of the contending forces, it would be well to curb your enthusiasm."

As he rose to leave, she noticed his uniform had an iridescent appearance, and the insignia on the pocket was a triangle – point up – with three little circles and a crescent moon inside. He told her that he would return, but she didn't see him again.

About a month later, again one night during a heavy storm, there was another knock on her door. This time it was a handsome couple, wearing unusual clothing which indicated some form of quasi-military origin. The woman, who had shoulder length blond hair, was exceptionally beautiful.

They explained that they belonged to the same 'Guardian' group as her previous visitor. She did not confide in everything they told her, except to say they were pleased she had used restraint when trying to reach out for contact with extraterrestrial visitors. As of 1965, she had no further interaction with these people, although she occasionally saw their saucers in the sky.

Mrs C. Lived near Coventry in England, and her experiences were investigated in 1968 by 'Contact UK.' By this time she was an honest and reliable forty-five year old housewife with several children.

In 1940, during World War II, when she was in her early twenties, she was walking down a country lane at Meridan, and inadvertently came across a dome-shaped object and its crew. It was quite solid, giving off a bluish-grey light.

There were several tall men, all wearing one-piece garments, standing around it, apparently adjusting something on the perimeter. They looked quite normal, except for high foreheads and unusual eyes. Mrs C. walked past, and then retraced her steps to find the craft and its crew had mysteriously disappeared.

A few months later she was at work, and went into the section where 'lifting' work was done by the male employees. One young man seemed to be performing his tasks with relative ease, compared to the strain being shown by his workmates. His overalls were also much cleaner, and when he saw Mrs C., he came over. She immediately recognised him as one of the men she had seen at Meridan.

He had no foreign accent whatsoever, and started a conversation. He said that our war was upsetting his world, and when she reminded him that it was his world also, he said that he did not come from this world. He, perhaps jokingly, asked her to take him to her King and Queen, and she said that was not possible.

He was more serious when he asked if she would accompany him to the country homes, head scientists and other leaders, so he could talk over their differences with each other. Mrs C. told him it was no use her going along, as she was a very insignificant person.

She worked at the factory for three years, and didn't recall ever seeing him there again. She felt depressed and miserable, and one of her 'escapes into dreamland' was to remember this unusual man and yearn for a meeting with him.

Then, one day in 1951, she arrived home to find she had a visitor. He explained that he was a 'Messenger', and had signed on for the job. He said that unless she really wanted to meet the person she had met at the factory, she must refrain from intruding on his thoughts.

She commented; "I was completely bewildered, and recall thinking he must be mad as it was impossible that I could have done this.....but I was taken several times to the craft, which was usually situated on some lonely grassland plot. I got the impression that these people had got something for erasing your memory from the time of contact until you were on the craft." – (Obviously they didn't want her to remember their exact location.)

She described it as somehow being well lit, and about the size of 'four double bedrooms', with what looked like rows of meters along one side. In the centre was a 'fibre glass' table which slid into the floor. One interesting feature was a black screen, on which white lettering would appear, and seemingly self-erase.

Mrs C.'s report continued as follows; *'Most of the crew looked similar to us, averaging six to seven feet in height, high foreheads with greased black hair to neckline, and smaller noses. They came and went from the craft. The others, who stayed in permanently, were very different.*

'They had a bluish complexion, and slightly different facial bone structure. They had larger mouths, and their large eyes had side vision as well as frontal. They wore either brown or blue one-piece garments.

'I thought the most intriguing thing about them was the way in which they were able to transfer their thoughts to one another. This seemed to be a natural gift for them.'

She explained that they tried to teach her how to do it, but she never really mastered the art. It required deep concentration on the person you were thinking of, to the exclusion of all other thoughts. They told her that she hadn't tried hard enough, and that anyone could do it. Strangely enough, when she didn't wander off, and just stared, she found that she could read their thoughts, and answer them.

They asked her many questions, about everyday life, medical procedures, household gadgets, everything she had done or witnessed, and what she believed to be right or wrong. If they didn't understand what she said she had to visualise the answer.

'One time I got rather tired of all the questions, and cursed my interrogator. I didn't mean any harm, but they insisted I retracted it because, "we don't understand the power of thought". If we wish someone ill, it can bounce back on ourselves. They said it didn't harm them, but may have adverse effects on me and my children.'

The Space People seemed to be Christian in their attitude, but had no religious ceremonies. They said that we were immature, and still had to grow up, forecasting that there would be trouble among the races before we could live together in equality. In later years we would be ashamed of our behaviour.

'Whatever my space friends may think of us, they will not harm us. They were very kind and patient, and I always felt at complete ease with them. The elder members of the crew told me that it wouldn't help to tell the story of my encounters as it would be of no benefit to me personally. I was told that in order to have success, (making open contact), a great number of people had to believe that it is true, and can be done.'

She said that some of the crew had signed on for the mission without really knowing what it entailed, however their leader always knew the purpose. He was responsible for the craft, and never left it unless there was a replacement.

Mrs C. finalised by saying; *'On board the spacecraft were people from different planets. The older ones didn't particularly want to be involved with our planet, but the younger ones did express a wish to make contact. They asked me whom they should contact. I was bewildered, and so were they, but they said they would keep on trying. There would be a lot of misunderstanding and errors, but we will understand in the end.*

'They wanted an exchange of ideas and trading with us. They also wanted to help us grow up, but as one of them pointed out; "It involves a great deal more than you think." It will come.'

Anyone around the Space Brothers, has to be careful to monitor their own thoughts. Once, when entertaining someone in his home, Adamski also issued this caution.

Fred Stone reported on a controversial case from 1954, when Mel Noel, a retired Air Force pilot was flying north towards Canada. Over Idaho he was accompanied by several flying saucers. The Colonel on board instructed him to switch to another radio channel, and Mel could hear the captain of the saucers talking to him in slow English.

When they landed, they were told to fill out forms detailing exactly what they had seen, but nothing about what they had heard. The Colonel later told Mel that he had made arrangements to meet the saucer occupants in a motel room in Phoenix, Arizona. Two men met him there, and drove him into the desert where a landed saucer was waiting.

They went inside, and found both male and female crew on board. The Colonel said that two 'gorgeous women' came into the room. His mind went into overdrive with what he described as 'progressive thinking' and a possible overactive imagination. One can only guess his extreme embarrassment when they started giggling. He realised that they were both much older than he originally assumed, and furthermore, they could read his thoughts.

Mel didn't know all the information which was imparted to the Colonel, but when he returned he was a changed man. He later disappeared in a jet during a flight over the Atlantic Ocean, and was never found. One can only wonder!!

Thought Transference and Knowledge

Some contactees I am acquainted with have experienced an inexplicable transference of information into their minds. They claim to 'know' things without understanding 'how' or 'why'. This mysterious knowledge usually proves correct, whether in relation to current events or something in the future. They are sure this aptitude is not due to any rational deductions, and does not involve any 'voices in the head' or telepathic communications. It is more comparable to a 'data' dump from a computer.

In other cases, some witnesses have experienced an overwhelming compulsion to go somewhere or do something out of the ordinary. The capability to control a person's thinking or actions, no matter how well intentioned, is disturbing.

The Space Brothers have often alluded to an individual's brain frequencies, which are as unique as a person's DNA or fingerprints, and which they can easily access. When one considers some witnesses describing automatic writing or 'channelled' music, the remote transference of information or 'compulsions' may also be possible.

Some scientists have also claimed each person's brain has an individual frequency. That is why identical twins, because of their mutual genes, have a great ability for psychic communication. If somebody is tuned into the desired frequency, they can achieve complete thought transference.

Contactees, who from the mid-fifties, worked with the Amicizia group of visitors, claimed that telepathic thought transference did not come naturally. The aliens used specific methods to induce telepathic abilities in their human counterparts.

Usually this consisted of a small, black implant, called an 'ania'. Once inserted under the skin, immediately behind the ear, it dissolved into thousands of minute biological robots that dispersed in the body. That way it couldn't be detected by X-rays or any other conventional methods.

Following George Adamski's telepathy lessons, groups all over the world tried to master the art, however it was not easy, and many fell into the trap of psychic, spiritual and paranormal phenomena. Often it would just be participants accessing their own subconscious or wishful thinking.

Brinsley le Poer Trench jumped on the bandwagon with his 'Contact' groups, where at specific times several people together would concentrate on the space visitors. Whilst often a lot of mumbo-jumbo would come out of these experiments, sometimes meaningful and intelligent communication would eventuate.

In 1970, he published a report from Carol Halford-Watkins of 'Contact Canada'. This message was of great interest to the Dickesons in New Zealand, as it tallied with one given to Mr. X.

Carol Halford-Watkins wrote; *'At the appointed time period we tuned in telepathically to the Space People with welcoming thoughts. My personal experience when, after this, I made my mind receptive to telepathic communication was that I received the following message:*

'The time is not yet right, nor is your world yet ready to receive us in any numbers for friendly personal contact. Isolated landings for contact with specifically selected Earth people, and the inevitable, odd accidental confrontations will continue to take place, but under cosmic law, we cannot present ourselves en-masse until there is a better spiritual climate on your planet, and a far greater sincerely expressed desire to meet with us on the part of Earth people.

'Do not be discouraged or give up these attempts to make contact with us. Rather, concentrate on building them up to the massive proportions required for a successful meeting with us. Your welcoming thoughts are being well received, and we are pleased with your efforts which are the first and necessary steps towards your desired meeting with us.

'Some of you are disappointed at the present apparent lack of our presence in your skies. Be not deceived; we have not deserted you, but are near you in great numbers although invisible to your earthly eyes. We have first a specific mission to perform, vital for your survival, but later we shall make ourselves known to you visibly in a spectacular manner. In the meantime, 'Contact' has our special blessing, and we ask you to link up with us in earnest prayers for planet Earth and its people.'

There are many words of warning to people wanting to communicate with extraterrestrials or any other entities. This can be very dangerous, and must only occur between two conscious consenting minds. In 2004 Katrena Rose reflected upon the cases where abductees have felt their minds and bodies being 'controlled'. (Something the Space Brothers don't practise.)

'You wouldn't open your door to a bus full of strangers, and you wouldn't approach a large, ferocious looking animal to make friends, so don't do it with aliens. Be observant and cautious, observe from a safe distance, keep your head down, and don't take unnecessary risks. Trust your own inner instincts, hide or run if you feel even remotely fearful within. If you hear a loud, repetitive voice in your head screaming 'run', then do it!

'If you feel any sort of heaviness, probing or tugging sensation, start talking to yourself loudly in your mind and repeat phrases. Say the alphabet or nursery rhymes and get as far away as possible as quickly as you can. If all else fails, pray to your own angels, guides and God-force to protect you and help you find a way of escaping.' Even with telepathy – it is your life and your choice.

CHAPTER THIRTEEN

MORE CONTACTEES

Contactee reports were continually being received from around the world, although as time went by, not so many involved the Space Brothers. The British *'The Flying Saucer Review'* included a Danish report, with an unusual and somewhat humorous ending, from the summer of 1961.

An Albort farmer and his wife were sitting down to their meal, when they heard unfamiliar noises from their cattle, which were grazing nearby. He went outside, and saw that a twelve metre, round 'machine' had landed on his property.

A small 'door' opened, a ramp came down, and two individuals emerged from the craft. They appeared to be normal humans, and one raised his arm as if indicating a greeting, or sign of peace. They spoke to him in perfect Danish, and invited him to come for a trip, as they wanted to show him something.

He accepted their offer, and climbed on board. His astonished wife watched through the window, and became alarmed when the craft took off and sped away. She contacted the local police, who in turn brought in the military. At first, they all thought she was hysterical, and wouldn't believe her report.

Several hours later, with the authorities still present, the saucer returned, and the farmer alighted, excitedly racing down the ramp to tell everybody how his hosts were very kind. They wished to demonstrate that they weren't hostile, and didn't intend to hurt anyone. They had taken him away from Earth, and he was able to see our planet from outer space.

During the uproar, with the farmer relating his experience, and everyone milling around, the two 'spacemen' stepped back into their craft, and quietly departed. The authorities were annoyed that they had missed their opportunity to meet the unexpected 'space visitors'.

The farmer had enjoyed his wonderful experience, but he was not so happy when the Danish military took him away for two weeks, and subjected him to intensive interrogation regarding every detail of the incident. The results were noted in a NATO report.

In 1963 Gordon Creighton reported upon Italian Bruno Ghibaudi's photographs of saucers, and contact with their occupants.

Bruno had not really given the subject much thought, until in 1961, his bosses asked him to prepare a TV programme about people who claimed they had seen flying saucers.

He had heard about accounts of sightings and contact from other parts of the world, but as he travelled around Italy, was astounded at the number of cases being related by people from his own country.

He said his job was not easy. Many people who had previously taken pictures, or related their experiences, regretted being outspoken. Some had lost their jobs, others subjected to ridicule, and a few endured hours of intensive questioning by 'officialdom'.

Suddenly, his TV producers told him the documentary was cancelled. By this time Bruno was fascinated, and conducted further investigations on his own initiative. After a while, he was recognised as one of Italy's leading experts.

One breakthrough occurred in the summer of 1961, when he was invited to meet some of the 'space people'. He has always refused to divulge the location of the house where the rendezvous took place, or the name of the 'go-between' who issued the invitation.

Along with other witnesses, he learned much about the Space Brothers, and their reasons for visiting our planet. He said that some of them are so much like us in appearance, many have infiltrated our society and live, incognito, among us now. If they ever wish to identify themselves, it is usually by gesture or telepathy, or sometimes in the language of the people they meet.

Bruno states emphatically, that they are only men like us, and not omnipotent deities. They are however, thousands of years ahead in science and technology, not to mention morality. They have an 'exact estimate of our natures and the level that we have reached'. While their intentions are benevolent, we must not rely upon them to get us out of our difficulties.

There are cosmic laws which prevent the more evolved races from interfering, beyond certain limits, in the evolution and development of the more backward races. For every race must be the maker of its own progress, paying the price for it with its sacrifices, its failures and its victories.

One of the principal reasons for their coming is to prevent nuclear disaster, however they are not infallible, and their efforts and concern might not suffice in preventing disaster if something went wrong, or some accident nullified their plans to avert the worst. While they are capable of destroying such weapons, mankind would still retain the ability and intention to build fresh nuclear devices. For this reason, extraterrestrials are working in a more subtle manner to influence the minds of men.

Bruno said that there are other reasons for the Space Brothers visiting and sometimes revealing themselves, but he had been forbidden to speak of them.

In 1964, South Australian researcher, Fred Stone, published the following abridged account of his experience the *'Panorama'* Newsletter. Were they actually extraterrestrial visitors? We may never know!

'I am writing this in my diary, ...so that I may not forget it. On July 14th 1962, I was on my way home after attending a lodge meeting, and was being driven by a friend, who was witness to the entire incident.

'Just outside of Adelaide,...we were proceeding up Montefiore Hill when he suddenly turned to me and said; "There were some fellows fell off a motor bike back there. Did you see them?"

'I hadn't, but we thought we had better go back, and see if they were alright. We stopped, and walked back to the other side of the road, where the scooter was lying on the ground. The two men were standing up against the railing of the fence surrounding the track down the hill.

'We asked the men if they were hurt in any way, and could my colleague or I help. The older man answered, "No", in good English, but with a slightly unusual tone of voice. During the whole conversation, this man always answered in monosyllables of 'yes' or 'no'.

'We were a little taken aback by the appearance of the two men, who appeared to be in their twenties and one a little younger than the other. They were oddly dressed, and neither had headwear or helmets, which was usual for bike riders at the time. The older man was wearing some sort of suit, with a jumper and short jacket over the top, and both had very unusual soft leather boots. I noticed the one man had torn his pants, and underneath, instead of underwear,

he had an undergarment of material, dark-reddish in colour, similar to what I had seen occasionally on airmen.

'They were both just over five feet tall. One had tidy, shoulder length, long, fine red hair, and a small, fuzzy beard, and the other younger man, had very fair blonde hair and very pale skin. Their demeanour was calm and controlled, and not what one would expect from people who had just had a bike accident.

'The older man was rubbing his wrist, and I put out my hand and held it, his skin was soft to feel. I asked him if it was badly hurt, and he replied in the negative. Then he made a movement with his hand and arm, and in my concern for him, I did not, at that moment, consider anything unusual or recognise a very well known and definite sign to me. It was not until I got into the car that I recalled it. My fellow driver would not have recognised the sign because he was not taught along the same lines as I. Reflecting afterwards, I regretted I did not pay more attention to both of them.'

(The Space Brothers had secret gestures, used to identify themselves to contactees. When Fred chaperoned Adamski as he toured Australia, he would have been made aware of these recognition signs.)

'The man then lowered his arm and hand, and I looked down and said; "You've torn your pants. Is your leg alright?" He said; "Yes", and at that stage my attention was drawn away by my colleague, who was speaking to the younger fellow, who still looked very pale, seemed rather shy, and only nodded in response.

'They still leaned against the wall of the fence, looked grateful, but didn't seem to want us to help further. We returned to the car and proceeded homewards, continuing to discuss who they might be, as they did not fit into a 'normal' pattern. After I got home, it struck me like a 'bolt out of the blue'.

'I saw the young man making the gesture and movements with his hand and arm, and immediately recognised what I had failed to do before. He had given me a definite sign, to which normally I should have replied, and failed to do so in my own stupidity. Was I deceiving myself, or was it a definite effort on his part to make himself known to me?

'The next morning I went to church, and when in meditation I seemed to see the man again. It was as though he mentally projected himself into my mind. He said; "We had to do it that way to alert you, being dressed that way was the *only way to appear among your people and not draw too much attention in the time allowed us....But we will come again – wait – we will contact you again."*

Fred contacted his friend from the previous night. He admitted he had not seen the men fall off the bike, and just assumed there had been an accident because the bike was lying on the road. Further, neither of them had said they were involved in an accident. Fred, of course, said nothing about his thoughts on the matter.

Some days later, his colleague said to him; "You know, I can't get those chaps out of my mind. They were not real foreigners, but it just seemed as though they did not belong here!"

Fred kept his counsel. He was very much a 'nuts and bolts' ufologist, and although he later privately admitted to meeting the 'space people', he never said if he encountered these two particular men again.

In 1965, Jerome Clark wrote of a little known encounter, which he considered worthy of more significance than it had previously been given.

A newspaper reporter, named House, had been driving near Lake Huron, in Wisconsin, when he stopped at a service station. After filling up with petrol, he decided to have a coffee, and got talking to the proprietor.

The conversation got around to UFOs, and the garage owner told him that a craft had been landing regularly on a small island, just offshore. He said that he had met with its occupants, who numbered about twenty-five, and looked just like humans. He had only spoken to one, whose English was good, but in a slightly 'sing-song' manner.

He then added that they were tall, strong and live for hundreds of years. They had advance technology, and kept equipment on their 'plane' which would amaze an Earth scientist by its perfection and material – however, he was not permitted to reveal what these instruments were.

The crew apparently 'had friends on Earth, whom they visit with, and have been selected by a method known only to them.' He said that the beings were here to promote 'everlasting peace', and had not made their objectives known to more than a few people.

The contactee's wife and son also confirmed seeing the craft, on several occasions, as it landed on the island, and men in 'shining clothes' would disembark.

In August 1969 the *Portland Flying Saucers Club* published the following article in their *'Bulletin'*.

A REASONABLE SPACE CONTACT

By Ellen Zigler

'We have been asked to write a short synopsis of our experiences with what most folks refer to as UFOs. In 1965 my husband became involved in a series of events which led eventually to contact with flesh and blood personages from another Solar System. Ours has been a continuing and very revealing friendship with these people whose home planet is more than four years distant. Their world has a written history of more than thirty thousand years, compared to our six thousand. Even so, they long since have been required to live more simple lives because all, or almost all, of their minerals, oils, coal, etc. have been used up. They are plagued by over-population and must utilise all of their land resources in order to provide for their people.

'From the beginning these people have impressed on us the fact that the laws of physics are constant throughout the universe, and that if something does not meet all the requirements of the laws of physics it is impossible. They also point out that each planet was made of the same materials and in the same manner. There are no mystery minerals or materials on some other planet. Space is orderly, they say; and when one has learned this secret, space travel is safe. Our space effort is, as was theirs in the beginning, far too complex. When we have learned to simplify, we will enjoy much more success in our space travels.

'These people are very much like us in appearance, with subtle differences not easily recognised; but they cannot mix with races of this world. It is genetically not possible.

'Their first landfall in this world was about 1745. Our world was of little interest to them because it was peopled by crude and cruel people. Samples of ore, water, soil etc. were taken for study. They next came here about 1870, when more samples were taken. In the mid-twenties another ship arrived, as

forerunner of one which came about five years later, equipped with certain minerals from our seas. They arrived with a force of men and women numbering less than five hundred, and do not exceed that number today. They brought with them a number of small craft resembling a straw hat. They are but another type of 'helicopter' and are not capable of high or fast travel.

'We are assured, and it has been well proven to us, that certain men high in our government circles are well aware of their presence here and of their nature and purpose.

'As a matter of courtesy, and they are most courteous people, they refuse to take part in our religious, political or social life in such manner to bring about change. If change is to be made, it must be our acts which bring it about, independent of theirs.

'They refuse to use their craft either to entertain us or to educate us. Their craft are used for their own purposes and needs. At the present time, not one of their craft has been within the boundaries of the United States since 1968.

'One of our friends says this; "We are not angels. We are not devils. We are man, nothing more nor less. We are not something to fear; if we were it is now many, many years too late. We are required to live in accordance with our own laws; and when we have done this, we certainly have broken none of yours. Besides, it would be most discourteous of us to transgress your law in such manner to wreck havoc or terror upon your people. It is not our nature.

"There are some questions we cannot answer because we do not know the answers. There are some we do not wish to answer because we feel it might endanger our friends."

The editor of the *'Bulletin'* mentioned a 1952 report from another contactee who said; *"Visitors from other solar systems occasionally come to this one for various purposes. If their purpose is not malicious, they are permitted to proceed. Otherwise they are usually intercepted and turned back in the outer limits of this Solar System..."*

This may have been true in 1952. Given the 'Two Friends' parting messages to Mr X, and more recent abductee reports, this 'protection' of Earth and its people does not seem to exist now!

In 1978, Harold Salkin, an American ufologist, had been a military correspondent for Associated Press during World War II, and considered the witness, Sid Padrick, to be an honest and reliable. Salkin wrote about this interesting case which occurred in California on January 30th 1965.

Sid Padrick, a forty-five year old radio and television repairman, was taking his customary walk on the Manresa beach, near his home at Watsonville, at 2am one morning. He suddenly heard a noise, like a jet, and turned around to see a huge craft on the ground. It looked like two really thick inverted saucers – about fifty feet in diameter and thirty feet high.

He panicked, started to run, and kept running, even when a voice from the ship called out; "Don't be frightened. We are not hostile."

The voice repeated its message, and then added a reassurance that it meant him no harm, and invited him to come aboard. Padrick doesn't really know why, but he went back, and when he saw a door on the side of the craft open, he stepped in.

The door closed behind him, and he found himself in a small room. Another door slid open. He walked through to meet a normal looking man standing there. Padrick said he had clean-cut features, and a type of flying suit which completely covered his body. Padrick said the man spoke perfect English; "and seemed as curious about me as I was about him."

His host showed him around the ship, which had fourteen rooms on two levels, with a small elevator between. As with many other reports, the light inside the craft was 'indirect' and seemed to come from the walls themselves. There were several other crew on board, including one woman. All were about five feet nine inches tall, and normal build with very pale skin, and except for the woman, who was shorter with dark auburn, wavy hair. The only feature, slightly different from ours, was that their faces came to a point – sharp chins and noses. They wore similar plain, pale bluish-white flight suits, and were working at many highly complex instrument panels. None of them spoke to him, and barely glanced up when he went past, however, he was sure they were normal people, and not robots. He wondered if the whole crew were communicating telepathically, as his host always paused for about twenty seconds before he answered Padrick's questions. His guide, who introduced himself as 'Ziena' said his crew could speak most languages, but he was the only one fluent in English.

As they toured the craft, Padrick had a lengthy conversation with his guide, and he related much of what he had been told; "They are here for exploratory reasons only, or for observation. They did say that they would come back for further observation. I think they were mostly watching people. There was no mention of anything political or government-wise, or anything which would affect our future." Padrick also recalled him mentioning their contact with a group of people in New Zealand.

They said they had been here before, but not how many times, or when their most recent visit was. When he asked if they had ever attempted contact with the government or military they said not. They do not come armed, but; "Your nation, and all nations, will attack an unknown object for purposes of destruction, without cause."

The 'spaceman' explained that they were from a planet 'many lights' away, and he was shown, through a large lens, a cigar-shaped 'navigation craft', or 'mother-ship', which was hovering out in space.

Although Padrick felt no movement, the craft must have been travelling, as it landed on a hillside, and stopped for a short time, allowing Padrick to walk outside and examine the hull, which was about fifty feet long and thirty feet high. He said it looked metallic, but was soft to the touch. He was told that they had landed in a spot where they couldn't be seen. Apparently it was used by a large house-trailer in summer, but deserted during winter.

By 4am, two hours later, the craft returned to the beach, and Padrick walked home.

The Air Force came, did a lot of checking around the area, and confirmed that a craft had been present before and after the incident. They were the first people Padrick told about the incident, and they questioned him extensively, wanting a 'word for word' account. However, they asked him not to publicly reveal anything about the visitors' craft, technology or way of life.

Padrick said that although he had not met the space people for a second time, they were observing him. If he wished to contact them, it would be on his own initiative by an action they had prearranged.

CHAPTER FOURTEEN

THE SCIENTISTS

Leo Noury and other investigators have also discussed the controversial case of the 'Ummo' visitors at length. Some debunked the whole episode as a hoax, and others thought it was a genuine case of aliens among us.

Hilary Evans was one of the researchers who looked into these reports, and he was still left with many unanswered questions. He wrote about how the Ummites arrived in 1950. They said that having detected signals from planet Earth, they had decided to investigate the possibility of intelligent beings living here. They were part of a group of visitors who were specially selected to come on an exploratory mission.

They once said; *"We are not here to bring you a new doctrine, as prophets descending from the skies, to preach a new physics or mathematics, or preach a new religion, or offering you panaceas for your social or patho-psychological ills."*

In March 1950, they had landed near La Javie, in France. Gordon Creighton's French colleagues advised that later investigations discovered that they were possibly based in a lonely, dilapidated farm in the area. The previous owners were found to be living in 'great opulence' on the French Riviera. – *'Their mouths were as tightly shut as clams!'*

The Ummites were apparently as human as we are, and came from a planet fourteen light years away, although it only took them a few months to get here. They claimed they had lived among us, undetected, for fifteen years, establishing their bases and acclimatising themselves to our way of life. Then, in 1965 they started contacting a variety of people.

At first they sent documents to high-ranking scientists in different countries, hoping to arouse their curiosity. Having received polite but clear rebuttals, they tried a different strategy. They approached members of the public, such as journalists and UFO advocates and researchers. Their initial contacts included Fernando Sesma and two of Spain's leading ufologists, Antonio Ribera and Rafael Farriols.

Another person contacted in 1966 was engineer Enrique Novoa, who got a telephone call one night from a person who said he was an extraterrestrial. They spoke for two hours about various technical matters, and a couple of days later Enrique received some follow-up documents in the mail.

Many of the Ummites' contacts belonged to a secretive Madrid group – 'The Society of Friends of Space', which the Ummites said had affiliates all over the world. This of course, substantiates the reports of 'Friendship Clubs' in Italy and many other European countries, which I discuss in *'The Alien Gene'*.

They certainly did not want to attract the attention of the government or military, and resisted attempts by a couple of their contacts to 'go public'.

'Some of you keep saying that we must give you proof. We continue to repeat, until you are tired of hearing it, that we are not concerned whether or not you believe us. We can operate much more effectively in anonymity, and we are not going to be so naive as to introduce ourselves to you openly, simply to satisfy your need for proof.'

Obviously, in the future, they needed to operate in a more covert manner. In Madrid, during the 1960s, a young dactylographer had been advertising for work. In 1967, two 'Danish' doctors asked him to type some scientific articles. Both were tall and blond, no different to any other human being. One day they asked him to type out scientific material for them on a regular basis, plus papers about their 'home world', the planet Ummo, fourteen light years away. He took this at face value, and questioned the men, who eventually admitted that they were extraterrestrial visitors and not 'Danish doctors'.

He thought they were pulling his leg until one pulled a small transparent ball from his pocket. It started to levitate, and in it was a recording of all the scenes from the dactylographer's home the night before. They advised this was just a sample of their technology.

That was the only face-to-face meeting, and from then onwards everything was by letter or telephone. Most of the letters were in Spanish or French, and posted from London, Germany, New Zealand, Austria, Canada and Yugoslavia. They also rang some scientists and discussed engineering matters. (Oddly enough, French physicist Jean Pierre Petit claims that part of his work on Magnetohydrodynamics (MHD) propulsion systems was made possible through the Ummo letters.)

One report offered a revolutionary view of Space, based upon a physics that has no relation whatever to terrestrial physics. The Ummites described our conception of Space as simplistic, and not corresponding at all to the true reality of the Cosmos, being based on mathematical and geometrical abstractions.

The Euclidian three-dimensional space is, they say, a purely mental creation. Our Theory of Relativity added to that Euclidian Space a fourth dimension called *Time*, but even so, our conception of Space is too superficial. They said that Space consisted of at least ten dimensions, some of which they utilise.

One item of their technology was purportedly lent, temporarily, to a Professor of Medicine at Madrid University. He was sent a small package containing a smooth, black metallic cube, with instructions to repeat certain vowels in a specific sequence. Once he did this, a little screen became illuminated, and inside were several live specimens of nerve cells.

It was, as he was told, only a loan. One day a young man, with a beard, turned up and said he had been commissioned to take back the apparatus, however he left a colour film with the professor.

Over the next nine years, about twenty people in Spain alone had been receiving enigmatic 'Ummo' reports through the post. A lot of the information provided related to physics, space travel and other aspects of science and technology. Researcher Antonio Ribera claimed to have seen blueprints of a number of useful devices which originated from the Ummo interactions.

Enrique Villagrasa told Antonio Ribera of several telephone conversations he had with 'a man from Ummo'. The first, in November 1966, lasted just over two hours, and covered many diverse topics including history, science and various technologies. His caller spoke clearly, and without hesitation, as if he were 'reading the answers out of a dictionary'. Enrique wondered if he was talking to an electronic brain.

Other people also had long conversations with our mysterious visitors, but it was always a one-way street. There was no known way to reach the Ummites. They always initiated the contact.

The entire scenario is still contentious today. Some sceptics have suggested it was a deception perpetrated by British academics, and claim the theories resemble some of those proposed by earlier British, Russian and other scientists. In 1993, in order to try and debunk the affair, a Jordán Peña tried to 'confess' to perpetrating a hoax, without providing any evidence to substantiate this. Omar Fowler, in his *'Ovni'* publication, disputed the 'confession'. He pointed out that there is physical evidence, in the many letters in the possession of investigators, where the contents contain a high level of scientific knowledge, which has helped many earth scientists with their research. Further, letters were still being received in 2005, forty years later, in countries as diverse as Spain, Great Britain, France and Latin America.

The authenticity of photographs of an Ummo spaceship landing in Spain is still argued, as are the Ummites' plans to shelter in a secure base if nuclear war broke out on Earth. Even today, we may never know the truth of this matter!

The Ummites once told a contact that, besides themselves, there were other humanoid type visitors on Earth. This lends some credence to a report from the Soviet Union, featured in the *'New York Times'* in 1979; *'Another writer says he was visited by extraterrestrial beings in his home in the forest. As a token of good faith, he says, they gave him a mathematic formula that they said unlocked the secret of space flight by tapping the energy from stellar light. The writer said he himself did not understand the formula, but he gave it to scientists who examined it and pronounced it genuine.'*

Roger Laithwaite

Among the many scientists who claimed to have been influenced by extraterrestrials was British Professor, Roger Laithwaite.

Researcher Jenny Randles was just a very young novice researcher in 1976 when she and Peter Warrington were contacted by a man claiming to be an alien, living as a human here on Earth. He wished to prove himself by meeting a certain scientist. The 'alien', who looked like a normal middle-aged man, was insistent, and Randles was surprised when the scientist, Professor Eric Laithwaite, actually invited them all to meet him in his Imperial College University laboratory in London.

The alien proffered suggestions as to how Laithwaite could further his work in the development of magnetic-field based propulsion systems. During the afternoon the professor produced a small gadget, which resembled a gyroscope. It proceeded to rotate and rose vertically into the air over the top of the table. It reminded Jenny of the 'flying saucers' reported by so many witnesses. The UFO researchers did not understand the science, but the professor took copious notes and taped the entire interview. Jenny later remembered it was around that time Laithwaite announced the solution of a fundamental problem he had been struggling with.

When the researchers apologised for bothering him, Laithwaite smiled and said: "This is not the first alien I have met!" He added that some ideas for his magnetic levitation propulsion system had been offered some years earlier, in another meeting with a man claiming to be an alien. He later asked Peter and Jenny not to divulge what he had told them as it may affect his research funding. They kept his secret, and did not write about it until just before he died twenty three years later.

Eric Laithwaite was highly respected at the Imperial College, where he taught electrical engineering, but some of his contemporaries did not like him. One of his projects included developing magnetic levitation for hovertrains. In the following years he collaborated with another inventor, Edwin Rickman, and they were granted several patents.

The circumstances surrounding Rickman also give rise to some speculation. Before joining up with Laithwaite, he had recurring dreams about attending a scientific meeting and seeing an antigravity device being demonstrated. That meeting came to pass, and Rickman was in the front row of the lecture theatre when Laithwaite gave his demonstration.

Laithwaite also believed in a 'benign influence' and claimed that there was an invisible 'father-figure' watching over and encouraging him when he gave a lecture to the Royal Institution in 1962. He spoke of this to others – some believed him, others didn't.

The conservative members of the Royal Institution were not happy when the media reported the invention of an antigravity device, and accused him of 'party tricks', and 'stepping outside of his field'. They denied him his rightful Fellowship, and refused to publish his papers in their Proceedings.

Wilbur Smith

In Canada there were also some high ranking officials who had more than a passing interest in extraterrestrials.

(Wilbert) Wilbur Smith was born in 1910, and gained a Master's degree in electrical engineering. From the late 1940s he had an interest in ufology, and in

1952, he was a member of the Canadian Government special committee to study the UFO problem and recommend a course of action. It had been formed after Smith, in 1950, proposed a project, within the Canadian Department of Transport, named *'Project Magnet'*, to explore the possibilities of new technology, including anti-gravity.

The project's purpose was twofold: To learn as much about UFOs as possible, and to use this data to duplicate their performance.

In a Memorandum to the Controller of Telecommunications he wrote; *'We believe that we are on the track of something that may well prove to be the introduction to a new technology. The existence of a different technology is borne out by the investigations which are being carried on at the present time in relation to flying saucers.'*

'........I made discreet enquiries through the Canadian Embassy staff in Washington who were able to obtain the following information;

- a. *The matter is the most highly classified subject in the United States Government, rating even higher than the H-bomb.*
- b. *Flying Saucers exist.*
- c. *Their modus operandi is unknown, but concentrated effort is being made by a small group headed by Doctor Vannevar Bush'*
- d. *The entire matter is considered by the United States authorities to be of tremendous significance.*

The project was set up in a shed at Shirley Bay, Ontario, but due to unwanted publicity, *'Project Magnet'*, which was unfunded and unofficial, was short-lived. The participants continued their work secretly, often getting information from contactees. My colleague, Rosemary Decker, was also a close friend and supporter, and often quietly liaised between Wilbur and other researchers and experiencers. Much of their work remained confidential.

In 1956 Wilbur was promoted to Superintendant of Radio Regulations Engineering, and was responsible for allocating radio frequencies, even to the intelligence agencies.

In 1956 he also founded the Ottawa Flying Saucer Club, and made several 'telling' statements along the way. In 1961 he said; "As far as I know, our group in Ottawa is the only group that has actually taken the info from 'the boys topside' and translated it into hardware that works."

He was only interested in the scientific and technological aspects of alien visitations, and had little time for those that placed religious or paranormal connotations on the subject. He did, however, seem to understand the motives and ethics of 'the boys topside', and claimed to have been, through a contact, in touch with UFO occupants himself.

He often passed data onto the appropriate people in his department, without saying where he got the information. He was also concerned that nuclear explosions caused a very serious gravitational disturbance. Wilbur was convinced that we were being visited by extraterrestrials, whose science and technology was far more advanced than our own.

In 1958, at a lecture on March 31st, he said; "....Our civilisation here on Earth is only one of many that have come and gone. This planet has been colonised many times by people from elsewhere, and our present human race are blood-brothers of these people. Is it any wonder that they are interested in us? To orthodox thinkers this may seem strange, but not nearly so strange as our own orthodox ideas on evolution. This question might be asked – if these people are our brothers, and are interested in our welfare, why do they remain so aloof?

"There is a basic law of the Universe which grants each and every individual independence and freedom of choice, so that he may experience and learn from his experiences. No-one has the right to interfere in the affairs of others – in fact our Ten Commandments are directives against interference. If we disregard this law we must suffer the consequences, and a little thought will show that our present world state is directly attributable to violation of this principle."

He admitted that they tried to get as much information as possible from witnesses and contactees, and this effort was at first directed towards science and technology; "But it soon became apparent that there was a very real and quite large gap between this alien science and the science in which I had been trained. Certain crucial experiments were suggested and carried out, and...in each case the results confirmed the validity of the alien science. Beyond this, the alien science was just incomprehensible."

He went on to explain that a society should not be given advance technology until it had progressed sufficiently to be able to use it in an ethical and responsible manner.

In 1968 the Ottawa New Sciences Club wrote a lengthy article about their founder, Wilbert Smith. Since he had passed away in 1962, his colleagues felt that they were now able to discuss his interactions with the 'Space Brothers'.

At first Wilbur, being a pioneer scientist, was originally very sceptical regarding UFO and other reports. He finally became convinced of the reality of extraterrestrials visiting Earth in spacecraft of superior technology, capable of performing feats which defied our present knowledge of physics. In 1961 he admitted to examining a piece of metal from a UFO, which he was told had had fallen off a small glowing disc. He said that although it had come from the US Air Force, he had to return it to a much higher classified group.

During a 1961 interview with C.W. Fitch and George Popvitch, Wilbur also revealed that a large amount of unidentified material was recovered by his group in July 1960 in Canada; *'There is about three thousand pounds of it! We have done a tremendous amount of detective work on this metal.*

'We have something that was not brought to this Earth by plane, nor by boat, nor by any helicopter. We are speculating that what we have is a portion of a very large device which came into this Solar System – we don't know when – but it had been in space a long time before it came to Earth; we can tell that by the micrometeorites embedded in the surface....We have it, but we don't know what it is.'

(Whilst I was not able to discover the actual composition of the metallic samples Wilbur referred to, an interesting case occurred in San Paulo State, Brazil in early September, 1957.

A group of fishermen on a beach near Ubatuba sighted a disc, just off-shore, flashing towards the sea. It exploded, showering fragments and sparks everywhere. Dr. Olavo Fontes, from APRO, had the metal examined by experts from government and military laboratories. – Their conclusion was that the fragments; *'consisted of one hundred percent magnesium, which is not within the technology of our times.'*)

Eventually, when Wilbur privately admitted that he had personally met the 'visitors', he publically stated that most information was transmitted telepathically. This caused him to be accused of involvement with Spiritualism or the Occult, something he emphatically denied.

His concept of the Cosmos had also expanded. In 1958 he said; "I began, for the first time in my life, to realise the basic oneness of the Universe – science, philosophy, and all that in it. Substance and energy are all facets of the same jewel, and before any one facet can be appreciated, the form of the jewel itself must be perceived."

He claimed that the 'Space People' were concerned about our welfare and had a philosophy to enlighten mankind on Earth and prepare it for the wider horizons of the New Age.

His colleagues wrote; *'Let it be categorically stated that Wilbert Smith, first and foremost a scientist, never wasted his valuable time dabbling in spiritualistic activities...and he secured invaluable scientific and philosophic data from the Space Brothers.*

'In regards to the scientific data obtained from 'The Boys Topside', he was able to test their genuineness and practical workability by protracted tests and experiments in the laboratory. It was against Cosmic Law to drop unearned answers into the laps of Earth scientists. What Wilbur received were certain guidelines and suggested avenues of research.

The Space Brothers were helpful, quick to point out when he was on the wrong track, and offering further suggestions of approach to the solution of a problem. Never once did they spell out the complete answer. They said that this would have been contrary to the Universal Law that there is no virtue or merit to anything that is not achieved by personal merit.

'By diligent research and many experiments on a trial and error basis, Wilbur eventually proved much of the truth of the scientific data conveyed to him by the Space Brothers. Many of his unique inventions remained unacceptable to Earth scientists because of their unorthodox origin, but the day may dawn when they will be used for the benefit of humanity.'

There was one particular contactee who also passed messages on to Wilbur. Some of the information was scientific, and some which seemed completely unintelligible, but Wilbur said it was pertinent and he clearly understood it. Since Wilbur's death the contactee has not received any more messages.

Wilbur wrote several articles on advanced physics, and was continuing his experimentation on his own anti-gravity device when he died early, at the age of fifty-two. Unfortunately, many of his papers were never published. He was often controversial, but always respected for his integrity, and was posthumously awarded a much coveted Canadian Engineering Award for his important and significant contribution to the development of the technical side of the Canadian broadcasting industry.

Paul Hellyer

At the time Wilbur Smith was promoting his research into visitors from space, Paul Hellyer was already a member of the Canadian parliament, and it stands to reason that their paths must have crossed.

Hellyer was born in 1923, and graduated in aeronautical engineering at the Californian Curtis-Wright Technical Institute of Aeronautics in 1941. He also gained his private pilot's license and went on to earn a Bachelor of Arts at the University of Toronto in 1949. That same year he was elected to the Canadian Parliament. In the 1960s he was the Minister of Defence, ruling over the Canadian armed forces during the 'Cold War'.

It wasn't until after his retirement from public office that he started to speak out about his belief in UFOs, even though he had only admitted to seeing one, from a distance, himself.

In 2014 he said; "I've been a sceptic for quite a while, but I've been exposed to more and more information, and have just decided to take a stand, because I know that UFOs are here. As a matter of fact, they've been visiting our planet for thousands of years...During the 'Cold War', in 1961, there were about fifty UFOs, in formation, flying south from Russia across Europe, and Supreme Allied Command was very concerned and about to press the 'Panic Button' when they turned around and went back over the North Pole."

Hellyer said that they decided to do an investigation, and concluded, after three years, that at least four species had been visiting this planet for thousands of years, and there had been a lot more activity since we invented the atomic bomb; "Because the Cosmos is a unity, and it affects not just us but other people in the Cosmos, they are very much afraid that we might be stupid enough to start using atomic weapons again, which would be very bad for us and for them as well.

"They are here among us, and I'm not afraid, because in most cases, as far as technology is concerned, they are light years ahead of us, and we have learned a lot of things from them....We could get a lot more too...if we would go about it peacefully."

The *'Huffington Post Canada'* said that Hellyer had been speaking out since 2005, and he told the Citizens' Hearing on Disclosure that *'aliens are living among us, and it is likely at least two of them are working with the US government.'* He also believed that many, who look like us, are integrated in our society.

Hellyer suggested that we need to switch our priorities. We should stop spending so much time and effort on weapons to kill or dominate each other, and spend a lot more time on how to help each other to have a better life and a more just society. His main thesis was that we have to start right now.

One researcher commented; *"Yet another example of a public figure who has come forward despite the potential for ridicule, to support the UFO reality. It's a pity though, that not many are prepared to say anything until after their retirement."*

Wilbur Smith used to talk about the 'boys topside' and I wonder just how much contact some of our scientists had with their Space Brother counterparts. Lucy McGinnis wrote to Hans Petersen about a conversation she had with a young pilot in 1952/53.

'He told about piloting an American plane to Australia, where he landed at a vast airport, but did not give details as to its location. He said that a gigantic spacecraft was already there. He was introduced to a group of scientists from other planets, and told he was to take them to a scientific meeting in Scotland. The reason given for them having to travel in one of our planes was that there was no landing field in that part of the world, (Europe or British Isles), large enough to accommodate their ship.

'The young pilot said that all of these men were very good looking, friendly and intelligent. He liked them very much and was very impressed by them and their conduct. He remained in Scotland with his plane while the visitors attended the conference. Little publicity was ever given to this scientific conference although, we are told, scientists from every nation in the world were present. When the conference ended, the young man returned them to their ship in Australia, then returned to the States.'

He immediately went to tell George and Lucy, but had to leave again for another flight, and didn't say where to. It is very likely he was involved in other top secret missions and flights.

In those days there were large abandoned airports in the far north of Australia, where a landed spaceship would not attract the unwanted attention it would receive in Europe or Britain. One was Carsons Base, built during World War II. It remained deserted until 1960, when it was taken over and later became RAAF Base Tindal.

Arthur Matthews

A more controversial figure is Arthur Matthews, who purportedly worked with Nikola Tesla during his lifetime. Tesla was a genius, whom I discuss at length in *'The Alien Gene'*.

Matthews claimed that in 1941, while continuing Tesla's work on a property at Lac Beauport, Quebec, Canada, a huge 'Venusian' spaceship landed. Two men, both nearly six feet tall, with blonde hair and blue eyes, said they had come to see how he was progressing with Tesla's inventions. After they inspected his workshop, they gave him a detailed tour of their craft, where he met some of their companions. He was also shown visual 3D-images of their home planet, which of course, we now know could not have been Venus. (A common deception on the part of the 'Visitors'.)

Matthews claimed many contacts over a period of time from 1941 to 1961. In later years wrote copious articles about his experiences. It is impossible to know whether they are accurate, embellished or the product of a fanciful imagination.

Matthews did mention one item of interest. He claimed that in 1938 Tesla gave him a design for an Interplanetary Communications Set. This immediately reminded me of all the ham radio operators, around the world, who had modified their own equipment in order to communicate with the 'Space Brothers'.

CHAPTER FIFTEEN

PUZZLING AND UNUSUAL REPORTS

Sometimes, even though we speculate, we will never know the truth about a mysterious happening. One such event occurred in Germany, at the end of World War II. In 1961, the witness wrote a letter to New Zealand ufologist, Henk Hinfellaar, who was allowed to publish it without mentioning names.

'In January 1945, a few days before a heavy bombardment, the following took place in a central German city:-

'During an air-raid warning, when a large community gathered in the air-raid shelter, suddenly three young men, roughly of the ages between twenty and twenty-five years, appeared and desired to inspect the shelter. The striking part of their appearance was that they were wearing dark, tight fitting, high necked interlock suits. In spite of a temperature of eight degrees below zero, they wore neither headgear nor scarves. Their footwear reminded one of gym shoes, which on no account suited the occasion, since snow lay outside. Everyone present was struck by the fact, that in these shoes, they moved about in a completely noiseless manner.

'A further striking feature was that they did not speak to one another, and that only one of them spoke at all. This man had a strange sounding accent, and he stood always slightly more in the foreground. All three men had beautiful symmetrical features, dark hair, and were similar in type. The spokesman was slightly taller than the other two.

'Since, from the start, it was assumed this was a case where inspectors wanted to test the air-raid shelter's facilities, no suspicions were raised. With the others, the spokesman briefly looked around in the shelter, and then only remarked that people should take note that in the event of an air-raid warning, everyone should be in the shelter. Then the three men disappeared without anyone ever hearing anymore about the affair.

'Later, during a heavy bombardment, their apartment house was completely destroyed, but nothing happened to any of the people concerned. They had all heeded the warning and were in the air-raid shelter.

Investigations, conducted later, revealed that these three men had only been seen by the persons present in the shelter. A search, carried out by the authorities, determined that no inspectors had been sent to test the shelter, and produced 'no clues as to whence the men had come'. Their footprints were visible in a small clearing nearby, but no trails of any vehicle tracks leading to or from the spot. Some of the witnesses thought that they may have been English spies, but this was discounted because spies would not have made themselves so conspicuous in behaviour, language, clothing etc.

The Argentine newspaper *'Diario de Cordoba'* reported an inexplicable incident which happened to a well-known businessman in 1959. He got into his car one morning in the city of Bahia Blanca. As he started to drive away from his hotel, a strange cloud enveloped his vehicle.

The next thing he knew, he was standing alone in a deserted part of the countryside. He hailed a passing truck, and asked the driver if he could give him a lift back to Bahia Blanca. The puzzled driver explained that they were over one thousand kilometres away in Salta! He took his confused passenger to the nearest police station, who confirmed with their colleagues in Bahia Blanca that the businessman's car was still outside his hotel with the engine running. How had he been transported over six hundred miles in just a few minutes?

A similar incident occurred nine years later. Dr. Gerardo Vidal and his wife reported how they had been driving one night, over one hundred kilometres south of Buenos Aires. Their car had been surrounded by a deep fog, after which they remembered nothing. They regained consciousness, in daylight, on an unfamiliar road. Their watches had stopped, and their car, although in perfect running order, was badly scorched. After seeking help, they discovered that forty-eight hours had passed, and they were over six thousand kilometres north in Mexico.

The Argentine Consul, Rafael Pellegrini, asked them to remain silent about the incident while it was being investigated. Their car was sent to the United States, and they were given a similar replacement vehicle.

It is not known if either of these cases involved an alien abduction. We may never know the answers.

Sometimes our alien visitors are not as benevolent as we think, or is it that, in time, they succumb to more human tendencies and emotions? In 1993, *'Samizdat'*, a publication mainly for Spanish speaking people, carried a most interesting account by Salvador Freixedo.

It all started in the 1970s, when Lula, a Venezuelan woman who had a wealthy older husband, was on holiday in Spain. She got talking to a tall, handsome man while in a museum. He told her his name was Jorge, but it disturbed her a little when he guessed her correct name and nationality.

She thought no more about it until years later, when he appeared on her doorstep in Caracas. She was giving a party at the time, and all her guests thought him to be a very charming man, who discussed the UFO flap the country was currently experiencing. From that day on, he harassed Lula to leave her husband and marry him, which she did the next year.

Friends of the couple noted he possessed an extraordinary power of prediction, and an almost super-human physical prowess. He was a great husband to Lula, and although she had no complaints, he refused to tell her anything about his family, where he came from, or what he did for a living. She concocted a story for their inquisitive friends, and once in jest suggested he was an extraterrestrial, something he neither confirmed nor denied.

Despite appearing to be physically fit, Jorge suffered from almost catatonic trance states, and respiratory problems, which he relieved by taking a sniff from a small crystal vial. He always carried it with him, and nobody was allowed to touch it. He would complain to Lula that the 'atmosphere' was killing him.

One day he did not recover, and lapsed into a coma. He was rushed to hospital, and the doctor ordered immediate X-rays. He and the medical technician were so stunned they thought their equipment was faulty. It wasn't! Jorge did not have any lungs. His organs were bizarre, and foreign to human anatomy.

When he died, his crystal vial rose from the bedside table and smashed on the ground. Not a single shard of glass was found. Beforehand, Jorge had forbidden any autopsy, and had ordered a servant to wrap his body in bandages, like a mummy, with silver coins between his fingers.

Lula complied with his wishes, but eight years later, she contacted a researcher and contemplated exhuming Jorge's body. Before this could happen, Lula mysteriously disappeared, and was still missing when Freixedo wrote his report.

In 1947, a young seventeen year old Mexican lad was struggling to maintain the farm he had inherited from his father. One day a stranger, who looked like a local peasant, arrived. He claimed that he had been held captive by tall, fair humanoids in a tunnel beneath a volcano.

His captors, who spoke an 'unintelligible gibberish' had lived on giant vegetables, and before he escaped he memorized a magic formula, which he sketched on a piece of paper. He told the young Jose Garcia that if he concentrated on the symbols, after a while the message would become clear.

After several sleepless nights, Jose understood the message. Soon his gigantic vegetables were the talk of the province, being three times larger than any others. The Agricultural Ministry organised a study, where Garcia and other farmers cultivated areas of a test farm.

The results, and Garcia's giant vegetables, were proven beyond doubt. He was disappointed and had thought the officials would take him to Mexico City, to reveal his secret. Instead, they thanked him and said he was allowed to sell his produce.

This incident had all the indications of assistance being offered by an incognito Space Brother to an impoverished community. We will never know – what a missed opportunity!

STRANGE DISAPPEARANCES

Reports of unusual 'disappearances' are not new, but are people and objects actually disappearing, or merely becoming invisible?

In the early 1980s military technology was already available which, by use of reflected light and radar wavebands, made objects appear to be invisible. Often called 'cloaking devices', some inventions bend electromagnetic rays so that they flow around the object, like water around a rock, but these are still visible to the human eye.

It stands to reason that an advance civilisation may have perfected the ability to still be present, but unseen by us.

Mexico's *'El Universal'* newspaper reported an incredible encounter an Aeromexico airliner had with a UFO on 6th March after departing Mexico City for a late night flight to Monterray. The passengers were nodding off, on what was a comparatively short trip, to suddenly see the night sky and stars above them. It was 'as if the entire fuselage had been blown away!'

One of the witnesses said; "We were flying in space, seeing the skies and stars without the barrier of the cabin walls, which were still there, detectable to the touch, but completely invisible. We could even see the pilots in the cabin, at the controls of the aircraft, that none of us could see, only touch."

The startled passengers could see a glowing object, shaped like two inverted bowls stuck together, flying alongside the plane. For ten minutes there was a gap in communications, and the aircraft disappeared from radar screens in both Mexico City and Monterray. Once the UFO departed, everything returned to normal.

New Zealand investigator, Hamish McLean, reported on an unusual phenomena in the Waimata Valley, where, at times in a certain area, there seems to be a strange force field. One person put her arm into it. The watching witnesses were astounded when the arm disappeared from view, only to reappear when she withdrew it.

One lady in Britain told of a case in Weston-Super-Mare in 1920. Her grandmother was elderly, and rather frail, so friends escorted her to the bus-stop to catch the local bus. She just 'vanished' into thin air! She couldn't be found on the bus, nor had she alighted elsewhere!

Vehicles, as well as people, have been reported to instantaneously 'vanish'. On 4th March 1964, the Japanese newspaper, *Mainichi*, carried a story about a car disappearing from view on a crowded highway.

Three officials from the Fuji Bank saw a black car, ahead of them, and travelling in the same direction. They could see the driver, and an elderly man in the back seat, who appeared to be reading a newspaper. Suddenly there was a puff of something like white smoke or vapour, and five seconds later the cloud dispersed, and the black car was 'gone'.

The bankers were so disturbed by what had happened that they immediately reported the event to the police. It is assumed they were believed, but very little was said publicly.

British researchers, Jenny Randles and Derek James, reported an incident, in 1971, which cannot be easily discounted. The witness to an insignificant white light in the sky, told them that he had received a call from someone claiming to be from the Ministry of Defence, who told him that all he had seen was a Russian satellite.

This was unusual, as the government rarely contacted witnesses, especially where minor sightings were concerned. Even more disturbing were the two men, sitting in a black Jaguar car, outside his home in the following nights. Derek James asked a friend in the local police force to look into the matter.

A patrol car was sent to check, using the excuse that the suspicious vehicle and its occupants may be planning a robbery of a nearby factory. On October 19th and 20th, they watched the suspicious vehicle, and then drove off. At 9pm on the 21st, their superiors noted that the car had a false registration number, and instructed them to detain the two strangers for questioning.

They parked their patrol car at the side of the road, and walked back towards the Jaguar and its occupants. When they reached it, and were about to knock on the window, the car and its two occupants simply vanished – melted away in front of the two astonished policemen. Neither the two men nor the car were ever seen again.

In World War I there was a controversial case of a battalion of soldiers disappearing into a strange cloud, but this was not the only case involving the British Army.

In August 1957, troops from London's Southern Regiment were conducting exercises on the Salisbury Plain. They were equipped with five Centurion tanks, which were deployed in a guarding role, and were to engage half way through the manoeuvre. While preparing for this task, one of the crew reported to Command that they had sighted a large silvery, cigar-shaped object, and that the tank was about to open fire.

Nothing further was heard from the tank – it had vanished, along with its crew, without a trace! Even though they interviewed everybody present at the time, the Army could not explain what had happened.

In 1968, Mr. Scarah, an Englishman, from Hull, was making his way to work in the early hours of the morning. Suddenly he saw an unusual man, who was nearly six feet tall. His hair was brushed right back, and he was dressed in a boiler suit, which was tightly fitted at the ankles. They came face to face for a moment, and as the stranger confronted Scarah, he looked surprised, stared at him for a few moments, then turned around and just vanished.

Scarah insisted that he had never had any psychic experiences, and the man was quite solid. There was nowhere he could have disappeared to!

In his journal, *'Understanding'*, Dan Fry wrote about a couple of similar cases: Harvey Campbell, a taxi driver, experienced a strange occurrence on 12th July 1966. Hoping to get a fare, he was cruising down the street in Merced, California, when a very 'stately', well dressed gentleman hailed him. He got into the cab, and asked to be taken to the perimeter of the city. The driver asked in which direction, and his passenger said the north would suffice.

He then asked; "Might I borrow your etching pad?"

The driver, thinking the man must want to write a reminder note for himself, handed him the pad on which he recorded his calls, and it wasn't until later that he discovered the stranger had written on a sheet in the back of the pad.

When they were on the outskirts of Merced, and reached the ramp leading to the freeway, the driver asked him how much further he wished to go. His passenger said; "This will be adequate – what is the tariff?"

Upon alighting, he gave the driver a one dollar bill, which looked in pristine condition without a wrinkle or bend, saying; "I hope this will suffice."

The driver thanked him, turned around for a second, then looked back. His passenger had 'disappeared into thin air'. It was not possible – he could not have gone onto the freeway, or over the side where there was a high fence, topped with barbed wire.

Harvey became a little more reticent during the remainder of his report. At the time he hadn't understood what was written on the pad. Further, the stranger *'came by later in 'his vehicle' and told me what the writings contained – their message....It may not be destined to convince you of the presence of flying saucers or the beings they carry.....I hope that the same enthusiasm be used to explore the understanding of our fellow man as was used in the past few years to investigate flying saucers. If this is done, in a very few years planet Earth would be a much better place in which to live.'*

There was another case in 1973, in Biana Blanca, Argentina. Eduardo de Deuce was driving home, and not far from Mendanos, when he picked up a hitch-hiker from the side of the road. The man behaved rather 'oddly'. He said very little, and did not speak, answering questions in some unintelligible whispers.

They had travelled about twenty-five kilometres when his engine started malfunctioning. The car came to a halt after another fifty kilometres. When Eduardo got out to investigate, he saw a huge object, about forty metres away, on the road. At first he thought it was an overturned bus, but then realised it was a strange craft with blue and two white lights. There was a row of small windows, emitting a greenish type glow.

At that moment he was blinded by a hot, intensely bright, blast of light. He took shelter behind the car door, and saw the object move slightly to the side, touch the ground, and then shoot away at full speed. He got back into the driver's seat and saw his passenger was gone. His motor started without any trouble, and Eduardo, thinking the man had run away in fright, drove back looking for him. He was gone. Eduardo drove to a neighbouring town and reported the matter to the local radio station. Later the police asked him about the incident, and whether he thought there was any relationship between the stranger and the UFO. Later, the Federal Police got him to make a formal report and 'Declaration'.

New Zealand researcher, Bryan Dickeson, told me of an unusual case Prudence Buttery had unearthed after an interview with a local woman.

In 1975, at 6.30am, Mary was driving to work, along Buchanans Road, Yaldhurst. She noticed a huge sphere approaching from across the fields on her right. It was wider than her car, and had a turquoise blue centre, and a white aura all around.

She wasn't afraid, just puzzled. She backed up three times, but the object seemed to be following, as if observing her. In her mind she was asking; "What are you, and what do you want?"

Eventually it moved over the road and into a field of cabbages, finally disappearing from sight. She was nearly half an hour late for work, but didn't think much of it at the time.

Two weeks later, she was working in her front garden at 7am one morning, when she heard a voice saying; "Can I speak to you?"

She stepped onto the drive where a man, just over six feet tall, was standing. It was a hot summer day, but he was dressed in common farm working clothes of herringbone serge. He was wearing long pants, a trench coat, scarf, gloves and a wide brim hat.

He showed her a drawing of a red sphere, and asked her if she had seen it? Mary told him the sphere she had seen was blue, and she didn't think anyone else had seen it. She said he could ask at the Yaldhust hotel when it opened later that morning. He moved away, and wanting to ask more, she looked over the hedge. He was gone - no car, no bike, nothing!

In front of her property was a four kilometre open side road leading to the main thoroughfare. She told her husband about the two events, but he just laughed. Three weeks later the local newspaper printed a story about a cylindrical 'mother-ship' above the airport near Yaldhurst. It was seen by other people, and had smaller spheres going in and out.

'Omni' magazine detailed an interesting case, which happened in Dunstable, England in about 1982. The investigator on the case felt that Roy was a sane, sober and reliable man.

Late one night, Roy Dulton was driving home from a darts match. A gaunt, long jawed man hailed him from the side of the road. He stopped and offered the stranger a lift, but when the chap got in, he said nothing, and merely pointed straight ahead. Roy was concentrating on the winding road, and when he turned to offer his passenger a cigarette, he was gone!

In 1991 researcher John Pinkney reported a strange case of a New Zealand man – 'Fred' - who was on holiday in the USA in 1986. Wanting a quiet drink, he popped into a bar in Montana. An Indian sat down next to him, and whilst they were talking, he directed Fred's attention to a very attractive Caucasian woman. She was sitting alone, sipping a beer, at a nearby table.

Fred noticed her face seemed to be expressionless, and his drinking companion told him that he had once tried to 'chat her up'. She informed him that her race had not indulged in sexual activity for ten thousand years or more! She then touched his hand – her skin was icy cold!

Fred was so intrigued, he decided to approach the woman himself, but when he looked across at her table she had disappeared. Fred said there was no way she could have got up and left. She had just vanished into thin air. Maybe she could read his thoughts.

In 1995, the Australian Paranormal Research Foundation reported an unusual case from Adelaide. Toni Ottens was going to the supermarket one afternoon, when she noticed an old derelict man on the footpath. After she had parked her van, she took a ten dollar note from her purse and made her way over to him.

When she got close, she put one hand on his shoulder, and took his hand, tucking the money into it, saying; "Buy yourself a nice, hot meal."

"Thank you. That's very kind," he replied. "Tell Dani, in 2010 you'll prove what you know."

Toni said that his hands were not those of a street person. They were long and slender, with soft white skin. His voice was 'so beautiful', and when she looked into his eyes, they were sapphire blue and ageless. She was stunned, and glanced away for a moment, just for a couple of seconds, to rapidly collect her thoughts. When she quickly looked back – he was gone!

He had simply vanished as if he had never been there at all. It was impossible for him to have disappeared, almost instantaneously, from her field of vision. She asked a woman, nearby in the carpark, if she had seen the old man who had been sitting near the garbage bin on the footpath. The woman hadn't seen anyone.

A 1972 edition of *'Saucers, Space and Science'*, edited by Gene Duplantier, published an interesting story about Susan 'X', a registered nurse from Ohio.

Susan was about eighteen or nineteen, when she and Paul were returning from a trip on July 14th 1963. They were not travelling very fast when a man stepped out in front of their convertible. They apparently knocked him over, so they stopped the car and ran back to the fellow who was getting up and brushing himself off. He was nearly six feet tall, about 160 pounds, with dark hair and light skin. He was wearing a pale shirt and black trousers and shoes – no different from any everyday man-on-the-street.

Although he didn't seem to be hurt, they sat him in the back seat, and headed towards the hospital. They asked him why he had stepped in front of their car, and if he preferred they would take him home. Where was he from? Three miles from the hospital, they looked around – the back seat was empty!

They could not understand what had just happened. He appeared to be uninjured, yet the damage to the front of their car cost several hundred dollars to repair.

Later that month, Paul and Tom were driving across town to pick up Susan and her friend Janice. After three hours, when they still hadn't arrived, Susan got a distressed phone call from a drive-in restaurant. Could she come and pick them up instead. She borrowed a car, and she, along with Janice, found the two men in a dreadful state.

Their car was a mess of stains and residue. Both men appeared to be in shock, and Tom was sitting on the curb and wouldn't talk. A shaking Paul detailed what happened.

They were driving over to pick up the girls, when the same mystery man, 'dressed like anyone in the street', suddenly appeared in the back seat. He assured them they would come to no harm.

The next thing they knew, they were standing in a desert-like area, surrounded by several humanoid figures. They were verbally told they were on the strangers' planet, and would be safely returned. Before Tom, Paul and their car were returned to near the restaurant, the mystery man who appeared to be their leader, asked them a lot of questions about procreation and how we live and die.

Sometime later, they were going to a Sunday picnic. Paul and Susan were in the front seat, and Tom in the back with the picnic basket. Tom started stuttering, and when his two friends turned around, there was the mystery man.

They stopped the car, and the unexpected passenger said something before disappearing three or four minutes later.

Another time all four friends were riding on a ferris wheel when the same stranger suddenly appeared in the chair behind them. In 1971, when Susan made her report, she said Tom disappeared in about 1966, and nobody knew where he was.

Paul was still around, and he said the mystery man told them they were here for observation only. He told them to be very quiet about what they had seen and knew, as they only revealed themselves to certain people, to make them aware of their presence, and observe our reaction when under stress.

UP IN THE AIR

During the days of the Space Brothers, our own pilots sometimes experienced inexplicable events.

There have been cases of unidentified objects saving our pilots from crashing. Keith Flitcroft advised of a close encounter as early as 1942, when he crossed the Normandy coast while flying a Wellington bomber. Due to cloud cover, they were at an extremely low altitude, and had to veer off course because of continual harassment by a small ball of green fire. It was only when he returned to base that he learned that his sudden forced deviation had prevented him from flying straight into a mountain dead ahead in the low cloud.

One hot day in 1953, Fred Reagan took off in his Piper Cub plane, and quickly climbed to eight thousand feet. He saw what looked like a traditional flying saucer at the same altitude, and instead of taking evasive action, banked and headed towards it.

By the time he realised he was on a collision course, it was too late. He threw his plane into a tight, diving turn, but the unknown craft tore away his tail. As his plane plummeted towards the ground, Fred was thrown clear. He could feel himself falling, alongside his plane.

Suddenly the wind stopped rushing past him, and he was hovering, motionless above the farms and fields below. He said; "Far below I could see the wreckage

of the plane, dropping away. But I floated there....like a human cloud, thousands of feet in the air.

"How long I couldn't tell. Time had stopped for everything but me....I was afraid to move lest I disturb the mysterious balance which held me there."

Fred sensed an invisible force, like a giant suction cup, and felt himself rising upward at an ever increasing speed. Looming above, his could see a monstrous, brilliant object, which 'swallowed him up'. He found himself suspended in a dark room, and through a round opening underneath could see the countryside thousands of feet below.

He looked around in the dim light, and screamed in terror when he saw three short 'alien' type figures moving below him. He thought he must have fainted, because the next thing he remembered he was lying on his back on a metal type 'bed' which was soft to the touch.

He felt stunned, but strangely calm, and didn't know how long he lay there before he heard a 'click', like a switch being turned on.

A sudden voice, speaking in an expressionless monotone said; "How do you do, man."

It continued, in perfect English, but hollow and muffled, as if coming through a loudspeaker; "Do not reply. Only I shall speak. We, from outside your planet, regret extremely the unavoidable circumstance which caused our vehicle to collide with yours. We are here only to observe your primitive....your civilisation.

"We do not wish our activities to interfere with man-living in any manner. We cannot replace your vehicle, but we have examined your body and assured ourselves of its undamaged condition. We have also corrected an abnormality in your body which we have found is most common in your species. It is called ....". Again there was hesitation, as though the speaker was groping for the word, ".....cancer. We offer this as slight reparation for the loss we have caused you.

"We shall return you to the surface of your planet. We caution you, for your own peace, not to reveal your experience with us. You will not be believed...Think of us in kindness." Fred heard a humming noise, and everything went dark.

Fred was found lying in a field, besides the wreckage of his aircraft. Whilst he had not been wearing a parachute, he was uninjured, with not even a bruise or a scratch. His plane, however, was totally demolished, and buried six feet into the ground.

He woke in a hospital bed, with a doctor and nurse and several men peering over him. When he told them what had happened, nobody believed him. It was just as his rescuers had predicted.

Fred's experience did not have a happy ending. The authorities committed him to a State Asylum for the Insane. The next year he died from a degeneration of his brain tissue 'due to an inexplicable exposure to extreme atomic radiation.'

In October 1956, Jeff Brown a young private pilot from Milwaukee, Wisconsin, found himself in trouble at 11pm one foggy night. His engine started spluttering, and he realised that he had forgotten to check his fuel before he took off.

He saw the gas gauge was showing empty, and as he started to panic, he felt 'some sort of force' pulling him back into his seat. Through the fog he could see something which scared him even more. There were blue and green lights whirring about fifty yards off to the side of his plane.

His engine ran out of fuel and stopped. Instead of going out of control, the aircraft started descending smoothly, almost like a glider. The lights, at the side of him, were descending parallel to his plane. He landed smoothly in a cornfield, and scrambled out.

Through the fog he could see the strange lights hovering about one hundred yards away. After about a minute, they quickly took off. He was grateful for his rescue, and only wished he had been able to meet and thank them.

Until we had surveillance satellites capable of monitoring all of the Earth from above, we were not always aware of what was flying, or entering the atmosphere, over the poles at the extremity of our globe.

The *'APRO Bulletin'* documented an interesting report from a former member of the US Coast Guard, who was serving in the Antarctic as part of Operation Deep Freeze. Preferring to remain anonymous, I will call him 'Mr. B.'

In the early hours of April 20th 1964, he and five other crew members, were on a C-130 transport fight, inbound to the naval base at McMurdo Sound. There was a Russian plane, on radar, flying parallel about five miles off their starboard wing.

Nine glowing white UFOs, which did not appear on anyone's radar, approached at a speed of about four hundred knots. They then reduced their pace to match the plane's speed and altitude of about thirty-five thousand feet. The objects were flying in a 'V' formation, and close and visible to the crew as they tailed their plane.

Their plane began to lose all electrical power, and they attempted a 'May Day' call, but their radio was dead. An effort to switch to auxiliary power was also unsuccessful. It was if the entire electrical system had 'shorted out'. The turbo-props gradually began to grind to a halt.

Mr. B. commented that at this time the plane should have been 'falling like a rock', but it continued maintaining a steady speed and course. They flew along, in silence, as if someone or something else was in control.

The UFOs were still there when the plane entered strange haze, similar to, but not the same as a 'white out'. After twenty minutes the haze vanished, and the flight continued, still being shadowed by the unidentified objects.

Suddenly the electrical power came back on, and the crew began restarting the engines, one by one. As soon as all systems were functioning again, the UFOs departed. Their plane had flown for fifty minutes without engines or electrical power. During that time they had not only covered an amazing two hundred and sixty-five miles, their tanks had too much remaining fuel.

The crew were questioned for over two days, and seven of the nine rolls of film they had taken were confiscated. Mr. B. said when he developed the two rolls he had kept, they turned out very foggy. All the crew were told, 'in very strong terms', to keep their mouths shut about what they had seen and photographed.

Mr. B. had a second experience on 3rd January 1965, when he was on board another transport flight. As a huge, elongated glowing object, which did not appear on radar, passed their plane 'with a bang'. They were buffeted around in the 'wash', and temporarily lost power and radio operations. The crew also managed to get a few photos, which were all turned over to the Navy, and apparently much clearer than those from the first incident.

He said whilst he was not aware of any other incidents at the time, the Russians often complained about 'unknown aircraft' buzzing their installations.

In *'Contact Down Under'*, I discussed another case in the Antarctica. In 1979 a New Zealand airliner, on a sightseeing 'joy' flight, crashed into Mt. Erebus in the Antarctic. Some ham radio operators claimed they had picked up transmissions from the doomed aircraft, saying it was being 'buzzed by a UFO'. As I pointed out in the book, it may have been trying to warn them they were on the wrong course – we will never know.

CHAPTER SIXTEEN

STRANGE, HUMOROUS and SUSPECT INCIDENTS

Sometimes a UFO is not extraterrestrial. On 12th March 2017, residents of San Luis, Colombia, saw a UFO streaking across the sky, and crashing nearby. They called the police, claiming this was an alien invasion and not the usual drug smugglers. By the time the law arrived, not much of the debris remained. It had been souvenired by the local community, and very little was left for Google to retrieve from their high-tech balloon!

I don't know the authenticity of this following report, but considered it too amusing not to include.

Neil Armstrong, the first man to set foot on the Moon, made his famous statement – *'That's one small step for man. One giant leap for mankind!'*

Upon re-entering the capsule, he was heard to murmur – *'Good luck Mr Gorsky!'*

For twenty-six years he never explained this comment until a reporter brought it up after a speech he made on 5th July 1995, at Tampa Bay. He explained that since Mr Gorsky had died, he was now free to explain the reason for his comment.

In 1938, when he was a kid in a small Midwest town, he was playing baseball with a friend in the backyard. The ball went over the fence, and landed in the neighbour's backyard, below the bedroom window.

As the young Armstrong was leaning down to pick up his ball, he could overhear an argument going on inside. Mrs Gorsky was yelling at her husband; - "Sex! You want sex?! You'll get sex when the kid next door walks on the Moon!"

John Maybury, a New Zealand radio host, made a rather costly mistake in mid-1952. Years later, he told the *'Star Sports & Magazine'* how, for a couple of hours one morning, he faked a broadcast of pre-recorded fictitious eye witness reports of a UFO hovering over Hagley Park in Christchurch. A prominent local Anglican priest, with a lively sense of humour, had helped him with the scam, so it seemed a really great idea at the time. Unfortunately, it backfired.

He had got away with a few silly pranks in the past, and only two weeks earlier the Managing Director had told him to 'give radio a lift – inject more personality into your broadcasts!' John took him at his word. At 6am had the fictitious UFO travelling across the countryside and hovering over the park. By 8.30am he had crashed the saucer and reported little green men running for the trees.

Thousands of people flocked to the park. Some came from twenty miles out of the city, causing one of the biggest traffic jams Christchurch had ever seen. The city was in an uproar, and the telephones 'went mad'. All the time John was sitting in his 3ZB radio studio, blithely broadcasting his ill-fated hoax.

Maybury was ordered off air, and banished to the radio station's programme department. He resigned, and didn't get another radio announcer job for another eighteen months.

We often hear reports of aliens abducting humans, but occasionally the roles are reversed!

Claude Raffy, a French researcher, wrote about an interview he had with an eighty-two years old lady, who was quite intelligent and lucid. In fact, she didn't look her age, drove at some speed around the countryside, and had a husband much younger than herself. Quite a feisty no-nonsense woman! She told of an incident which happened in mid-February 1956.

She was a forty-one years old business woman at the time, and was driving along the road from her parents' home, at Choisy-le-Roi, to Fresn, just south of Paris. At about 9.30pm she noticed a bright, white, shining phosphorescent object hovering just above the ground. It was over an area of vacant land.

As she pulled up, she could hear a slight hissing sound, and noticed a small person, about one and a half metres tall, moving about near it. The thought of flying saucers came into her mind – there had been talk of them in the newspapers.

"I got the sudden idea that maybe if I could grab an occupant, and take him to the newspapers, what a fine thing that would be for me! The little chap appeared to be small and thin – he would not be hard to carry!

"So, there and then, I opened my boot and got it ready to put my precious captive into it. By now, around the machine, there were eight of them, engrossed at looking at something or other on the ground."

The object itself had the shape of a 'flattened pumpkin', with luminous facets she thought may be windows. She could see two more beings inside the machine, and the others still seemed to be concentrating on the waste area around them. When they saw her approaching, without any signs of fear, they were 'off', like scampering rabbits, into the opening at the base of the craft.

"The last one of them – the one I was aiming to grab – turned around and fixed his big back eyes on me, intensely, as if wanting to say something. Just as I thought I was going to get him, a beam of light shot out from one of the windows on the upper part of the machine. It engulfed me, paralysing me on the spot. I couldn't move anything except my eyes."

It was only then, for the first time, she began to feel scared. She was not sure how long this lasted for, but once they had all disappeared into the craft, the light surrounding her started to fade, and she was able to back away and stumble back to her car.

She got in, but was unable to drive away. For the second time she felt unable to move. After a while there was a 'scraping sound' – like a door closing. Later, the 'hissing noise' increased in intensity, and the craft slowly rose to treetop height. It stopped, momentarily, then took off at 'top speed'.

"To start with, the entire craft turned orange, and then passed to red as its speed increased. Immediately I was able to start the car, and didn't even stop to see in which direction the machine had gone.

"Panic had now caught up with me, and I decided to turn back and return to my parents in Choisy. When I arrived there, still gasping, I poured out the whole story. My father told me not to tell anyone about it. I had my job to think of. Everybody would laugh, and the police would question and harass me."

She said after that she felt 'different'. She had dreams and premonitions which would come to pass, but there seemed to be no indication of an abduction or 'forgotten memories'.

She described the beings as being humanoid in shape, but slim, with heads proportionally bigger than ours. They had large protuberant black eyes, nostril holes and a slit for a mouth. They were clad in greyish-blue tightly fitting one-piece combination garments.

She confirmed the description of the craft as being circular, and flattened on top and below. The central parts were luminous and white – not glaring – and the rest of the machine a 'metallic grey'. Her estimates of size were a bit vague.

Because Granny could not recall the exact date in 1956, Claude Raffy searched the records and data for occurrences at Orly Airport, which was not far away from her encounter. On 19th February 1956, radar operators detected the presence of a flying object, twice the size of the largest aircraft of the time, which came down slowly, remained stationary, and later departed suddenly at a fantastic speed. The radar operator reported that it was behaving in a fashion totally different from anything he knew of.

The pilot of a *Dakota* reported that he could see the object for over thirty seconds. It was enormous, lit up with red luminescence, no navigation lights and a hazy outline.

On September 19th 1975, the Canadian *'Toronto Sun'* reported bizarre events which occurred in 1968 during broadcasts at Montreal's radio station CKGM. Their 'shock jock', Pat Burns, was notorious for his less than pleasant treatment of bureaucrats, 'nuts' and 'phonies', often hanging up on people.

He was hosting a hotline show, and was used to all topics from marriage proposals to bomb and death threats. Nothing had prepared him for the 'space men'.

He recalled one regular caller, a lady with a European accent, who sounded as if she was in her forties, and only wanted to talk about her 'friends from space'. She claimed that you could identify them by their eyes, which 'are a brilliant mauve, and turn bright pink when you talk to them'.

He said that he used to humour her because the listeners enjoyed the comic relief, but one day he was in a bad mood.

"Doll," he growled, "I can't let you talk about your little men from outer space."

"Don't cut me off," she threatened, "or the little men will cut you off!"

Pat just laughed. "Honey, call me tomorrow and explain why your little spacemen let you down."

When he pressed the button for the next call the line was dead. Everything was dead. Station CKGM was off the air. It was six hours before they could broadcast again.

The next night the little lady called again; "Well, Mr Burns, I told you the little spacemen would cut you off. What do you say now?"

"You and your rotten little spacemen," Burns snarled. "Try for two in a row! Goodbye!"

The station immediately went off air – 'as dead as a doornail'. This time it only lasted for fifteen minutes, and was put down as an inexplicable power failure. The station manager rushed in and demanded to know what Pat had done this time.

"Honest," Pat pleaded, "I don't know how this dame does it."

Pat Burns was a very sceptical man – but two freak co-incidences? He was not prepared to put them to the test. The next night, when the little lady rang again, he was much more accommodating.

"Honey," he said, "I'm not going for three in a row. Now, you were saying about the little men from outer space......"

It is not often we hear about the stupidity of some people, especially these two police officers.

In 1983, when interviewed by Art Buchwald, two highway patrolmen could not understand why they were fired from their jobs. One was now working at a gas station, and the other had turned to drink.

In about 1980 Officer Dunning and Sergeant Redondo were driving along Route 21, near Sorrowful Bluffs, USA. It was 2am, and they were surprised to hear the overhead roar of engines which came from a strange object with two giant beams of light.

It was travelling at about 250 miles per hour, and the two patrolmen gave chase until it landed on the runway of the now abandoned Abel Hill Air Force Base. Redondo said the craft was cylindrical in shape, except for a wing, with a motor attached, protruding from each side. Why, on earth, at that stage did they not realise that it was probably not from outer space?

They approached, with their guns drawn, and after about ten minutes, a door at the back of the object opened, and a 'strange apparition' appeared. It wore dark coveralls, brown rubber boots, and something like a baseball cap. There were three more similar 'beings' who had hairy faces and 'funny things which looked like sunglasses'. Each of them carried something the patrolmen thought were 'laser weapons'. In fact they also resembled Thompson machine guns!

The patrolmen moved closer, and Redondo shouted; 'Don't shoot – we are friends!"

Dunning told investigators; "The leader of the group said something in a strange language to the others, then spoke to us in English. *'Buenos noches'*. We come in peace from the planet Sirius. Where are we?"

The sergeant said; "You are on planet Earth. Welcome!"

"*Caramba!* We have made a navigational error. Our mission was to explore the planet Pluto. We have got to be going – pronto."

'Wait!" Redondo replied. "Why not stay, and explore our planet?"

"We must follow the orders of our great Cyclone Bolivar. Perhaps some other time."

During his debriefing Dunning said he asked the 'things' if they could at least look inside their 'spaceship'. After some quiet argument and discussion among the group, the leader said; "*Si senor,* we will even take you for a short ride."

The two patrolmen were escorted into the craft. It was like nothing they had ever seen before, and not like the spaceships they had seen in the movies. It was empty except for large bales of what appeared to be a 'grass-like' substance.

Dunning asked what it was, and the leader, who was sitting opposite, with his laser gun pointed directly at them, said; "It is our food. One bale keeps us sustained for every million light years that we travel."

When Dunning wanted to taste it, the leader shouted that it was poisonous to Earthlings! The cabin lights dimmed, and the craft zipped along the runway and took to the air. Both the patrolmen were air-sick, but their companions just sat back, smoking and giggling.

Soon they landed back on the runway. Our naive patrolmen wondered how skilled the pilot must be when he hadn't been to Earth before. The engines were still running when the leader pushed them out of the door.

"Tell the people of Earth Sirius will never make war on them, unless they make war on us!"

Dunning and Redondo immediately went back to base, and made a full report to their captain. He called the Air Force who grilled the two men for two weeks. Soon after both patrolmen were sacked, without explanation.

When Art Buchwald was investigating the report, I can't believe why he didn't understand why the Air Force referred him to the Drug Enforcement Agency. Dunning was not happy; "I know what I saw, and told it as it happened."

Redondo had taken to drink, and had moved into one of the empty barracks at the abandoned airfield. "I know they'll return," he said, "and I'm going to wait here until they do....and then I'll bring the whole country to meet them. We'll see who gets the last laugh on whom!"

Whilst one can see the humorous side of the event, they were lucky they weren't killed or injured. Afterwards, the effect on their lives was quite sad.

Over one hundred years ago there was a great deal of publicity regarding mysterious 'airships', many of which were most probably the newly invented dirigibles. One case of mistaken identity was an advertising balloon for a Christmas chocolate promotion.

Captain Penfold was a 'ballooning aviation' hero in his own right. This particular day, in 1912, he was dressed as Father Christmas, and piloting the balloon above Parramatta, in Sydney. When it strayed off course, he grabbed his parachute and sack, and jumped out, landing on his head in unfamiliar terrain.

Local children discovered the unconscious Santa Claus, surrounded by boxes of chocolates. When he regained consciousness, he merely dusted himself off and started distributing the chocolates, which contributed to the promotion.

Within a couple of weeks he was fully recovered, and back in the air!

On 26th November 1977, at 5.12pm, when the scheduled newscast was going to air, a strange, calm but strong, unknown voice over-rode and took over or super-modulated the TV signals from five British transmitters that were monitored by the Independent Broadcasting Authority in England.

Surprisingly, despite being heard by many thousands of people over southern England, none of the authorities detected the intrusion.

"This is the voice of GRAMAHA, the representative of the Asta Galactic Command, speaking to you. For many years now you have seen us as lights in the skies. We speak to you now in peace and wisdom as we have done to your brothers and sisters all over this, your planet, Earth.

"We come to warm you of the destiny of your race and your worlds so that you may communicate to your fellow beings the course you must take to avoid the disasters which threaten your worlds, and the beings on the worlds around you. This is in order that you may share in the great awakening, as the planet passes into the new Age of Aquarius. The new age can be a time of great peace and evolution for your race, but only if your rulers are made aware of the evil forces that overshadow their judgements.

"Be still now and listen, for your chance may not come again. For many years your scientists, governments and generals have not heeded our warnings, they have continued to experiment with the evil forces of what you call nuclear energy.

"Atomic bombs can destroy the Earth, and the beings of your sister worlds, in a moment. The waste from atomic power systems will poison your planet for many thousands of years to come. We, who have followed the path of evolution for far longer than you, have long since realised this – that atomic energy is always directed against life. It has had no peaceful application. Its use, and research into its use, must be ceased at once, or you all risk destruction. All weapons of evil must be removed.

"The time of conflict is now past. The race of which you are a part may proceed to the highest planes of evolution if you show yourselves worthy to do this. You have but a short time to learn to live together in peace and goodwill. Small groups all over the planet are learning this, and exist to pass on the light of the dawning new age to you all. You are free to accept or reject their teachings, but only those who learn to live in peace will pass to the higher realms of spiritual evolution.

"Hear now the voice of GRAMAHA, the representative of the Asta Galactic Command, speaking to you. Be aware also that there are many false prophets and guides operating in your world. They will suck the energy from you – the energy you call money, and will put it to evil ends, giving you worthless dross in return.

"Your inner divine self will protect you from this. You must learn to be sensitive to the voice within that can tell you what is truth and what is confusion, chaos and untruth. Learn to listen to the voice of truth, which is within you, and you will lead yourselves on to the path of evolution.

"This is our message to our dear friends. We have watched you growing for many years, as you too have watched our lights in the skies. You now know that we are here, and that there are more beings on and around your Earth than your scientists admit.

"We are deeply concerned about you and your path towards the light, and will do all we can to help you. Have no fear, seek only to know yourselves, and live in harmony with the ways of your planet Earth. We, of the Asta Galactic Command, thank you for your attention. We are now leaving the planes of your existence. May you be blessed by the supreme love and truth of the cosmos."

The authorities and TV executives tried to deflect the immense publicity by claiming it was a hoax, but none of their engineers could explain how it was done. There were vague accusations that an engineer had cut into satellite transmissions to allow the mystery broadcast through. Despite the message echoing the sentiments of the Space Brothers, nobody would ever admit that maybe, just maybe, it could have been from the extraterrestrials.

If they were indeed, leaving our planet, with only a few remaining, what better way to reach a large number of people, rather than relying on a few individual contactees? This was not the first time such methods had been attempted.

Another incident also occurred three months earlier in August 1977. Residents of the entire town of Chester, Illinois, reported that one of the local UHF television stations went 'off the air' for several minutes. The screen went blank, and then the image of a male seated behind a control panel appeared. It looked like something out of 'Star Trek', and the man who had his hands clasped in front of him, looked straight at the camera.

"Attention earthlings. I am speaking to you from inside a spaceship circling high above your planet. We come in peace with good intentions, and wish to speak to you about a matter of utmost importance. At this very moment, hundreds of our craft are flying above the surface of your world attempting to clean the air of radioactive particles which have been placed there over the last decade by your scientists bent on testing nuclear weapons.

"These tests are very harmful, not only to your own people but ours as well. STOP THEM IMMEDIATELY BEFORE IT IS TOO LATE. WE BEG OF YOU. PLEASE WE BEG OF YOU....."

The face faded from the screen, and the regular programming resumed as if nothing unusual had occurred. Even though several other viewers confirmed seeing the transmission, the TV station denied any knowledge.

In 1978 Bill Winters wrote an interesting article regarding the use of radio and TV to plant subliminal messages into the minds of the viewers. Surprisingly, he raised the subject of alien communications, and how the authorities were trying to 'jam' any signals. At the same time, our own scientists were attempting to send friendly messages back.

'There is a vast and complex network of early warning devices on this planet that can warn of a UFO's approach many hours before it actually enters

Earth's atmosphere. When such a warning is received by the agencies responsible for the security of our world, the data is immediately fed into the most modern computer system in existence anywhere.

'The machines can plot the exact time it will take for the UFO to approach Earth, and in most cases they can successfully predict where the UFO will visit. The visits of such interplanetary craft are always very brief. Their method of operation is to enter our atmosphere and hover over individually chosen 'targets' for unknown purposes.'

One scientist said that the aliens can get away with a lot more at night. Their ships could hover closer to cities without being visually detected by many people. There certainly seemed to be a much higher incidence of transmission problems during the evening and night-time hours, when messages could be run for longer periods of time.

Since then, nearly forty years have passed, and our current technology would be much more adept at detecting intruders and unauthorised broadcasts.

In 1971 author Rex Dutta was invited to participate in a broadcast over one of the new Very High Frequency official radio stations in England. The producers had already categorised Dutta as being part of the 'lunatic fringe', (his own words), and after they discussed some facts, sightings and government response, he was to state that he believed in the reality of the 'Saucers', and then to answer any telephone calls which came in from the radio listeners.

The enthusiasm and response was enormous. Just after the conclusion of the program another call came through from someone who claimed they were from outer space. It was switched through to the studio's internal speaker, where it was heard by twenty people and tape-recorded.

The message was essentially the same. 'There are men among us who would guide us in our earthly affairs, but that every creature must help himself and use his own intelligence. For a time there will be trouble on Earth, but if man will find justice, then there is hope for man.'

Sometimes journalists also have to be careful of what they say. Hungarian Gyorgy Tarnavolgyl wrote, in part of his article published in the Hungarian weekly '*Hatarszel*', a criticism of UFO reports;

'The press blows up UFO reports in an absurd way. People see comets or polar lights, then go scuttling into their houses to hide, believing, oafishly, that space beings have invaded. It's time these fools were made to see the truth.'

Three days later, he had cause to change his mind, and published the following article the next week;

'I was driving along the Debrecan road at about 4am. The sky was clear and glittering with stars. Suddenly, in my rear mirror, I saw a dazzling yellow light approaching very fast. It stopped and hovered above my car, whereupon my engine went dead. It was an oval object, about ten metres in diameter, changing colour from yellow, through to orange and violet.'

Gyorgy watched as it moved away and hovered over a swamp. His car started again and he drove towards it for a better look. The next thing he knew he woke up behind the steering wheel in a foetus type position. His notebook was on his lap, he was freezing cold and over half an hour had elapsed.

When he got out of the car he experienced nausea, neck pains and a blinding headache, and to this day doesn't know what happened.

Some unusual reports also come from the Aboriginal communities in Australia. When John Glenn made his first orbital flight around the Earth, there was a group of people gathered at Muchea, south of Perth. They had turned on all their lights as a signal to him.

Among the people crowded around the communication's receiver was astronaut Gordon Cooper and a group of aboriginals, including one who was considered a 'holy man'. He told Cooper that he had 'been in space', which everyone assumed must have been some 'mystical' experience.

Suddenly, on Glenn's second orbit, there were indications of a malfunction with his heat shield, which was essential when he re-entered Earth's atmosphere. The aboriginals, sensing the problem, started chanting and dancing in a strange ritual.

It was around this time that Glenn reported 'yellow fireflies' swarming around his craft. These strange little 'sparks of light', in some ways, resembled the sparks of flame from an aboriginal camp fire. Minutes before he successfully returned to Earth, the natives quietened down, and Glenn noticed the lights were receding. We will never know if the ritual saved the astronaut's craft and life - or was just a co-incidence?

THE SUSPECT

Just because researchers classify a report as being suspect, does not indicate that the incident never happened. Some reports may well be quite genuine. Either we are not sure, or just don't know, whether it is extraterrestrial related or not.

Reinhold Schmidt

This unusual episode occurred at Kearney, Nebraska, where Reinhold Schmidt was a grain buyer. At 2.30pm on 5th November 1957, after inspecting a field of milo and corn, Reinhold noticed a bright flash near an abandoned farmhouse. He was curious and drove further, towards a riverbank.

One hundred feet ahead was a large, silvery metal craft. It was at least one hundred feet long, thirty feet wide and fourteen feet high. A thin beam of light shot out, striking Reinhold in the chest and paralysing him. Two men came out, and once they determined he was not armed, allowed him to go on board their craft, provided he did not touch anything.

From the outside the ship seemed to be one solid piece of metal, without portholes or windows, but from the inside the walls looked more like thick glass which one could see straight through.

Now we come to the interesting part of this report. There were six ordinary looking humans inside – four men and two women. All were wearing normal 'street clothes', especially the women who had light coloured blouses, dark skirts and medium heeled shoes. The desks and equipment they were working on were similar to those available on Earth, and Reinhold saw regular and Roman numerals on the instrument panel. Although they spoke English to him, it was with a definite accent. Further, they spoke perfect German amongst themselves.

Reinhold said that the one man looked and talked just like a fellow who had been watching TV with him in the hotel lobby the night before. He left the craft before it departed, and the crew told him that they would meet again.

Thinking that this was a Russian ship, manned by German scientists, he first went to his church minister and then to the local sheriff. The sheriff, having already received a report of a strange object in the sky that day, decided to go straight out and investigate the landing site.

When he and Reinhold arrived, they could see evidence of where the craft had been. When they returned to the town, the chief of police assembled a party of five, including the city attorney and a newspaper reporter to return to the area for a more detailed investigation. That night, without Reinhold's knowledge or permission, the incident, including his identity, was broadcast over all the TV channels.

He was besieged by reporters and photographers, many of whom went to the landing site that night and the next morning. Two Air Force officers arrived, and it was during their interview that one of the local officials wondered out loud how the ship could go straight up. One of the Air Force officers blurted out; "Oh, we know what makes it go straight up!" It was after that the 'officials' asked him to change his story, something he refused to do unless it was for the security of the United States.

What followed was a nightmare. Attempts were made to discredit his report, by the planting of false evidence. He was locked up, incommunicado, in the local jail for two days, then transferred, under guard, to a mental hospital. He was not allowed any phone calls, and neither his employer nor his family could contact him. He was kept there for two weeks before family and others obtained his release.

This was not the end of Reinhold's experiences. The following February, he saw the same craft hovering over a meadow. He stopped his car and walked over, to meet the same crew member he had seen before. He said they wanted to talk to him, but could not stay where they were, in full view of the road.

He got into the craft, which took off, and landed in a more remote spot. The man asked him a few questions, including whether we would accept their landing on friendly terms, and what would the United States do if other planets set off atomic bombs or launched satellites to orbit the world? They also told him that they could contact him whenever they wished because our brain impulses are similar to individual fingerprints. When he mentioned the intimidation he had experienced, they said they knew about it, and if he hadn't been released from hospital they were going to do a mass display over Kearney.

He then contacted a 'Flying Saucer' group, who persuaded him to give a talk to some of their meetings. After that he claimed the visitors took him on a four day trip to the Arctic Circle, where they explained the damage out nuclear testing was doing to Earth's ecology.

Whether or not this last excursion actually happened is a matter of conjecture, but there seems to be little doubt about Reinhold's first experience. We must then ask the question if these 'space people' were actually extraterrestrials, or the crew of an experimental craft from our own planet?

Raechel's Eyes

Jean Bilodeaux, a MUFON field investigator, conducted ten years of extensive and thorough research into this fascinating case from 1971.

'Callie', Marisa's mother, was concerned, because her blind daughter was, despite her impairment, continuing her studies, and moving into a college-sponsored apartment. Marisa had been raised in an isolated part of Nevada, and needed to interact with the general community. The school counsellor arranged for a girl named Raechel to be her room-mate, and assist Marisa with social skills and day-to-day living.

Marisa was puzzled about Raechel's background. It was if she had no past life or childhood. She never had a boyfriend, knew nothing of music or popular songs, and used no slang or colloquialisms, common for young people of the day. She didn't talk about any usual teenage activities, and Marisa thought she must have been raised in a very isolated environment, or be suffering from amnesia.

Marisa asked Raechel to help her choose matching clothes to wear each day, but it seemed that Raechel had no sense of dress or colour at all. Marisa's tutor told her that Raechel always wore a jumpsuit, scarf, long sleeve shirts, and wrap-around sunglasses, even when in the apartment.

One day, when 'Callie' was visiting, Marisa introduced her to Raechel. 'Callie' noticed she had a small face, wispy hair, exceptionally long arms, and looked very skinny and frail. She thought perhaps her total cover of clothes may have been simply due to a skin condition. As Raechel walked across the room she stumbled, and 'Callie' caught her mid-fall. Whilst her skin felt cool and smooth, it was not that which startled Marisa's mother.

Raechel's glasses had slipped forward, and 'Callie' heard a buzzing in her ears, and found herself staring into a pair of 'large, avocado-green eyes'. There seemed to be no whites, and 'something wrong' with her pupils. Raechel looked frightened, and hurried away.

It wasn't just that which made 'Callie' determined to find Marisa another place to live. Marisa told her that every week Raechel would get a visit from some men. Marisa's eyesight, which she had lost through diabetes, sometimes enabled her to see fuzzy shapes and colours, and she said these men always wore dark suits.

They brought specially mixed food and drinking water for Raechel, and although she would stay in her room while they were there, Marisa was sure she sometimes heard them hit Raechel during their visits.

Raechel didn't have any friends, only her father. Marisa asked her about this, and since Raechel knew 'Callie' had seen her eyes, she arranged for her to meet her father, who was a Colonel in the military.

What he told 'Callie' and Marisa came as a complete shock. Raechel was the product of a genetic hybridization experiment, originating on Earth. She was moved 'off Earth' to grow, and then returned to an isolated military base in Nevada. The colonel felt an affinity towards this young girl, and after adopting her, a decision was made to attempt to integrate Raechel into society.

Selecting an appropriate room-mate was the first step. Marisa, being blind, would not notice Raechel's unusual appearance. Once the truth was known, Marisa and 'Callie' kept the secret, and the two girls became more like sisters rather than just best friends.

One afternoon, Marisa came home from classes to find Raechel was gone. She had left nothing behind except a note, taped to the dresser; *'Dear Marisa. You are my first and only friend. I will miss you very much, but I have left you a gift to remember me by. Love, Raechel.'*

Marisa looked around the room, but could find no present. It was only then she suddenly realised that she could see. Raechel had left her the gift of sight.

Unfortunately, Marisa died a few years later, and when Jean Bilodeaux's report appeared in the *'MUFON UFO Journal'* it elicited a flood of correspondence, some critical and some supportive.

Jean Bilodeaux wrote a book about her decade of investigations into these events, and details not only the memories of Marisa's mother 'Callie' – Helen Littrell in real life – but also those of Marisa's brother, husband, roommates and friends. Special attention is given to Harry, Raechel's adoptive father, and his work with the clandestine 'Four Corners' Base in Nevada.

We are left with the following unanswered questions. Was Raechel a gifted human, a hybrid, or an extraterrestrial visitor, 'incognito' on Earth?

The Space Seeds

In the 1960s, whilst the 'Space Brothers were the main extraterrestrials being reported, every so often researchers heard some very strange stories.

One came from a seventy year old Seattle man, living in a ramshackle cottage. He said a group of short men had arrived at his hut, claiming they had come from another planet. He wasn't scared, but got worried when they told him they wanted him to accompany them back to their home world.

He protested that he was too old, and suggested that a younger man would be more fit for the purpose. His visitors tried to reassure him, saying that one of them was three hundred years old and another over five hundred. Their longevity was due to a plant which grew on their planet, and prolonged life for up to over one thousand years.

One of them offered the old man a double handful of seeds, and encouraged him to eat them, saying it would give him strength to withstand the long journey. When he still refused to go with them, two of the men tried to pull him off the bench he was sitting on. He resisted by throwing everything he could find at them, and his violent reaction caused the visitors to leave and not return.

At first he thought he must have been dreaming or hallucinating, but when he looked down, there were the seeds at the side of the bench, where they had been dropped during the struggle. When investigator, Lucius Liotto, arrived there was a great mess and holes in the walls from where the semi-hermit had thrown everything from pots, pans, china and eggs at them.

Lucius was naturally sceptical, but he took some of the seeds and planted them in his flowerbed. The plants that grew were beautiful, with small yellow flowers. They were also very vigorous, and soon dominated the whole bed. Lucius, thinking that they looked similar to marijuana, was concerned that they may be narcotics, and contacted the local drug squad. They said that whilst they couldn't identify the plants, they were not illegal.

Various colleagues of Lucius obtained some of the seeds, which they sowed and grew. Despite consulting botanists, for years no-one could identify the plant, which did prove to be edible and non-toxic. Eventually, a Swiss botanist claimed he had solved the puzzle, and that the plant was a weed which originated in Mexico. Since no other experts had been able to identify the seeds, we can only wonder. Perhaps this case will always remain a mystery.

CHAPTER SEVENTEEN

UFOs – A MYSTERIOUS AND RISKY PURSUIT

Sighting a UFO, meeting the Visitors or investigating the subject can be fraught with difficulties, and sometimes danger.

EDGAR JARROLD - A MAN OF MYSTERY

In 1952, Edgar Jarrold founded Australia's first open civilian UFO investigation group in Sydney, *'The Australian Flying Saucer Bureau'*. It was, at first, very much a one-man affair, with limited public involvement and impact. Jarrold published a newsletter, *'The Australian Flying Saucer Magazine'*, which, in later years, Phillip Frola would incorporate into an excellent book titled *'The Jarrold Listings'*.

Edgar included other researchers into his group, including 'D', W Clifford and Dr. Miran Lindtner. In January 1954, he appointed Andrew Tomas to be AFSB's 'Sydney Observer' and assistant in the production of their magazine. He also expanded his organisation by appointing State representatives across the country, including Fred Stone in South Australia.

In 1953, Edgar Jarrold formed close contacts with Albert Bender, and other researchers around the world, including Harold Fulton in New Zealand. They formulated 'Project X', which focussed on the idea of a saucer base in the Antarctica. Bender claimed 'inter-dimensional' type abductions to a huge saucer base buried under the icy cover of the southern continent, and at the end of 1953 Jarrold felt he had 'confronted the solution to the saucer mystery'. He said the 'secret' could only be shared with a select few!

In October 1953, Albert Bender's *'Space Review'* published the following; *'Statement of Importance: The mystery of the flying saucers is no longer a mystery. The source is already known, but any information about this is being withheld by orders from a higher source. We would like to print the full story in 'Space Review', but because of the nature of the information we are sorry that we have been advised in the negative. We advise those engaged in saucer work to please be very cautious.'*

Albert Bender claimed he was being harassed by 'Men in Black', and mysterious visitors and threats. Jarrold claimed one visitor had told him something that 'amazed him beyond belief', but he was sworn to secrecy.

In July 1955, *'People'* Magazine published a six page article, discussing flying saucers in general, and highlighting the research of Jarrold and Tomas. During that period, there was also some controversy over Edgar Jarrold and fellow researcher, Fred Stone, obtaining copies of a 1953 UFO film, taken over Papua New Guinea by Tom Drury the Deputy Director of Civil Aviation. In 1955 Edgar Jarrold wrote an analysis of the prints from this film, which I suspect were not meant for public perusal.

It also detailed how, in 1954, Edgar Jarrold had attended a meeting with Sqn. Ldr. Birch at Air Force Intelligence in Melbourne. It is not known whether Jarrold was supposed to have divulged this connection, however he suddenly seemed to disappear from public view.

For six months nobody heard from him. Mail and phone calls went unanswered, and in the end, Andrew Tomas managed to arrange a meeting with the elusive Director. He arrived at Jarrold's home to find a note on the door – 'Gone for the weekend.' Tomas was very embarrassed and distressed, as Jarrold had personally handled all correspondence and subscriptions. Tomas was left with the unpleasant task of having to answer mail, refund money and generally pull the group back together.

UFO researchers, world-wide, were speculating as to the reasons for Jarrold's sudden and mysterious silent withdrawal. In 1958, American investigator, Coral Lorenzen, wrote; *'After a conference with RAAF officials in Melbourne, Mr. Jarrold abruptly ceased his activities, closed up shop, and has not been heard from since. Some say he was 'hushed-up', but in my opinion, knowing Jarrold as I did, is that the military officials with whom he conferred in 1954, convinced him that it was in the best interests of the people to keep the truth under wraps, and that he couldn't fight City Hall. That pattern of intimidation was evident from that point, and it has become increasingly evident ever since.'*

John Auchetll, PRA Director, reported that, in a 1954 interview, Jarrold said; *"I don't like the subject, it scares me to death, and since I have started asking questions, I have had endless troubles from all types of people....I do not know what I have done wrong, but it is something very important to someone..."*

One must ask – if he didn't like the subject – why did he found The Flying Saucer Bureau in the first place?

The first person to start raising questions was South Australian researcher Fred Stone. In 1960 he wrote about looking into old files and records which may throw new light on the happenings some years earlier. At that time, he thought Jarrold may have been intimidated. Maybe he was, and maybe he wasn't. Fred noted that four researchers, Bender, Fulton, Stuart and Jarrold suddenly ceased all communication with their colleagues, and withdrew from ufology. There was a total of seven investigators who had experienced disturbing paranormal events of varying degrees. Six had withdrawn from the field. Fred was the only one 'left standing'. He suggested that all investigators should keep away from the 'dark side', not get involved with 'groups that dabble in the negative occult', and stick to the factual side of the saucers.

It took several decades before more of Jarrold's actual story was unearthed. Researchers, Bryan Dickeson and Frankh Wilks, started digging deeper about twenty years ago, and were astounded when they learned the truth after contacting one of Jarrold's sons, and accessing the Australian Defence files in the National Archives.

Edgar Jarrold was born in Queensland in May 1918. His parents were later divorced, and after his mother, Florence, was widowed by her second husband's unexpected death, she married Reg Wallace, a railway guard. In 1938, the young Edgar travelled alone to Sydney, and the next thing his mother knew was when she received a letter from him, in early 1939, saying he was working on the docks in England.

This is where the story gets very strange indeed. In England, he was using the alias 'Roy Peter Simpson' with no proper identification, or record of how he arrived in Britain. He later told authorities that his parents were dead, and that he had stowed away on a ship from Australia. There was no record of any such crew member or stowaway in the Captain's log, but in 1938 a British citizen could sign on as a crew member without a passport.

Bryan Dickeson wrote that he had been told that Jarrold was involved, militarily, during World War II, and afterwards in some mysterious capacity. His one son said his father could be very distant, and was always reluctant to discuss his World War II experience. He believed he had joined the Australian

Navy in Brisbane a year or so before the war began, but had several photographs of him in Navy, Army and Air Force uniforms at different times.

Bryan came to the conclusion that Edgar had been involved in Military Intelligence, and had actually spent some time training in the US and then embedded in Europe before the war began. He later arrived in England under a false identity, and set about getting himself detained in an internment camp, in order to assess whether the alien and enemy detainees were spies or foreign agents.

It took him some effort to be placed in the required detention camp. On 1st August 1940, he was apprehended trying to enter the docks with a stolen pass. After he told the court he was trying to stow away on a ship, to get back to Australia, they set him free with a £2 fine. Two weeks later, on 15th August, he smashed a shop window, and when he wasn't apprehended, turned himself into police.

This time, he was sentenced to three months jail, and whilst there, told another inmate that, although he was a loyal Australian, he hated England. Once he was free, he was going to signal the position of a nearby airfield to the German planes. He repeated this to the Chief Constable, and this got him to where he wanted to go. At the end of his sentence, he was moved to an internment camp on the Isle of Mann.

Edgar kept using the alias of Roy Peter Simpson, and of course, the Australian authorities could find no record of him. Jarrold wrote to his stepfather, Reg Wallace, using his false identity, and Wallace kept up the pretence. After some time Reg Wallace wrote to the Australian Government requesting 'Simpson's' repatriation back home. Despite saying he was a 'good, but misguided young lad', that he had only met a couple of times, his request fell on deaf ears.

Eventually, Jarrold revealed his true identity, which his stepfather confirmed. Surprisingly, very few questions were asked about the reasons for the deception. Jarrold was eventually released, and arrived back in Sydney in August 1943.

We may never know the true reason Edgar Jarrold founded the Australian Flying Saucer Bureau. He claimed it was because he saw two UFOs himself, one night in May 1951, but he was obviously a good pretender. Was he actually an intelligence agent, setting up groups where they could monitor sighting reports from the public? We will never know!

However, another thought came to mind. He was on the Isle of Mann from 1941 to 1943 – the very years when some contactees suspected there was secretive UFO and alien activity. (See my book *'The Alien* Gene') A mystery to which we do not have an answer!

During his period as Director of the Australian Flying Saucer Bureau, Edgar Jarrold felt threatened. He wrote to a South Australian colleague and told of a frightening incident, which occurred late one night at Sydney's Wynyard Train Station.

He was standing, alone, on the near empty platform, and as he heard the train approaching, he moved forward to his customary spot, ready to enter his usual carriage. Suddenly, without warning, he felt a violent push in the back, which propelled him over the edge of the platform and onto the line.

Luckily, the train was slowing down, and Edgar was able to scramble back onto the platform before the train reached him. He looked around, and the nearest person was over twenty feet away, and very unlikely to be the culprit.

Edgar Jarrold's experience on a railway platform, brought to mind a similar incident which occurred to Dr Miran Lindtner, many years later, in July 1969. Dr Lindtner was the President of the NSW UFOIC organisation, and highly respected by all who knew him.

He had been a fighter pilot in World War II, and was also a talented musician. He was in Europe to attend several UFO meetings before he proceeded to a World Veterinary Conference in Yugoslavia. He was killed when he 'fell under a train' in Rome. Was it an accident? His family didn't think so, and later told me that they thought his death was due to his involvement with UFO research.

In *'Contact Down Under'*, I mentioned that the fate of Lindtner's files was a bit of a mystery. Alan, one of the witnesses Lindtner had interviewed, went in search of them. His efforts proved fruitful, and he found, in a University basement, a couple of dusty bins containing some paperwork and letters, dating back to the 1950s.

Alan took some, and later told his friends that he 'should have kept quiet about it'. He was being followed by cars, and his credit card had been 'blackened'. A short while later, he moved to South Australia, and just 'disappeared'. Nobody heard from him again!

After Lindtner's tragic death, Fred Philips succeeded him as President of the UFO Information Centre in Sydney. Some years later he was knocked down by a car in the centre of Sydney, and whilst he survived, both he and Bill Moser, another long time organiser of UFOIC, died within three weeks of each other in the early 1980s.

Fred Stone, another leading Australian investigator, also survived a suspicious accident. His injuries slowed down his previous enthusiastic pursuit of ufology, although when I knew him in the early 1970s, he was still an inspiration not just as an active researcher, but also a poet and musician. He fully never recovered from another accident in 1976, and passed away in early 1977.

TONY DODD and GRAHAM BIRDSALL

Whenever a ufologist dies of cancer or a heart attack, everybody cries 'foul play', but these are probably the most common natural causes of all human deaths.

While in Australia, Graham Birdsall told me about a military encounter, involving several countries, with UFOs, some underwater, which occurred over the Arctic during the Christmas-New Year period 1992/93.

British colleague Tony Dodd followed up with further details. He reported that at least four UFOs had been seen descending and entering the sea in that area. The incident involved the Icelandic, British and American military, including submarines, warships, gunboats and Coast Guard vessels. Despite a great deal of secrecy, it was said they were searching for a surface vessel which had reportedly gone missing.

In February 1993, after an American contingent of three destroyers had told all ships to keep a distance of three nautical miles, sixteen airborne objects were seen hovering over the US flotilla. Tony then reported that on 15th April 1993, only two US warships could be seen. The Russian Navy joined the operation, which was purportedly to search for the missing American destroyer. One radio operator advised overhearing a communication between the Russian ships to the effect that they were 'engaging unknown underwater craft'. The press reported it as 'joint military exercises', which later moved on land to Tiksi in Siberia.

Tony didn't just restrict his investigations to those recent events. He started digging into the suspicious death, involving a car crash, of a man involved in 'Operation Aeneid', some twenty-five years before, in 1970/71. Some of the UFOs involved had been over Iceland and the Arctic area.

In 1997 Graham Birdsall wrote in his *'UFO Magazine'* of further reports received from terrified Icelandic fisherman, about numerous UFOs in the sky, some of which entered or exited the sea. The most amazing was a telephone call he received on 23rd April 1996. The fisherman claimed they were working fairly close to a group of American warships, when there was a sudden blinding flash of light, and 'one of the warships just disappeared in front of our eyes!' The Americans ordered all fishing boats out of the area, and the caller's captain 'retired to his cabin with a bottle of whiskey'.

These were not the first reports from the Arctic area. Some Scandinavian pilots claimed that flying discs had landed in the Arctic during snow storms, when their own planes were unable to intercept them.

In early 1952, a UFO crashed near Spitzbergen in Norway. In 1956 Colonel Gernod Darnbyl, chairman of the Norwegian General Staff board of inquiry stated; "Some time ago a misunderstanding was caused by saying that the disc probably was of Soviet origin. It has – we wish to say this emphatically – not been built in any country on Earth. The materials used in its construction are completely unknown to all experts having participated in the investigation, and at any rate only to be obtained after physical and chemical processes still unknown to us."

In *'The Alien Gene'* I discuss the British and American military expeditions to the Antarctica immediately after World War II. Most investigators have assumed that the hostile reception they received, and the advanced craft they witnessed, were due to alien activity, and possibly a base in the area.

In the 1960s military personnel from Chile, Argentina and Britain were still reporting anomalous flying objects over the Antarctica. The Commandant of the Chilean Air Force's Antarctic Base, Don Mario Jhan Barrerra made the following statements to the *'El Mecurio'* newspaper;

"It is rash to say that we all saw a flying saucer, like those in Science Fiction. But, nevertheless it was something real, an object travelling at a staggering speed.....what we observed was no hallucination or collective psychosis....That

it could be an aircraft constructed on this Earth, I do not believe possible. I belong to the Air Force, and to my knowledge the machines built by man fall far below this in respect to shape, speed, manoeuvrability in the air etc.'

Only a few months before his untimely death in 2003, Graham Birdsall again started digging into the possibility of aliens in our Polar Regions - this time in the Antarctic. Along with Dr. Richard Sauder, he published an interesting article, concentrating on the Lake Vostok area, occupied by the Russians. Perhaps this was not a wise topic to tackle, given the previous difficulties Jarrold and Bender encountered.

Lake Vostok occupies a three hundred square mile, ice free region, containing many warm water lakes. It has always been assumed that this anomaly is due to volcanic activity under the continent. Do we really know?

Graham said that following a filmed interview with Valery Uvarov, from Russia's Department of National Security Academy, he asked him about any curious activity around Lake Vostok;

'Valery stopped dead in his tracks and his face visibly paled. He put a hand on my chest, looked around, and with a look of genuine concern and fear etched in his eyes, quietly said; "Please, please, I can't talk about that. You must not talk about that. The Nazi's'

'Struggling to come to terms with the remark, and in a knowing matter-of-fact fashion, I said; "But everything is being contained, right?"

"Yes, yes, everything is fine. But please, we must not talk about this."

'And at that, Valery increased his pace and disappeared into a waiting elevator.'

Certainly many countries have bases in the Antarctica, and Graham also mentioned being told of one called *'Europa S8',* which was apparently top secret. Graham Birdsall never discovered the truth of what was really happening in the Antarctic. If he did, he never had the chance to say. A few months later he died following a brain haemorrhage.

Tony Dodd
Tony was a British police officer, a tough competent police sergeant, for twenty-five years, and exceptionally well-trained in standard investigation procedures and psychological profiling. Completely trustworthy, he served in

the Diplomatic Protection Squad. In 1983, whilst driving near Addingham, in Yorkshire, he and his wife, Pauline, saw and photographed a disc-shaped object in the sky.

When he retired, Tony Dodd relentlessly pursued information on humanoid aliens, and the reasons and intention for their activities. He travelled the world, speaking at many international conferences, and liaising with other leading investigators. As a result, he became involved with several contentious cases both in the UK and overseas.

Tony had previously helped with research on the Holy Grail and been in contact with the British contactees, such as Elizabeth, Lydia, and Vera, whom I personally knew, and have discussed in *'The Alien Gene.'* He once claimed researchers and those who got too close to the truth often meet with fatal accidents or suspicious deaths.

He once commented; "Out of the four different groups, all humanoid, one group was so human looking, they could sit next to us in a restaurant, they could sit next to you in a theatre, and you would never know." Tony also said that teams of agents, including those from the UK, USA and Russia, were trying to track them down. He was concerned that if captured these 'visitors' could suffer imprisonment, death or even worse.

One of his contentions was that the humanoid aliens were who they said they were, and had been associated with us for a long time. He considered that a more malevolent Reptilian type had formed a liaison with some 'authorities' and were trying to locate, capture, or eliminate those with Visitor connections. He had ignored warnings not to continue writing about these activities and infiltration of our society.

His research was always thorough and meticulous, and he left no stone unturned. He was not a person to be fooled by hoaxers, or fanciful witnesses. He supported genuine contactees, and once commented: "Instead of conducting a witch hunt, sceptics and debunkers would be well-advised to remember there are more things in Heaven and Earth than perhaps science will ever be allowed to understand."

While Tony never openly claimed to be a contactee, he wrote the following words, which echoed the message of those who came before him;

'My telepathic communication with the aliens has helped me to solve a lot of questions about what they are and why they are involving themselves in the life of this planet. Here, in the words given to us, is one of the messages I have received in response to my mental questions.

'Our presence within your Solar System is to observe the evolution progress and environmental changes occurring not only in your planet, but to its people.

'Using this observation technique enables us to foresee potential future difficulties which may arise, and if necessary, give you a view on the course of action needed to overcome them. To achieve these aims we employ the use of many types of monitoring equipment, each with a responsibility for a different area of scientific investigation.

'The problems facing your race are many, and largely due to the act of your technology being turned towards the hostile aspects of humanity. You have the ability to turn the world into a place of harmony and plenty, if you direct your abilities and enterprise towards sharing with not only your own people, but the natural laws of the universe. You can advance technology, but only for the good of all, otherwise it will destroy you.

'We are here with the hand of brotherly leadership, to teach you as you evolve. Each one of your kind has the ability to grow in cosmic consciousness. The answer lies within the fabric of you all. We hold great love for you and know that the direction is now turning towards the path of cosmic understanding.

'But, we can only advise, the future of your race must be determined by your own free will. Our view of you shows great hope and expectation, and we wait, with anticipation, the day when you aspire to the Federation of Cosmic Brotherhood.'

(Tony Dodd researched many facets of ufology, and I do not know if it was this, or some other aspect he disclosed, that upset US officials.) Graham Birdsall, in an article, *'The Watchers'*, detailed the intense pressure and threats Tony and his wife were subjected to when attending a conference in Tuscon, Arizona in May 1991.

In 1994, when attending the annual UFO Congress at Mesquite, Tony was again threatened by a couple of men who told him: "You are a very dangerous individual...and don't think we can't get at you when you're back in

England...we can and we will." (In 2009 Tony was diagnosed with a rare and aggressive form of brain cancer and died six weeks later.)

He was a beautiful soul, and admirable investigator. We will never know whether his untimely death was due to natural causes.

"Allow modern science to evolve and take its course, albeit through a narrow and open mind to the amazing possibilities and probabilities all around us.

"We all arrive on this Earth with nothing, and we all depart with nothing, except the learning of a lifetime. Before we can begin to understand the truth of who we are, and where we come from, we must first begin to know ourselves. In truth, we are all alien to this planet, our real home is amongst the stars."

......Tony Dodd.

Was something happening in both the Arctic and the Antarctic all those years ago? Certainly we did not possess the technology to monitor the area as we do now. In my book *'The Alien Gene'*, I also discussed the ill-fated British and American expeditions there after World War II.

In 2015 Linda Moulton Howe published information from a retired US Flight Engineer stationed in Antarctica during the summer season of 1995-96. On several occasions he saw silver aerial discs darting around over the Trans-Antarctic Mountains. One area was designated a 'no-fly' zone, which he was told was an 'air sampling' area. Once, when traversing it for a medical emergency, he and his crew saw a very large hole, like an entrance, going down into the ice. The debriefing they received indicated a lot more than an 'air sampling area'.

They were told 'they had never seen it', and never to talk about it. After their flights they would have a few beers at the bar, where they heard scientists talking about 'guys at the South Pole working with strange-looking men', and confirming a future trip to the 'air sampling area', (ie. big hole in the ice!), 'to meet-up with the ETs that were there.'

We have to ask where did the unusual craft, seen over the last sixty or more years, originate? Were they ours or 'Theirs'? More recently, there have been reports of secret visits to the Antarctic by some of the world's influential leaders. Why? Did their knowledge and investigations of activities around the

Earth's Polar regions have any bearing on the fates of Jarrold, Bender, Birdsall and Tony Dodd?

Ken Phillips

Another British researcher, to meet a premature death, aged only 54, was Ken Phillips, who joined BUFORA in 1957 and for many years was a leading figure in their investigations and training programs. In 1989 he helped found a witness support group, allied to BUFORA and part of the RAPPORT organisation.

Ken was meticulous and scientific, especially when examining the contact and abduction cases he was considering and documenting. All experiencers trusted him, and were grateful for his assistance and understanding. Ken did not favour the use of hypnosis, and preferred to refer to cases as *'close encounter experiences'*. Often he raised the money for a witness to see a psychologist or specialist at one of London's leading hospitals.

On 19th July 1996, he was travelling with a colleague to give a lecture at the South Wales Conference in Cardiff, and suffered a sudden fatal heart attack. Friends in the UK said that, during the confusion, his travelling companion was hit by a car the same night.

It may be only co-incidental, but only two days before, he had intimated that he was going to look further into any connections between the 'Holy Grail' and the mysterious Isle of Mann. Further, there were plans for Ken to link up his research and findings with CUFOS – the Allen Hynek Centre for UFO Studies.

Although he didn't always agree with his contemporaries, he was well respected, and in an obituary, Jenny Randles referred to him as 'Lost Warrior'.

Pete Willisher

In 1972/73, Pete Willisher, originally a guitarist, often played with Country and Western bands that visited American Bases in Europe. In the early seventies he was playing with a group called 'The Muskrats', and Terry, another band member, was fascinated by the UFO issue.

They were appearing in an American Air Base in the north of Germany, and during a break, when he and Terry went to the bar, they raised the question of UFOs with some of the servicemen standing there. They didn't anticipate the nervous, almost frightened response to their questions.

One said; "We've encountered all kinds of things. There are things I'd like to tell you, some things that, if I told you, you'd want to commit suicide....Please, while you are here, leave it alone. We're enjoying your music, but there's no way....I'm in fear for my life, I can tell you."

A couple of years later Pete was appearing in a cabaret at an American Air Base in England, and this time he faced an unexpected interrogation when he broached the subject of flying saucers with some of the serviceman at the function.

They had happily been discussing music, but when he changed the subject to UFOs many looked uncomfortable and either turned their backs or walked away. An older American approached him and warned; "You're causing problems here!"

The next thing he knew, two enormous 'black guys', Military Police, took him by the arms, bundled him through a door and into a room where some Americans in buff coloured clothing were sitting.

There were a lot of screens in a line, with two 'guys' sitting at the consoles. What amazed Pete was one screen was displaying details of his and his family's history.

One man, facing him, asked him what organisation he belonged to. Pete said he was just a musician, and why were they asking him all these questions? Pete said he had always been fascinated by UFOs, and couldn't understand their reaction.

He was starting to get a little scared when a Colonel came through the door. His wife liked country music, and wanted the entertainment to start. Since Pete was now the band leader, the Colonel signed some 'release form', and demanded he be sent back to the dance floor.

The Colonel was much nicer than the 'secret service' type men, and since the band was staying at the Base to do a show the following night, he invited Pete to breakfast the next morning.

After they had eaten, he took Pete to his office and showed him some photos of UFOs taken from fighter plane gun cameras. He said that he could tell Pete this because no-one would believe him; "We've been dealing with these for years and years."

He stressed that there was no way they could tell the public; "This is connected with religion, it's connected with national security, it's connected with the entire planet. It is so bizarre, and I don't know it all. There are those who do, and I don't envy them."

He went on to explain that all the military authorities and governments had been in cahoots with the film industry for years. He said movies, books and magazines were all a small part of a slow information programme, and a way of getting the younger people to accept the fact that we are not alone, and all kinds of other things are going on. He finalised by saying some people can accept this, but most don't want to know.

Several prominent investigators' files and research have been lost to the flames. A lifetime's work of my colleagues Rosemary Decker and Millen Le Poer Trench was reduced to ashes when Rosemary's home was destroyed the Californian forest fires. There was nothing sinister to this event, but other cases are more suspicious.

Leo Noury wrote about how contactee Paul Villa's house burned down to the ground after his contacts. He went on to document another case, when the best friend of a contactee he had worked with, saw her house burned down entirely after she learned of her friend's experience.

'The fire began with a ball of light appearing in her daughter's bedroom. Although she tossed water onto it, she could not extinguish it. Within minutes, the whole house went up in flames. The firemen were shocked by the heat of the fire that had melted metallic objects. The family was very frightened, but unharmed.'

Dr. Andrija Puharich was writing a book called *'Time no Longer'*, which by all accounts included, among other topics, information on developing telepathic abilities. He claimed that the government had set fire to his New York home in the 1970s, and his manuscript was lost, along with many years of research. For a while, he was in fear for his life, and spent several months in hiding in Mexico.

New Zealander, Bill Startup had taken some important film footage of the 'Kaikoura Lights', seen from a plane at the end of 1978. Later, he visited the home of fellow witness, David Crockett, in Island Bay, Wellington, to show him the documentary film he had just made. Just after, Crockett's home was mysteriously burned down. Fortunately, the film was not there at the time, and it is not known if this event prompted the Crockett's decision to move to Hawaii.

In the 1990s, Dr. John Mack, a Professor of Psychiatry at Harvard University, conducted a controversial study of over two hundred men and women who had claimed alien encounters. In 1994, his book *'Abduction: Human Encounters with Aliens'* was published. The university was far from happy, as were government agencies. Harvard conducted an inquiry into the matter, but he escaped without censure.

In September 2004, Dr. Mack was speaking at a Symposium in London, and at 11.25pm, while returning to the home where he was staying, was struck by a silver Peugeot. He was rendered unconscious, and died a short while later at hospital. At the time, Dr. Mack was on a pedestrian crossing on Totteridge Road. It would have been well lit, but the police suspected that the driver was intoxicated.

Possibly just an accident, as the authorities said, but given all the other ufologist and scientist deaths, some people remained suspicious. Ufologist Leo Noury expressed his doubts, claiming that John Mack had suffered a crushed rib cage, indicating that he had fallen before the car ran over him.

Further, Noury claimed that John Mack was going to make important revelations in a conference which had been programmed for the Spring of 2005.

It was not just witnesses, researchers, scientists or members of the military who met with a suspicious demise. In 1971, Desmond Leslie commented; *'If memory serves us correctly, US Secretary of the Air Force, Quaries, suffered a sacrificial death of some kind, perhaps because he experienced a change of mind and wanted to tell the public the truth. Anyhow, he was found mysteriously dead in bed one morning, at the age of 49, by his butler, in his Washington D.C. home. Coroner's verdict: heart attack.'*

In 1979, New Zealand's Murray Stott was on a lecture tour of Australia, and had completed several successful talks in Melbourne, when his plans to address several Sydney meetings were cut short.

He told the *'Sunday Times'* he was walking back to the home where he was staying in Sydney, when someone waved from a car parked a few houses away. He walked over, and someone jumped out of the back and told him to get in.

There were three men in the vehicle, and they addressed him by name, and asked about his lectures. He demanded they produce some identification, or he was getting out of the car. (In my opinion, he should never have got in to start with! Perhaps we were all more trusting in those days.)

A ginger haired man in the front seat said; "We're telling you for your own good, you had better leave." They said they did not want anyone talking about UFOs in Sydney, and Murray thought they might be some sort of policemen, as they were all respectably dressed and groomed.

He was so shaken up, that when he quickly got out of the car, he didn't think to note down the registration number. He went back to New Zealand soon after, but told the newspaper reporter that since he wasn't physically assaulted, he was considering a return trip to Australia.

Australian ufologist, Fred Stone, wrote of the perceived threat to New Zealand author and researcher, Bruce Cathie. In 1970, his book, *'Harmonic 33'*, was quite popular, and they publisher had arranged for him to give a lecture at an Adelaide UFO Convention which was being held over the Easter long weekend holiday.

Bruce seemed very enthusiastic, and travel and accommodation arrangements were made on his behalf. Suddenly, without explanation, he could not attend the Convention. Fred contacted the publisher, who advised that Bruce's life had been threatened, and the New Zealand police had advised him not to come because of the danger involved. (In a further development, Bruce himself told me of how, without explanation, his publisher had shredded all the copies of one of his books.)

Investigators are not the only ones to be pressured into silence. Whilst any sane and sensible researcher knows that some people misidentify conventional objects in the sky, they also realise that the occasional 'abductee' has mental problems and is prone to fantasy. This does not excuse genuine witnesses being silenced and incarcerated in mental health institutions.

The New Zealand *'Kosmon'* publication published a letter from a distraught mother, who told of what happened to her son, Garry, in the late 1960s.

'My son was stationed aboard the USS Wasp as an airman apprentice in the newly formed space patrol. He had just joined the Navy, and wasn't quite eighteen years old. He has always been interested in the space program, so naturally he is interested in the flying saucers too, and wanted very much to learn all he could about space and space travel.

'...In between the No.2 and No.3 Gemini launchings the USS Wasp had an experience with UFOs. The mother ship hovered at about ten thousand feet, and four saucers flew in staircase formation in 'squares' around the carrier, and did ninety degree angles. There were eight witnesses, including the "Officer of the Day'.

She went on to say her son was called into the Chaplain's office, and told him it was all because he was 'talking about' UFOs. She said he was 'tricked' into seeing someone at Chelsea Naval Hospital, who immediately diagnosed him as being schizophrenic and having 'hallucinations'.

His mother contacted her local Congressman, who ordered a 'hold' on Garry's treatment, until the matter could be investigated. The hospital ignored the Congressman, and committed Garry to Philadelphia Naval Hospital, where he was also questioned by Naval Intelligence.

She believed what her son had reported because her husband, who had previously been employed by Convair Aircraft Corporation, and had seen UFOs over an airport where they had been doing test flights. They had been tracked on radar, and she had also seen them herself.

When is a Hoax not a Hoax?

We hear of many cases, especially in the USA, where witnesses have been pressured either into silence or recanting their reports. One such incident occurred to Carroll Watts in 1967.

On March 31st, at 10.30pm, he was driving home from his father's residence, in Lobo, Texas, when he noticed a light coming from what he thought was a nearby abandoned residence. He drove up towards the property, to investigate, and soon realised that the glow was actually a landed craft, about one hundred feet long and ten feet high, with no apparent windows or doors.

At first, he never considered an extraterrestrial explanation, and thought it must have been a new Air Force aircraft that had made an emergency landing. He wondered if there was anyone inside, possibly injured, and started hitting the hull with an old fence post, to attract attention and offer assistance.

Suddenly, a door he hadn't detected, slid open, and he peered into the interior. It was lit by a bluish light, and contained all kinds of machinery including lots of meters and dials, - but no crew!

Watts said; "There was a loud crackling, like the beginning of a Victrola record, and then a voice, sounding like it came from a machine, or was recorded, began talking to me. It knew my name and everything, and it told me it wanted to give me a physical examination. It said that no harm would come to me whatsoever, and that the examination would be completely harmless."

The voice told him that if he agreed, and passed the physical, they would take him on a short flight into space. The voice instructed Watts to stand in front of a machine against the opposite wall, but by this time he had become so scared that he fled from the craft, and jumped back into his car. As he sped off, the craft rose silently from the ground, and headed in a southerly direction.

In the following couple of weeks he could not put the incident out of his mind. He knew that there had been other reports of sightings in the area, and decided that if he ever got the chance again, he would hold his nerve, and try to discover more about the strange craft and disembodied voice.

Less than a fortnight later, on April 11th, a severe thunderstorm brought down a tree on Watts' property. When he went outside, to inspect the damage, he noticed a flickering light from the abandoned farmhouse. This time he was going to investigate without running away.

He set off, but before he reached the previous landing area, he realised a much smaller object was hovering behind his truck. He got out, and could see an open door on the craft, with four men beckoning him to come inside. Again, he could hear the electronic voice, urging him to take the painless physical examination.

He stepped through the door, which automatically slammed shut. The four occupants weren't exactly the stereotype 'Space Brothers'. They were about five feet tall, muscular, and wearing white overalls. Their ears and noses were 'superficial', with 'wrap around eyes', and slit-like smiling mouths which didn't seem to move, but he thought may be responsible for the electronic voice. One must consider that these initial beings were possibly biological robots, charged with safely collecting Watts, and delivering him to the main ship.

He was shown to a chair, and after he sat down, the craft's interior darkened, and he felt a slight sense of motion. After a couple of minutes, the light came back on, and the entry door re-opened, not to the outside, but into a much larger room. Watts thought this small machine had attached itself to the larger craft he had encountered the first time.

His escorts went into another room, and he was taken by what is assumed to be normal men for a physical examination involving delicate wires passing gently over his naked body. During this process, he saw what looked like a small green cube, sitting on a table. He surreptitiously slipped it into the pocket of his jeans, which had been left hanging nearby.

After he had dressed, one of the men reached into his pocket to retrieve the cube. When Watts grabbed his arm, he was immediately struck unconscious. When he came to, he was back sitting in his truck. (Obviously, he had been a 'bad boy', and didn't get his promised short trip in space!)

There were, however, subsequent contacts, where Watts managed to get eleven photos of the craft, and one of the 'beings' who spoke with an electronic voice. In several parts of the world, there have been reports of space people taking advantage of abandoned farmhouses to facilitate their movements. Perhaps it was to Watts' benefit that he lived in close proximity to one.

Soon the Air Force learned about the incidents in Loco, and after they referred it to the Condon Committee, Watts willingly told them of the events and sent them copies of all his photos. These were then forwarded to Dr. A. Hynek, who concluded that the photos were genuine, and all that remained was for the witness to undergo a lie detector test.

Watts failed the test, and said the whole thing had been a hoax. That may have been the end of the matter, but Dr. Condon was suspicious, and sent Capt. Robert Loftin, from the University of Colorado, to visit his previously rock-solid witness..

It was then that Watts told Loftin that he had deliberately failed the lie-detector test, and falsely admitted to a hoax, because he had been beaten, and his family threatened. He said that on his way to take the test, he came across a car stalled in the right-hand lane of the road. A woman was trying to raise the bonnet, and he stopped and got out, to see if he could help.

The next thing he knew, someone from behind hit him over the head. He fell to the ground, but was still conscious. Two men in dark suits, one holding a rifle, were standing over him.

One said; "If you pass this test, there's going to be a lot of daylight seen through you in more than one place. Now git!"

That evening, after returning from the failed test, he was explaining to his wife what had happened, and a car drove by his home, spraying it with bullets from an automatic weapon.

How much witness intimidation has existed in Australia in later years, and who is behind it, is something we may never know. In August 2015, the *'Sun Herald'* published an article about Liam Freaney, a Kiama family man, who had videoed several unusual flying objects in 2013.

He thought his activities were just a passing interest, but soon had cause for concern; "I would see and film an object, then directly afterwards I would get home and a helicopter would show up and sit over the house. So I started filming the helicopters as well as the unidentified flying objects. It happened over and over again, twenty or thirty times at least."

In 2014, he contacted UFO Research NSW. After speaking to our President, Marianna Flynn, and learning that we knew of several other similar cases, he agreed to give a talk, and show his films to our well-advertised monthly meeting. Two weeks before he was due to speak, he noticed a vehicle following him as he drove home. As it was a black Holden Statesman, with Canberra number plates, and flashing lights inside the front grill, he pulled over.

Two men got out of the vehicle, and one spoke to Liam through his driver's window. Liam said that the man told him that they would not like it if he gave his proposed lecture, and showed his films. Liam recalled the man saying that... "It would be better off for me to keep my mouth shut." They then wished him a good day and left.

At the time, although it was nothing as drastic as the Watt's case, he thought it might be wiser to take their advice. Later, he plucked up enough courage to tell his story in the documentary *'Australian Skies.'*

It is not just UFO researchers in the West who sometimes meet with suspicious ends. Valery and Roman Uvarov wrote about former Russian cosmonaut Aleksei Zolotov, who had previously seen several UFOs, and encountered his first extraterrestrial in 1933, when he was only seven.

He reflected on the subject saying; "Personally, I understand UFOs in this sense. Namely, I have seen them in flight. I have seen a living humanoid and have investigated the landing sites of these objects. If you understand UFOs from this standpoint, then they certainly exist. But there needs to be enough material, not only of an observational character, but also of an empirical and practical nature, which can be studied in laboratories. In a lot of institutes in Russia, they are studying samples taken from landing sites, including in our laboratory."

Zolotov had a lot to say about these 'Visitors', their motives, and their craft, much of which was consistent with other reports from around the world. Perhaps he had said too much for his own good.

On October 8th 1995, just a few days after his interview with the Uvarovs, he was found dead at the door of his house in the Russian town of Tver. It was alleged that he was murdered for daring to speak out about his involvement with the UFO phenomenon.

Scientists researching alien or secret technology, can be in just as much, if not more danger than the average ufologist. In the 1960s, Riley Crabb and his wife made a lecture tour up the Pacific Coast of the USA. During their trip they stayed overnight with a fellow researcher, who had a considerable technical background in the space sciences. Riley detailed the following in correspondence to a colleague in New Zealand:

'While there, he showed me a letter, a job offer, written to him by an engineering firm, with headquarters in the Denver, Colorado area. The letter was dated August 1961, and it outlined a proposal to set-up an anti-gravity research project, aimed at building flyable hardware using the radical new source of propulsion. This group of physicists and engineers were confident they had some sound theory, derived in part, as I recall, from the research of W.B.Smith, the late Canadian Flying Saucer expert; and they also had plenty of research money, freed by Congress after President Jack Kennedy's message to that body in May 1961.

'Our UFO researcher friend declined the job offer. I don't believe he even bothered to reply.'

'At a Reno, Nevada, UFO convention in 1965 this same friend was approached by a woman, obviously disturbed, who wished to talk to him alone. She identified herself as the widow of one of the engineers of the Denver project. She said the group was successful in taking theory right on through production. The finished product was designed, built, tested, and then disassembled. It was hauled secretly to a deserted spot in the New Orleans area, and then reassembled and secretly flown to a pre-determined landing spot in Florida.

'Within two days of the successful test flight of the man-carrying flying saucer, all the leading men in the group, including her husband, met with violent deaths. Since that time, several widows had also been 'bumped off' in mysterious or unusual circumstances. This woman was fleeing for her life!'

The Kennedy Brothers

Some researchers have stated that the American President and his brother were assassinated because they knew too much about UFOs and extraterrestrials. So far, I have found no evidence of this, however Riley Crabb's report, if correct, indicates their interest.

Brad Steiger wrote of the following correspondence, dated May 9th 1968, on United States Senate letterhead. It was addressed to, and published by Gray Barker, and demonstrated the late Senator's interest in the subject. Gray Barker could be both a serious researcher, but also a practical joker, so this must be read with some caution;

'As you may know, I am a card carrying member of the Amalgamated Flying Saucer Association. Therefore, like many other people in our country, I am interested in the phenomenon of flying saucers.

'It is a fascinating subject, which has initiated both scientific fiction fantasies and serious scientific research.

'I watch with great interest all reports of unidentified flying objects, and I hope that some day we will know more about this intriguing subject.

'Dr Marlow Shapely, the prominent astronomer, has stated that there is a probability that there is other life in the universe.

'I favour more research regarding this matter, and I hope that once and for all we can determine the true facts about flying saucers. Your magazine can stimulate much of the investigation and inquiry into this phenomenon through the publication of news and discussion material. This can be of great help in paving the way to knowledge of one of the fascinating subjects of our contemporary world.'

Sincerely,
Robert F. Kennedy

THE SUSPICIOUS SUICIDES

It is a sad fact of life that some people do commit suicide, but sometimes we cannot accept the official reports on 'face value'.

James Forrestal

James Forrestal was the US Defence Secretary in 1947, and knew, better than anybody, the importance of UFOs. He was often at odds with his contemporaries and the government, especially over funding issues. He was usually silent regarding extraterrestrial intrusions, however he was a firm advocate for studying 'unidentified celestial bodies', and for the US being the first country to put a satellite into orbit.

In 1949, James Forrestal certainly became paranoid and mentally disturbed, and was genuinely considered to be a security risk. He was taken to Bethesda Naval

Hospital, and not only did he attempt to escape the moving ambulance, upon arrival, he told a witness that he did not expect to leave the place alive.

His doctor was told by 'the people downtown' to place him in the VIP 16th floor suite. This was against the advice of his medical team, who wanted him placed on the bottom floor of a nearby annex. During his seven weeks hospitalisation, his condition was reported as being well improved, however several family members, and clergy, whom Forrestal had wanted to see, were denied entry by the hospital.

On 22nd May, the Navy corpsman, responsible for guarding his room, was a last minute replacement, as the regular guard had got drunk the night before. The new corpsman claimed Forrestal 'sent him on an errand' at 1.45am. When he returned, the bed was empty, and Forrestal's body was found sixteen floors below on the ground. He supposedly got out of bed, crossed the hallway, and jumped from a small kitchen window.

There was no autopsy, inquest or investigation into his death. Because it happened on a US Naval Reservation, the hospital immediately labelled his death suicide, the local coroner signed a death certificate, and the Naval Board rubber stamped the hospital's report.

After his death, fifteen loose-leaf binders, containing three thousand pages of notes, plus the partially completed manuscript of a book he planned to finish after he left hospital, were removed from his former office, and taken to the White House.

Richard Dolan has written extensively about the incident, and said that Father Sheehy, a former Navy Chaplain, had, on several occasions, been denied permission to visit Forrestal. When he arrived at Bethesda, the day after Forrestal's death another hospital corpsman approached him through the crowd. He whispered in a low, tense voice; "Father, you know Mr. Forrestal didn't kill himself, don't you?" Before Sheehy could ask any more, his informant disappeared back into the crowd.

Dr. James McDonald

Dr. James McDonald was a senior physicist at the Institute of Atmospheric Physics, and also a professor at the University of Arizona, Department of Meteorology.

He concentrated on proving these unknown craft were a physical reality, and his years of research were meticulous, objective and scientific, earning him the respect of all who knew him. During his most active period, from 1966 until his death in 1971, he encouraged many scientists to join him in his quest for the truth.

In 1966/67, he conducted a probe, on behalf of the US Navy, into the possibility of an alien base beneath Australia's Southern and Pacific Oceans. The research was not highly classified, however the results are not known. Later the US Navy conducted a more top secret investigation into Unidentified Submarine Objects in Australian waters. (It is worth noting that while all these researchers investigated different 'sensitive' subjects, the common denominator is that besides McDonald, both Edgar Jarrold and Albert Bender were investigating the possibility of an alien base in Antarctica, and Grahame Birdsall and Anthony Dodd were documenting UFO activity at the other end of the globe in the Arctic Ocean.)

While in New Zealand, he made mention of research being conducted into the propulsion systems of UFOs. He quoted a 'reliable source' within NASA as saying that the Hughes Aircraft Corp. had fifty men working on the UFO propulsion problem. He was quick to recognise that they would not employ all these men if there was not a reasonable chance that their research could be fruitful.

Paul Norman, an American UFO researcher, who settled in Victoria, Australia, remembered McDonald's visit to this country, shortly before his death. While he was officially researching atmospheric physics for the US Navy, he also spent every spare minute interviewing Australian witnesses, either in person or by phone.

Prior to his Australian visit, he had been in contact with U Thant, the Secretary General of the United Nations, requesting immediate action on the UFO problem.

In March 1971, McDonald ruffled a few feathers by attending a public Congressional hearing, and opposing government funding for fleets of SST planes. He claimed they would weaken the Earth's already fragile ozone layer.

In 1971, Dr. Robert Wood, a McDonnell Douglas Aerospace engineer, recalled meeting Jim McDonald only six weeks before his first 'suicide attempt'. He was excited, saying he 'thought he had got the answer', but couldn't tell Robert until he was sure.

Medical reports claimed that McDonald was allegedly depressed, and shot himself in the head. He didn't die, but his injury left him confined to a wheelchair.

If the official version of McDonald's death are to be believed, on 12th June 1971, despite being in hospital, confined to a wheelchair, and partially blind in both eyes, he drove to a pawnshop where he purchased another gun. He then supposedly drove into the desert where he shot himself again – this time fatally. There was purportedly a note, saying he couldn't bear being blind.

In 1994, during a lecture given to the Gulf Breeze Conference in Florida, Bob Dean commented that Jim was a family man, with a wife and six children, and he did not believe the suicide verdict. He noted that McDonald's widow said that Jim did not own a gun. Further, when his body was found, a gun was in the wrong hand, and the bullet hole in the wrong temple.

Gone at only 51 years of age, Jim McDonalds death was a sad loss to both the UFO and scientific communities. His papers on unidentified flying objects have been re-published in later years, and are a valuable portion of my own collection.

Colonel Uyrange Bolivar Soares Nogueira de Hollanda Lima

Many may not have heard of this Brazilian Air Force Officer. He had been commanding *'Operacao Prato'*, (Operation Plate), in September 1977, when he photographed numerous UFOs which had been causing panic in the Amazon region.

He waited close on twenty years, until after his retirement, before going public with his evidence, including classified documents and diagrams. Colonel Uyrange appeared on Brazil's National Television where he divulged all the details, including one incident involving a close encounter with an enormous unidentified craft. (Afterwards he followed up his testimony in a public lecture.)

Brazilian researchers Adamar Gevaerd and Marco Petit conducted an in-depth interview with Colonel Uyrange, and eagerly awaited his scheduled appearance at the 'World UFO Forum' to be held in Brasilia, but this was not to be. The apparently healthy fifty-seven year old Uyrange was found dead in his apartment. The authorities claimed he had committed suicide.

Phil Schneider

Phil Schneider was a controversial figure, whose suspicious death in January 1996 was questioned by many who had known him. The detective on the scene claimed he had suffered a stroke, but the medical examiner found a catheter tube, hidden under flaps of skin around Schneider's neck. It had been wrapped around three times before being double knotted, and an official determination of 'suicide' was made.

His widow, Cynthia Drayer, was furious and claimed he had been murdered, but an investigation was never conducted. She said he was about to write a 'tell all' book, and further, within days of his death, intelligence agents had thoroughly searched the premises and seized 'many assets' including photographs.

Seven months earlier, in a lecture he gave in May 1995 he said; "Eleven of my best friends in the past 22 years have been murdered. Eight of the murders were called 'suicides'. Before I went to talk in Las Vegas, I drove a friend down to Joshua Tree near 29 Palms. As I drove into the mountains, I was followed by two government E-350 vans with G-14 plates, each with a couple of occupants, one of which had a Uzi. I knew exactly who they were.

"I got ahead of them and came to a stop in the middle of the road. They both went either side of me and down a ravine. Is this what it's going to take? I cut up my security card and sent it back to the government, and told them if I were threatened, (and I have been), that I was going to upload 140,000 pages of documentation to the Internet about the covert government structure and the whole 'plan'. I have already begun that task. I have spoken nineteen times and have probably reached 45,000 people."

So what had he done or said to merit a possible assassination? He was very outspoken and had made many public accusations against the government which may, or may not, have been true. He was also a structural engineer and explosives expert, and publicly detailed various secret government underground bases. His most contentious claim was that in 1979 he was present at a facility in Dulce, New Mexico, where he witnessed 'grey-humanoid' aliens working alongside humans.

Apparently a 'shoot-out' occurred between the aliens and our own paramilitary. Many on both sides of the conflict were killed or injured, and Schneider himself was hit in the chest and wounded by one of the 'Grey's' beam weapons. (I have often wondered if there was any connection between these 'Greys' and the 'CTRs' the Amicizia described.)

Foreign Agencies

UFO investigators and witnesses also need to be aware of the interest of other countries, some not always our friends. They would like to know what is happening in our skies, whether the craft are alien, Western prototypes, or whether we have detected one of their own spy-craft. I am sure their agents must attend most of the larger conferences and meetings.

THOSE PESKY RUSSIANS

Following a trip back home to Britain in 1976, I had spent some time with UFO colleagues, including Betty Woods, the secretary of BUFORA, (The British UFO Research Association). She encouraged me to write an article for the BUFORA Journal, and I submitted my rather amateurish attempt, which they published in 1981.

When I look back on this article, discussing artificially induced amnesia in witnesses, and written about forty years ago, I realise that science has come a long way since then. I didn't think much of it until about a year later, in 1982, when I received a letter from Betty; "I thought you might like to see the interest your article has aroused in the USSR," she wrote. "I sent him a spare copy of the Bulletin as he requests."

She had enclosed the original Russian 'postcard', dated 31-7-82, which was addressed to me at Betty's BUFORA address.

'Dear Mrs McGhee,

I would greatly appreciate receiving a reprint or Xerox copy, of your articles on amnesia and the biological basis of memory, and Nigel Watson's pre-1947 UFO bulletin, published in: BUFORA Bulletin, 1981, No.2. (or the whole issue if you have by chance a spare copy).

Many thanks:

It was purportedly from a civilian Russian UFO group, and signed by someone at a Post Office Box address in Novosibirsk USSR. But wait – why did it have a postmark from Chelsea in London?

These were still the days of spies and counter-intelligence, something I did not want to get mixed up with. I had a couple of contacts who were 'in-the-know', and passed the card on to them. A few weeks later they got back to me. The Novosibirsk PO Box did indeed belong to the KGB. Perhaps the Russians wanted to know more about how to block people's memories?

They would certainly know more about it than little me! I decided I wanted no part of the espionage game, and never responded to the invitation. Imagine my surprise when I discovered that not only had New Zealand researcher, Harold Fulton received a similar card, requesting their publications, at about the same time, Fred and Phyllis Dickeson had received three cards during 1981/2. And yes – they were from the same Novosibirsk PO Box, and had been posted in New Zealand!

Many investigators have been threatened, including myself. I was told in no uncertain terms to *'be careful what you say,'* and guess what? I took the warning seriously – and I am careful what I say!

Many of my researcher/investigator friends and colleagues have also been threatened, or met with untimely and often bizarre or suspicious ends. The incidences are so prevalent, that in 2005, Rebekah Prole, wrote about the subject, and the necessity for all researchers to ensure that in the event of their unexpected demise, their notes, books and thoughts would be preserved for future generations. She composed this very moving poem;

Lest We Forget

They need more than just a minute's silence,
More than just respect,
The fallen will not fall away
Nor their work die from apathy, nor neglect.

To look and see, and question why
Strange things are seen, not just in the sky,
To search, and ask and question

Leaving no stone unturned,
Listening to every suggestion,
Teaching what they learned.

To build on what has gone before,
Whispers in the night,
Bringing what they know
Against all odds into the light.

What legacy will you leave behind
When it comes your turn?
Will your piece be added to the puzzle,
Or will it all be burned?

Let's honour them, remember them,
Those pioneering minds,
So that their work is built upon,
Not lost in sands of time.

EPILOGUE

The vast majority of the world's population either do not believe in visitors from space, or just don't think about it at all. Today's younger generation often know little about the 'Space Brothers', and only use the Internet to read UFO and Abduction Reports, many of which are neither proven nor adequately investigated.

Throughout history, man can only comprehend what his society and scientific knowledge dictate as being possible. Explaining interplanetary travel, or splitting the atom, to a fifteenth century scholar would be difficult. We must never forget that the ludicrous of the twentieth century may well be proven fact in the twenty-first.

There have been many researchers, world-wide, who have investigated the coming of the Space Brothers. Wendelle Stevens spoke at length about these visitors at a 2005 conference in Laughlin, Nevada.

He listed many common details prevalent in all the reports:
'They are human in appearance, and most speak our languages fluently.
Many limited their contacts to a select few individuals, and didn't allow it to be broadened.
They can read our thoughts, and make careful observations of Earth's affairs.
They use a variety of different ships, and use marvellous technology, including retractor and levitation beams, and intrusive surveillance to see anything we are doing.
They can also use our radio, telecommunications and computers at will.
Some have underground and underwater bases, and others bases on our Moon.
Their societies have no organised religion or money systems, and belonged to an organisation of beings from other planets or star systems.
Some gave false information, including of having come from Venus or Mars.'

In addition to Wendelle's observations, I would add that their message was always the same. They came with concern and love, emphasising that they could only advise, and were prohibited from interfering in Earth's affairs. They warned us of the dangers of nuclear testing and warfare, and the need to live in harmony, and care for the planet, before we reached the point of no return.

After the 1960s, their craft were not seen so often, possibly due to our own improved detection ability, and the presence of less benign aliens. They resorted to the alternative of integrating into our community. They are still here, and usually remain incognito, often due to the loyalty of their human supporters.

These days, many people when speaking of 'aliens', refer only to the 'Greys', and disregard any mention of the human looking visitors from the twentieth century. We ignore, at our peril, these peaceful Space Brothers and their message.

Fred Stone was a true pioneer in Australian Ufology, and not afraid to speak his mind. In a 1968 editorial of his magazine *'Panorama'*, he wrote the following words; *'Keep plugging away as a pioneer, watch for every angle where-in an answer may be found. Do not be satisfied with the accepted ones, maybe there is some greater answer than that generally considered the real one – an answer that perhaps you or others have avoided because it is offbeat, and you are afraid of being looked askance at or perhaps not so popular......'*

'Now to those who I know are true pioneers, those in some cases are leaders of groups, some of whom are deep thinkers, and are still pioneering on, still searching and digging......Continue your great quest, do not be deterred or swayed from it, and if age and health cause you to take a quieter way of life, continue giving all aid to youth, hand the torch on to them. Let the force and energy of their youth be your sword, and your mind and experience their inspiration to achieve what cannot be finished by you, so that it may be said of you, that to the end, you remained a pioneer, and scorned to be a settler or squatter.'

ANNEX A

GEORGE ADAMSKI"S PEACE AND PROSPERITY PROGRAM

In 1959/60 George Adamski was engaged in a World Tour and a multitude of public lectures. At the same time he released his 'Peace and Prosperity Program' to all his contacts and followers worldwide. It was succinct and closely echoed the views of the 'Space Brothers'. Adamski's English was not always the best, and he had a secretary or colleague to write his books and newsletters, which often rambled and included many of his own opinions. I could be wrong, but I think that this 'Program' may have come straight from Orthon and the Space Brothers. Not only were they suggesting our pursuit of more peaceful activities, perhaps they had in mind a possible threat from the CTRs.

'Space Economics Programme.'

'If you would like a lasting World Peace and Prosperity for yourself and your children, you will be interested in the following Programme. Many peace and security movements have been started, but none have offered a workable solution or replacement for war economy, which has kept the United States and the world out of economic depression.

'As we all know, economy is founded on the ability to produce and consume the product. In the machine-age we produce more than we can consume due to unbalanced conditions that prevail. Over production is the breakdown of economy. War and reconstruction have been the solution in the past.

'The Defence plants that have absorbed many of the otherwise unemployed, can also reach a saturation point. And then what? The only answer is a common enemy who threatens our right of survival. When our-way-of-life is endangered, allied countries are armed, and this provides an outlet for surplus material, and production continues. The Korean War was an example of this. Also, the state of emergency created by the Cold War causes the people of the world to live in fear of mass destruction.

'Every individual must realise that our modern weapons of annihilation would spare no-one. Nuclear and germ warfare could cause prolonged suffering before death. Sleeping gas would be the most humane, it would put a person to

sleep, never to awaken. It sounds stupid, doesn't it, to think that intelligent people would sanction the signing of their own death warrants.

'Should all Defence plants close? I am sure that you realise what the results would be; thousands of unemployed – hungry – panic-stricken people.

'Many industrial nations are faced with over-production. We now have two alternatives; Space exploration coupled with space craft for the defence of the world. This could be done by a change-over of the machines and would not interfere with our current economic system.

'The idea of an invasion from space will not be readily accepted by some, due to their idealistic thinking, but we must face the reality. Even the most orthodox astronomers admit there are perhaps millions of inhabited planets in our systems. Common sense tells us that surely we could not be the lowest in infinite space; that there must be systems far beneath us whose ships could come our way. On page 78 of my book 'Inside the Spaceships', the wise teacher said; "Also there are worlds where development has gone far in the field of science, even though space has been conquered."

'Is it better to be on the alert than caught asleep. A vast new horizon – Space Exploration – has been opened to all of the world.

'There is greater deal more involved in the production of satellites and spacecraft, and their myriads of instruments than the average person realises. The satellites and spacecraft will enable us to learn many things when we are geared for research. Look at the amazing discoveries that have been made with the limited appropriations that have been set aside for that purpose. Could you picture what the results will be when every nation has this same common goal?

'Past civilisations, when faced with the same problem that we face today, have retrograded and eventually destroyed themselves. But we are educated people.

'The Space Economy Program can be launched in only one way – by the insistent demand of the people – singly and united. Neighbourhood groups, civic organisations, churches – all united in a crusade for Economic Survival and Security from a World War.'

SPACE EXPLORATION IS OUR SURVIVAL FRONTIER

'Your part in the Space programme – if you feel this to be a worthwhile effort, write to your representative to insist that the NASA and also United Nations programme be given top priority. The NASA programme came into being on 29th July 1958, when the President of the United States signed it into Law. Many nations have accepted this programme for it can solve economic problems without war.

'Attempts have been made to unify the nations of Europe, similar to the United States of America. Now, for the first time, this unity has become possible for all the nations of the world. Small and large nations are involved in the space programme in one way or another. When all people take interest in one single objective – Space Exploration – they automatically become united.

'IT IS URGENT TO ACT IMMEDIATELY. Write to your representative and to the United Nations Economic and Social Committee.'

Less than a decade later, our Apollo Missions reached the Moon. Were the Space brothers instrumental in our great leap forward? In the following years our satellites, space stations and probes have increased in numbers, until by 2018 alone, nearly five thousand satellites were orbiting the Earth.

ANNEX B

MR. X's WRITINGS

Fred and Phyllis Dickeson, in New Zealand, published 'Mr. X's Writings' to a limited number of people. They were hesitant at first, saying that just what people would think about the information imparted would be very interesting. It was so different from the religious and political ramblings of George Adamski, they thought that many would not believe what was written. Others would know, deep down, that it was true. They also had difficulty digesting and assimilating everything, because much of what had been written was also new to them;

"If it really is Truth, then we have no hesitation in eventually believing that it will prove itself as time goes on, and we reach a better understanding of what is behind the mystery of Creation.....However we have our part to do, and so we print the information and leave it to the reader to digest it. It's for them to either accept or reject depending on whatever degree of understanding they have reached."

Some people, with deep religious convictions, wrote to them and condemned the printing of the 'X Writings'. Some copies were returned, and others burnt. Many other people were far more receptive. After the first two 'Writings' were printed and mailed out, Mr. and Mrs. X returned from a trip to the city, and found a note under their door;

'We have read your work and found it correct and now confer upon you the honour we have had in mind for you all through. Hence forward you shall be named Chief Scribe for us which you may use if it so pleases you. Your Two Friends'

To his credit, Mr. X was astounded by what he had written and never assumed this title. His material was published in four parts. Unfortunately, Part Three cannot be located, and after more than fifty years, it is not known if any copy is still in existence. The remainder, which is worth preserving, is very long, and sometimes repetitious. It is published here in a condensed form.

Mr. X's WRITINGS

'This work is not telepathic to you as this method of communication is prone to error, so we use the method of inspiring you to write, just as we have always done for you when we have given you all your musical inspirations. All good literary work is inspired, and it just does not come from nowhere, as you cannot make something out of nothing; there must be a source and a cause for every act and movement, or even thought. The source of your present action rests with us. Many will not believe what is here written, but that has always been so with many other great truths, and this your world already knows. How many have been put to death for saying things which later have been found to be Truth? You cannot find an answer to this question, yet we know the full story.

'There are so many facets to existence. No Earthling can possibly understand the implications to life's existence, yet there is still hope that the world will understand. Before that time comes, the cup of human suffering must be filled to overflow, which is still future. We know your suffering because we too went through it in times past, yet we are with you all the time in the knowledge that you too shall be as we are. Do not think that we have no troubles, on the contrary we have plenty, but not of the kind which trouble Earthlings.

'You have been wishing to know the answer to many questions which we could not answer with satisfaction by our past method, so herein you and others may find your answers, and if they are not here, then they shall be answered at a later time. All languages are represented amongst us, and indeed some of us speak ten to fifteen with ease. We are never at loss to converse with any Earthling anywhere in your world. We have answered questions on the state of other worlds in your planetary system, concerning which much fiction has been written by Earthlings, so there is no need to repeat all that here, but in order to complete this work, you may make copies to include, or be included, with this work. To make a point stronger, and to bring it out as more vivid, we may have to repeat some information even so.'

Some of the information transmitted contained more details of the Brothers' reasons for coming, both now and in the past;

'We have been visitors to your Earth for the past many thousands of years, and have been described in different ways by those whose good chance it was to see us. We have appeared to and spoken with many persons who have been afraid to tell of their meeting with us because of the fear of being disbelieved; we do

not blame them; we merely are sorry that society is such that it forces the isolated individual to keep silent. We know that many of those whom we have met would be very happy to tell about it if it were not for all this disbelief and suspicion. And so the world works against itself.

'We are the 'Messengers of Heaven', and you can never know at what moment you may be in our company, as it was with the writer of this message some years ago when we first approached him. We do not make ourselves known to any individual unless we have a special reason. Even you, as an individual, may at some time sit right next to one of us. There is no noticeable effect but one. When this happens to an earthling, he will notice a feeling of elation while in our company, but likely not know the reason for it. You will feel 'drawn' to our Messenger – the stranger at your side. You will feel that you wish to speak with him and will not be able to understand why. You may even suspect that he is one of us if you are so inclined, and may even ask the direct question if the opportunity arises. For your own safety, your question will be parried and turned to other pleasantries, but we would not lie to you. If you are watchful, you may be rewarded.

'We are scattered through many countries, enter your concert halls and chat at random with persons in your streets. Some of you are alert enough to know that there is something about us which marks us out as different to the average person. We encourage this interest, and recognise this alertness, for this is how we gain our contacts without being too deliberate. In some cases firm friendships have resulted and blossomed into further meetings, which in turn, as in the writer's case has developed into something more than firm friendship.

'It is through the writer that you will now learn about our true nature. Even the writer himself will learn facts here which he never knew previously. We have met him on more than one occasion, and know he is giving truth in the way we intend it. We have greeted him hand to hand, and all the time, he has said little to others about it because of the same fear – ridicule. Now he gets his chance which was all a part of our promise to him some years ago.

'The writer has no definite evidence nor eye witness to his meeting us; yet we gave him that evidence not long after the first meeting between us. We promised to show ourselves in the heavens on a certain night, and at a certain time, and in a certain position. He has witnesses to confirm that we kept our appointment to the minute. Various other evidence can be produced by him, which could not possibly happen by chance.

'Sometimes we have not been in touch with him in any way for long periods, yet he has always shown patience knowing that sooner or later he would receive a note from us, which shows chance does not enter into it. We have given him all his musical ideas in his musical compositions along with freedom to develop them to his own pattern, just as we give him that same freedom and choice of words in this inspired work.

'From now on, you shall hear of other inspired writers taking up this work, for we shall be contacting more individuals in other parts of your world. Each will have his particular part to play, and each shall write in his own particular language so that the whole world will receive the message.... This will begin very slowly at first, but as more writers take up the challenge on the side of truth, so it will grow, that is if you have not blown yourselves out of existence before that time arrives. Other writers are free to copy this into any kind of language they please, and without any kind of obligation, for in doing this, they will be doing a great service to all men.

'The writer intends not to make money out of truth, yet we cannot expect him to be the loser, so a way will present itself for release of this work to readers in general.

'It has been written that we, on isolated occasions, have taken certain earthlings on rides into outer space and to other planets in your system. This we have not done, and it is all mere sensationalism or literary window dressing because the plain truth is not exciting enough. Earthlings must gradually, and of their own free will, accustom themselves to our mode of travel. They cannot be just taken out there as easily as stepping into your conventional vehicles. Much rubbish has been written and we are more than surprised that there were so many who have been tricked by it. Long preparation is needed even for us before we are even allowed to travel away from our home planet. In this matter, we are far ahead of you because we have put all our energy into this instead of wasting it on useless war and destruction. You could have been much further ahead in this matter if your nations would pull together.

'In our world, there are no divisions or national boundaries; we find them a hindrance. Yes, we know all about you! We know too what is going on behind *the nations, but that is your business, and we can only look on. We cannot even intervene!*

'Earthlings often wonder why we do not reveal scientific information to them, but let us see first what they do with all the scientific wonders they have already acquired. Every 'could-be' blessing Earthlings receive is assessed according to its destructive value, and we have no wish to help them along these lines until they learn wisdom in the use of that which they already have. When you will have reached the point where you can be trusted, (and there is still no sign of that), then we shall gladly open up greater vistas to you. We have no desire to help you take your evils with you, and spread havoc among those who do not deserve it.

'Long, long, very long ago, we learned the secrets of your present atomic power together with its dangers, and we have always been afraid that Earthlings would eventually discover it for themselves. Knowing them as we do, we knew what they would do with it, and the signs are already becoming easier to read as the Un-Godly time of slaughter approaches. We have already seen them use their murderous weapons on their own kind, and of any sin that was ever committed, this is so far the worst that humans have ever committed.

'We, who leave our trails across your skies, have a grandstand view of all your man-made test explosions and we are afraid for your safety.

'The greatest could-be blessing ever so far acquired by you was used for evil purposes. We refer to the building material of which all things are made, yet further evil is at this time being plotted by nations – bigger and more powerful explosions are wanted, and we know that they are not wanted for constructive purposes. We know your weaknesses, and it would not matter what we revealed to you, you would value it according to its destructive force. Even if we gave you a plan of how to build our ships, we would be putting temptation in your way, thereby making our position unsafe, and why should we endanger our people? When you prove worthy, we shall willingly help. We have no more to say on this question, as we have said all that can be said.

The messages continued, condemning the social inequalities and injustice on our planet;

'At this point, we wish to try and shame you into some action, for the cries of the needy have and are reaching us in the High Heavens. While we are

listening to their cries, you are wasting valuable time and materials building great edifices to your strange God, the cost of which would feed and clothe many thousands of these unfortunates. Why do you do this? Your excuse, that the population of your world is growing faster than you can cope with it, is humbug of the purist kind, for it has not yet reached that state. There is still plenty of living space with the opportunity also of producing more food and clothing with that aim in view....

'*We have seen the pomp and vanity in the highest of places and the sins being committed in the name of the Creator – heard the Pagan rights given in a language not understood by the seekers of Truth, and garbled at such a speed that there is no meaning behind it. Did your Great Teacher do this? Truth has been replaced by ceremony until there is no room left for simplicity. Simple, honest prayer is all that is required from the faithful seeker after Truth.*'

The Space Brothers made it clear that we must change our ways. If we don't;

'*you shall remain in you present state of ignorance until your space scientists are able to catch up with us and prove for themselves the truth of all we have told you, which is still a long way into the future.*'

If we do improve as the 'Brothers' have wished;

'*We shall come to you in great numbers, and will fill your skies as soon as you are ready for us. We shall land, and gladly show you our ships and everything in them – teach you how to construct them and then with glee watch your advancement. We shall travel ahead of you, and lead you out there and away to our own home planet as well as to other Mansions of even greater glory than ours. We shall be one family with the seal of Love and Understanding in our hearts. And there shall be great rejoicing and singing. There shall be no veil of tears, and every man will say unto his neighbour; "Thou art my Brother."*'

Some of the writings described the Visitors' own home planet;

'*So here we are telling you all about ourselves – things you have always wished to learn. Now let us tell you of things more closely connected with us. We can only use words and meanings which are understandable to you, so we shall use the common language style which is yours.*

'*We use electricity for the same purposes as you, but discovered it thousands of years before you did, and we have a different method of distribution. It is beamed to great reflectors which pick it up and re-beam it over vast distances to where it is needed, thus dispensing with metal lines. These beams are also dangerous to our ships if any happen to pass through them, but they all have detectors and it is almost impossible that any should be caught that way. All public transport runs overhead by monorail for reasons you will know.*

'Other than what we have explained, it is not much different to the way you, yourselves, live. We are solid enough to touch, and we remain that way – no different to you physically, with the exception that we live longer and do not age as quickly as do Earthlings – two to three hundred years is quite common as reckoning by the length of your years.

'Material throughout all space is little different from what you see around you, although the elements are in some cases arranged differently, depending on environment or local conditions. We also have trees, shrubs and flowers which are quite different to what you have. One particular flower which might interest you is the same as your Musk, but unlike yours, this still has its scent, and its flowers are somewhat smaller in comparison to yours. But then again, we have a giant rose which has no scent, the flowers of which can reach one foot across. All varieties of grasses are represented, but we have varieties unknown to you.

'We have our weeds also, so do not think we live in a complete paradise and free from troubles. We too are sinners in as far as it applies to us, and we too must work in order to live, but there is a difference. We have learned to live with nature, to go along with her, to try to understand her, and above all not to try to upset the balance of nature. Destruction for good and Godly purposes is not a sin, as we must destroy the original form of something before we can make it suitable for the good and Godly purpose in which it is intended. So it is not so much what you destroy, as it is your purpose behind it, and this is exactly how we look at things on our home planet.

'Yes, it's not what you do, but why you do it that makes it sinful or otherwise. We too must destroy the original form of a tree if we wish to build in wood. Before doing anything, always inquire the reason for the act. Is it Godly or otherwise? Our building materials are again little different from yours, for as we have said, the same materials are fairly evenly distributed throughout all space.

'Both male and female are represented on our planet among all living things. We have our great rivers and seas with fish the same as yours, and here again

we have species not known to you. Our food is mostly vegetable, although some of us do eat meat and of course fish. Clothing is of similar materials, but much lighter because of the temperatures attainable over much of the planet's surface.

'We can visit seven planets, some of which are more glorious than either yours or ours. Indeed, we liken them to Mansions because of the very wonderful nature and make-up of all things which dwell thereon. Your planet, although Queen of your system, cannot compare with these. The inhabitants of these mansions can travel on visiting trips, as we do, and none of them support any kind of religion. They all believe in the Creator, as we have shown him to be.

'This will give you another Truth, which is that we do not know everything, as many seem to think, and being human, we have our limits. No human can ever have absolutely complete knowledge on anything. It does not matter how much you know about something, there is always more to be learned. Here you have still another Truth; He who knows everything, or thinks he does, will never advance any further, for he has met his Absolute and must be prepared to turn back. For what seems to be an end, is only temporary.

'All life is spontaneous and universal wherever the conditions are favourable. Some planets in systems many light years distant from you have low forms of life with still no appearance of intelligent beings on them. With regard to planets which have intelligent beings, these are very few throughout that area of space known to us. We can only surmise that since this is the case, the same Truth will follow in a general way throughout endless Time and Space. However, taking the immensity of endless space, there must be endless numbers of populated planets.'

They also made mention of their methods of travel through space, but did not divulge any meaningful technical details;

'Our travel techniques are a little different from those on which your world is now working, although it will require at least a further forty years before you begin to approach our present position in this field, which will bring you to your year 2000. Considering the amount of time you have wasted in wars and other similar pursuits, we think you have done remarkably well in this field. If it had not been for these setbacks, much of your energy could have placed you much nearer. Your atomic scientists have the right idea in slow fusion, which will undoubtedly overcome many problems for their long distance travels.

'Some of your fiction writers have made mysteries out of our method of propulsion; it is a little different from your jet system, but we are much ahead in the use of this – once out in space, we can travel at unbelievable speeds, as some of you have seen for yourselves. We will admit now that you are coming along, faster and faster, to be out there and travelling along side us in our own travel trips. We look forward to this time when we shall meet on common ground, so to speak.

'Some of us can levitate by a slower method, but even that must be instructed upon for long periods. As proof of this jet travel, many of you have seen the colour and heat from them when we have at times been sufficiently near, so there is no mystery about it. Nor do we use magic, which is the name given to things not understood. Just because there seems to be no sane explanation for some occurrences does not make it magic. As we have said, there is a reason and a cause for all phenomena, and it is because these causes were not known in the early stages of human development that fear was the result. Fear and ignorance have wrought havoc in the past, yet you are learning slowly that fear of something is caused by ignorance of its nature.

'We travel along well used lanes where we do not use any kind of propulsion fuel, because outside these lanes we are forced to contend with and counter gravitational interference from adjacent bodies. These lanes are very wide in comparison to the size of our ships, and can be thousands of miles in width. Our speed almost always takes us through an interference area without further resort to propulsion.

'Speaking of explosions, as we have just done, away out here in the vastness of space there are explosions of such magnitude that even we dare not approach to within many light years of them. This Natural-Law-Force must function, but it is for ultimate Good, and is the building material out of which other mansions are to be made. This is not destruction, but the changing of unsuitable material to make it suitable for constructive purposes, and these inevitable changes must go on forever, as they have always and forever gone on in the past. There was never a time when it was not so. The very nature of space shall never be known. We cannot see the end of space, no matter how fast we may travel to try and reach it, and it would be the height of folly to even try.

'All things must change. Change and decay is the order of everything which exists. That includes us, and even we do not know our ultimate future. So let us face it, for only man faces death because we know that we must eventually die. Other living things do not know this truth, for they cannot recognise it. On this matter we know little more than you. All we can do is to have faith in a rebirth, and take our lesson from birth and rebirth of all animate and inanimate things, for the new is built upon the old. This is the law.'

Some of the writings discussed the effect of the speed of light on space travel;

'We now wish to reveal something which your world has always wished to know, which is; What is the absolute speed attainable in space travel? Our answer is that any speed up to the speed of light may be attained, for that is one barrier through which nothing can go and yet still remain in existence. Perhaps we can make it more vivid by saying that it is quite impossible for any object to race its shadow which is inexorably co-existent with all solid objects. If you travel faster than light, you would while passing through the light barrier leave your shadow behind, just as your sound of travel is left behind while passing through the sound barrier.

'Now it is here where total annihilation takes place – where something is turned into nothing. Nothing left! Not even your shadow! You would not exist even to come back to tell of your experience. Even at your slow speed of breaking the sound barrier, a rough trip through is always experienced. You can leave your sound behind at the expense of a rough trip, but you cannot leave your shadow behind and continue to exist in any shape or form. This is Truth!

'We hope that even the writer himself has learned something here, as we have learned from bitter experience, and we pass it on for what it may be worth for the world. Some of us have completely vanished in these trial speeds, so we have no means of knowing exactly what takes place as nobody has returned to give us any information. We can only guess that here is the limit where the absolute can be attained, and from it we must turn back or perish. Yet here we learn another great Truth which says; "So far shalt thou go, but no further". But does this not apply to all things? There is always the danger point beyond which we cannot go.'

Mr. X was still a little confused about the speed of light, and he later received further information;

'We would now like to hark back to what we said about the speed of light, and would also warn you that what we have to say about speed and the Light

Barrier is only our theory as we believe that no man in the Heavens, nor on your Earth, will ever have an answer to what takes place on the far side of the Light Barrier, because we also believe that from the far side of that barrier, there is no return trip – once through, THROUGH FOREVER!

'On this side of that Barrier, we have our breaking systems with which to slow down, but on the far side of the Barrier all things are infinite, and therefore have no finite meaning. Intuition tells us that even if we were to send, experimentally, any object in the form of an instrument beyond the Light Barrier, in order to learn the answer, that instrument would become Infinite and lost forever.

'Putting it another way, we believe that on the far side of the Light Barrier there is a Dimension, the condition of which we can never hope to understand, for that Barrier is ABSOLUTE; Absolute in the truest sense of the word. We have discovered that any object approaching the speed of light begins to lose bulk and becomes shortened relative to the speed of its travel, until at the speed of light it becomes a condition, such as light itself is.

'We said that the above is only our theory, and as such it must always remain, as we believe there will never be any method by which the real truth will be known. Light, in its purest form, - that is where there are no reflecting surfaces, is invisible, for it is only the reflected surfaces that we can see. A beam of light is only visible because of the dust particles through which it travels, and it is here where condition produces effect. We believe that there is an absolute void on the far side of the Light Barrier. We know no more than you in this matter, even though we have been nearer to that barrier in our speeds than you have. No heavenly body can travel faster than light without reaching that Ultra-light Dimension of which we spoke.

'We have had much discussion amongst ourselves on the above matter, and many theories have been put forward, including some from our present Great Leader, yet in this matter we cannot do other than theorise. One theory is that there is a completely New Existence beyond that Barrier, but in this, as in other things which are unknowable, there is plenty of room for wishful thinking. That is something we cannot agree to, since it is truth we want, not wishful thinking.

'We can also theorise, that if there be Infinite Existence on the other side of the Light Barrier, then in that dimension there should be no limit to speed, as speed should also be infinite, but only in that Dimension. The Light-Speed Barrier is *one impenetrable 'wall' which divides the finite from the infinite, and much wishful thinking could have free play here, as it could be suggested that the Seat of a Personal God may be in that Dimension, even that He is Light itself. Let us hasten to mention, that Light cannot be a Personal Being, but is a Condition. A Condition is a state in which something exists, so there can be no misunderstanding of our intended meaning here. A changing of natural processes from one cause or another, brings about a Condition, which in turn produces Effect, which in its turn can be good or bad, or so on.*

When it came to discussing 'the Creator' or 'God' as we choose to call our Supreme Being, the answers were confusing;

'WE BELIEVE IN THE CREATOR, but we do not believe in religion as practised in your world at present. As for our reason, just take a look at the number of religions all claiming to be right, so we cannot be accused of being anti-God! But if we be accused of being anti-religious, then we bow to that accusation, for there is no place for religion amongst our un-numbered millions.

'The nature of the Creator has never been truly understood by Earthlings, although some have progressed more than others. So let us now try to tell you what you have all been wishing to know and for the first time ever revealed in this manner.

'He is above all things not a 'Person', but a 'Power'; This Power, or Natural-Law-Force permeates all space and affects both the good and evil amongst all men. It, and mostly referred to as 'He', has always been personified and this is where the confusion has become more confounded because His Nature, and this Natural-Law-Force were never understood to be one and the same thing.

'In our written notes to you, in the past few years, we could do no other than speak as we did, because you would not have understood our intentions, and we could not have explained all this to you by that method. Now it does not matter how you look at this matter of what the Creator is like. 'He', or 'It' must by very nature and logic, consist of the two opposites, otherwise 'He' or 'It' cannot exist. He would not, or cannot be complete! He must have, for His very existence, both qualities inclusive of good and bad, for completeness you must have both. The Creator cannot consist of a one-sided material only.

'This Natural-Law-Force is building and destroying all the time. It is both Creator and Destroyer because it can't be otherwise. Worlds are in the making *and in various stages of destruction. Creation and Destruction are going on right in your own world and it is called good or bad according to your needs. If it suits your purpose, destruction can be good, or construed as bad depending what is best for you. That would lead to another discussion and that is not what we wish.*

'Even we cannot grasp the meaning of the Infinite, nor do we expect you to grasp its meaning, because of the unending immensity of it, so why worry about things which do not concern us. Just live out your life in Faith and Truth, as we try to do, and you will receive your just reward. How this may come about, or what it will be, we do not know. Yet we do know that Earthlings pray to the Creator and feel all the better for it.

'Now this matter of prayer must be directed to some source, otherwise it would be aimless, and what better source than a very life-giving Power to which, or whom you can unload your troubles and feel all the better for it. Yes, it does something for you. It makes you feel good, and this is a good thing for we must have some aim, or we would be like a ship without a compass, so by all means keep up your prayer as it truly relieves one's conscience. If prayer is good, then it too is of God so to speak. Prayer is also an outlet for despair.

'You may be shocked at this kind of teaching – this asking you to pray to an impersonal God, or a God who has no soul – and well might you say that you may as well pray to the sun as a life-giving power, but you would be quite wrong, since the sun is not this Life-giving-Natural-Law-Force of which we have spoken. You are part of it for it is also in you; in other words you are a Oneness with it, as even is your sun, for neither would your sun shine nor give off its healing powers if it were not for the Greater Cause. Why, even your sun has the two opposite powers! It can kill! It can cure too! This great Truth prompts us to remind you of what your Great Teacher told you, for He said, "The Power is within You". It is so mighty that it is everywhere.

'In the very early stages in the history of Earthlings, (and we know this to be the truth), when cause and effect was a mystery to them, they solved the answer to many if not all puzzling events by believing that effect was caused by some supernatural 'Being' for want of a better explanation. They blamed or praised certain stars for their troubles or good fortune, whichever was the case until this too became a kind of religion and indeed is still so with many Earthlings

even to this very day; yet the world is now learning how wrong such a religion can be.

'Let us tell you, that there is always a perfectly logical reason for all events no matter in what way they happen. There is nothing supernatural in anything, and religion for religion's sake is evil. If your world would only try to understand what the Creator is, instead of putting prejudice before common sense, there would be no such thing as different religious bodies pulling in different directions. Many evil deeds have been committed in the past because Earthlings believed that their particular religion demanded such acts and that what they were doing was good and pleasing to the Creator. This was evil in its unadulterated form.

'Your world is fast emerging from its ignorance and becoming more secular in its beliefs, yet it will still be a long time before the true nature of the Creator will be fully understood. Right from the beginning of your existence, you have all been prisoners on a very minute island planet and in the early stages knew little or nothing about the limitless space around you, and so you built up preconceived ideas which became so deeply planted, is it any wonder that it was all so difficult to eradicate?

'All we wish to do is to point the way to better understanding of the nature of things around you so that you may get them in better perspective. Our brotherly love towards our kindred impels us to pursue this course. In the past, we have tried not to criticise and we hope you will take this not as such, but rather as pointing the way in order to make the journey easier and prove our love towards you who are so like us in form.

'We are sorely troubled as to how this Truth will be received in your world, but you are free to accept or reject this new teaching as you wish. Certain people among you already know the Truth as we have given it, but have been afraid to propound it because of the probable consequences. We can only hope that a new light of understanding will soon prevail. Right through all human history, a true understanding of the Creator has been sadly lacking.'

Some of the writings delved deeper into the mysteries of time and space;

'Now, it does not seem to matter where we begin to speak in Time and Space about anything away out there in boundless space since there is no beginning nor end to it, and we hope you understand the real meaning of what we just

stated; however, if you do not, then do not let it worry you, as we can still tell you the Truth even so. Earthlings in their writings have made genii of us, making it appear that we are capable of any wonders that they think up. This is quite untrue! We are certainly capable of much that Earthlings still cannot do and we know the fiction that is written about us. So let Earthlings try to understand us better and know that we are with them in order to help and not hinder. Let the world know that we do not dwell anywhere in your planetary system, but come from systems far removed from you. We are shocked by what has now become a religion, and like many religions containing wrong beliefs. We never wished it to be this way, but there lies the weakness of Earthlings; they are given a simple truth, and because it seems too simple, or not sufficiently exciting, they must dress it up to make it sell well. So Mammon clouds the vision, shutting out the Higher Aim, and those who wish to seek the Truth are beset by such a heavy curtain of half truths and untruths that the light of understanding cannot possibly shine through to the seeker after Truth. We ask you – is this not so?

'The big question always looms up in the minds of Earthlings on how and why matter is hanging in space in ever changing forms. The truth is that it was always there and there never was a time when space was empty. This will always be so. Nothing is constant because everything is ever changing be it ever so slow in the mind of Earthlings. We intend to tell you much in just the kind of language twists which are so familiar so that you will not misunderstand us.'

'There is always a temporary end to all things, but no absolute end to Time, Space and Movement in the wider sense. What we are trying to convey to you here, is that there has always been two of a kind, and believe us, it was never any different. It couldn't be, because of the very nature of matter and its movement in Time and Space.

'Past time can never return, for once a second of time is ticked away, it is gone forever. Other seconds of time can surely take its place, but never that particular second of which we just spoke. A rebirth of time can never occur – once gone, gone forever. Once an act is done, it cannot be undone. You may compensate for it by redoubling your effort, but you cannot rub it out. You may forget it, and the whole world may forget it, but that still does not erase it. Yes, this living is a serious business. Never will time return in order to allow you to undo something you may have done in the past. This is Truth! Like endless space, time goes on forever because it is Universal Law without beginning and without end because it was always so.

'However, before going any further, we would like to say that many good religious Earthlings will call us the Devil's Messengers using subtle words to trap them into evil. We have nothing to gain nor lose if such were our intention. Our intentions are good, and if they are good, then they are of God so misunderstood!

'The writer may well wonder why he is able to write in this way, for this is not his work, and that is sufficient reason, since we direct his every idea and trust him to use these ideas to the best of his ability and with words at his disposal. Through his instrumentality, let us tell you that Love will conquer worlds, but the withered hand of hate will blight everything it touches and therefore is of no avail to its owner. Do not try hate, for we know what you will receive in return.

'Much of what we are teaching is bound to be opposed by well meaning, deeply religious persons who will say that we have forgotten that man is a thinking being and free to choose. That he is free to accept or reject, and that this marks him out as something very specially different from the rest of Creation; but here again, there is a misconception of our relationship to the rest of Creation. Acceptance and rejection is universal, even in plant life, as any botanist knows. Even animals will accept or reject according to their likes or dislikes, and often for no apparent reason. Yes, this Law of opposites is everywhere. Affinity plays a big part in this Law. We hope that we have helped you so far concerning Truth. We do not apologise for what we have said, but just regret that we have had the unenviable task of saying it.

'We know how black we shall be painted by the doubters against whom we have not sinned. Yet, like your Great Teacher said; "Forgive them Lord, for they know not what they do," we too forgive them. Your Great Teacher was not understood, so perhaps there is still a chance for us to try and make ourselves understood; but with this difference, that we speak to a world advanced in knowledge and which is in a better position to understand now than it ever was.

"Now, we would like to go another step further to show you your complete misunderstanding in the matter of suffering. You have always believed that *human suffering was the result of disobedience to the Creator's command that the forbidden fruit must not be eaten, and it was through this disobedience that all your troubles began. Now just take a closer look at that belief in the light of what we have so far revealed to you, and your answer will be automatic without further explanation on our part. This is not all, because it is often believed amongst you that you bring upon yourselves all suffering.*

'This is not wholly true, and so we ask; "Did you bring upon yourselves earthquakes, floods, tornados and the like, all of which have killed millions? Do you really believe this?" You certainly do bring upon yourselves much of your suffering, and this is what some of you are pleased to call 'Poetic Justice', and we agree that your punishment for your own wrong-doing is also automatic and well deserved. There is one Great Truth throughout everything known and unknown, which is; 'Your Sins Will Always Find You Out'.

The final writing of Mr. X contained the following passages; *'At the beginning of the year 1964, we inspired your writer to commit to paper some verses of poem which we believe could be included at this juncture as appropriate to what we have just been telling you, and so we request him to do that.*

THAT FOR WHICH YOU SEEK

In the misty forest where footsteps are muffled by a mossy carpet,
And shafts of sunlight stab the mouldy earth,
In the bush-clad valleys where snow-fed streams,
Give great rivers their birth.

T'is there my friend where you will find that for which you seek;
For this to you may sound quite odd,
As we reveal to you this Truth,
That there, are you nearest to God.

He is less evident in bricks and mortar of which most edifices are made,
For these reveal not His Handiwork;
Although they are built to His glory,
Even then the Devil may lurk.

Go you then to the forest where the carpet is thicker and yet more rugged,
Where tree trunks stand like people,

For therein you will find his Glory
In a church without a steeple.

T'is around the mountain tops where clouds kiss the lofty peaks,
T'was on one of such – Mount Sinai, where God first gave his law;
For in the heights and these quiet places,
Reigns He for Evermore.

They then spoke of the Dickesons, who had risked both their reputation and friendships to distribute Mr. X's work. *'Your local Editor-Publisher is highly esteemed by us, for he, along with those nearest and dearest to him have remained faithful to our Cause. This we cannot, and will not, forget, and when opportunity presents itself, we shall approach him personally and press his hand. We have enjoyed every moment of our talk with you. Our time is now very short, and we have much to do. May our God be your God also.*

'So, with love and understanding in all our hearts, we say "God bless you all", for here endeth the final lesson. We shall always be – Your Two Friends.'

Some of the writings, regarding the nature of the Creator were a little incomprehensible, perhaps because Mr. X was confused, or perhaps because the 'two friends', although more advanced than us, still did not fully understand the 'Intelligence' of the Cosmos. Fred and Phyllis Dickeson added some thoughts of their own;

'There must be some purpose in life, we cannot imagine that the intelligence which constitutes you in you, or the me in me, is lost and cease to exist after our body has served its usefulness and returns to the earth from whence it came.

'It says in some writings that we have a loan of a small part of the great thought which upon death is returned to the Great Thought or Great Reservoir of the Living Thought, and there we imagine must be released later to some further manifested form to gain greater and more varied experiences. In other words, are we manifested in the shape of a human being, at the moment, to experience and carry out the expression of the Ever-Living Force or Power which we have been told is God? The more one ponders this angle the more fascinating and feasible it becomes, and bears out the saying that God 'IS', and nothing exists outside of God.

'Many a time we have, and probably you have felt too, that we are put here as this person, in this particular spot on Earth, for some specific purpose; we have some job to do, and that job must be done regardless. We feel that the stage has been set and we are the players. The plot is there, the play goes along, but how we act our set part, whether we make a good or bad job of it, rests entirely with us. Therefore, don't you think we should try and act our part well?

INDEX

A

Adamski-George. Chaps. 3-4
10,30,76,77.87-8,91,94,102, 117
145-46,148,150,153,157,174-5,
185,190,195, Annex A. 279-281
Afalov-Anton.14
Akon. 27-8
Akrij. 8,173
Amicizia. 105,145,167,170-1,190
Anderson-Carl. 176
Anderson-Lt.Col William. 132
Apraksin-Arkadii. 134
Argentina. 35,219
Armstrong-Neil. 229
Aston-Warren. 21,169,171-2
Australia. Chap.4. 41,138-9,266

B

Baileys-George & Betty. 122
Baker-Jerrold. 52-3
Barbato-Cristoforo. 73
Barnes-Bishop. 120
Bartholomew-Robert. 14
Beckley-Timothy. 151
Beers-Adrian. 52
Belize. 10
Bender-Albert. Chap.17. 247,252,257
Benito-Segundo. 74
Bilodeaux-Jean. 243
Birdsall-Graham. 257
Blodget-Charlotte. 51,59
Boyer-Father. 179
Brazil. 42
Breccia-Stefano. 171-2
Briggs-Frederick. 142
Britain. 140-1
Brown-Jeff. 226
Brunt-Tony. 60
Buchwald-Art. 233

BUFORA. 8
Burns –Pat. 232

C

California. 28
Carisson-Gosta. 26
Chile. 167
China. 137,153
Clark-Jerome. 196
Coe-Albert. 11
Cole-John. 12
Crabb-Riley. 267
Creighton-Gordon.
5,31,35,42,83,137,169,193,201
Crimean Peninsula. 14
Cronkite-Walter. 3
CTR. 8,105,145,170,172

D

Darnbyl-Col.Gernod. 253
Decker-Rosemary. Chap.5.
46,48,53,60,94,150,206,260
Denmark. 192
Diaz-Dr. Leopoldo. 181
Dickesons-Fred,Phyllis, Bryan. Chap.6.
60-3, 94,101,103,110,113-6,190,220,
249-50, 282
Dodd-Tony. 252-7
Dowding-Lord. 64-71,141-2
Duplantier-Gene. 222
Dworshak-Leo. 15

E

Edwin. 161-3
Evans-Hilary. 201

F

Farraudi-Orlando. 167-9
Firkon. 50-1
Fontes-Dr. Orlando . 208
Forrestal-James. 269-70
France. 10,230
Freaney-Liam. 266
Freixedo-Salvador. 215
Fry-Dan. 30,42,77,154-7,181,218
Fry-Margaret. 19

G

Galli-Luciano. 31
Gardner-Norma. 5
Gaulton-Sir Francis. 120
Ghibaudi-Bruno. 193
Giant Rock. 28-30,125-6
Glenn- John. 240
Good-Timothy. 11,54,67-8,70,133,147,150,160,172,175-6
Goodall-Medwyn. 109
Graham-Billy. 3
Greer-Steven. 7
Guimaraes-Dr.Jao. 42-3

H

Halpern-Steve. 109
Hamilton-Ronald. 133,135
Hellyer-Paul. 210-11, 232
Hilton-Alan. 182
Hind-Cynthia. 27,163
Honey-C.A. 68-9
Horton-Carl. 129
House of Lords. 87,143,146
Howe-Linda Moulton. 257
Hunrath-Karl. 52-3
Hynek-Allen.148,265

I

Illinois. 12
Italy. 31,71,193

J

Jarrold-Edgar. Chap.17, 247-257

K

Keel-John. 35.124
Kennedy-Robert. 268
Klarer-Elizabeth. 26-28

L

Laithwaite-Roger. 204
Leonard. 20
Le Poer Trench – Brinsley & Millen.
Chap.5, 2,141,143,146,190,260
Leslie-Desmond. 18,55-7.
59,66,68,71,74,141,261
Lindtner-Dr.Miran. 247,257
Lima-Col.Urange. 272

M

Mack-Dr.John. 261
Madau-Friar Guiseppe. 41
Marconi-Gugliemo. 120
Massie-Norman. 12
Matthews. 121,212
Mayberry-John. 229
McDonald-D. James. 270-2
McGinnis-Lucy. 54-7,59-60,66-7
Mendoza-Gertrudis. 139-40
Menger-Howard. 16-19,30,152
Mexico. 34
Middleton-Dave. 124
Mitchell-Helen/Betty. 128
Montana. 21
Mountbatten-Earl. 71,142
Mr.X. Chap.7, AnnexB,
27,88,90,94,163,198,282-300
Mundo-Laura. 69

N

NASA. 2,129-30
Nevada. 173
New Jersey. 16,18

New Zealand. Chaps. 4,6,7, 108,139,200,216,229,260,262
Nielsen-Olaf. 169-70
Noel-Mel.189
North Dakota. 15
Norton-Lord Hill. 141,146-8
Noury-Leo. 150,201,260-1
Novoa-Enrique. 202

O

Oliver-Douglas. 140-1
Orthon. Chap.3, 75-6
Ottens-Toni. 221

P

Padrick-Sid. 199
Pallman-Ludwig. 174
Palmeros-Rafael. 34
Palomar. Chap.3, 44,46,70,76,87
Petersen-Hans. 65,68,144-5,158,160
Puerto Rica.139
Phillips-Ken. 258
Pinkney-John. 180,221
Pope John XXIII. 72-4
Pope Pius. 71,73
Prole-Rebecca. 275

Q

Quaries. 261

R

Radio Contacts. Chap.8, 163
Raffy-Claude. 230
Ramu. 49-51
Randles-Jenny. 204,217
Raul. 11
Reagan-Fred. 224
Remirez-Armando. 34
Rendlesham. 146-7
Ribera-Antonio. 201
Rickman-Edwin. 205
Rizzi-Walter. 37-41
Roddenberry-Gene. 150

Ruppelt-Edward. 46,125-7
Rodeffer-Madeleine. 70-1
Roerich-Nicholas. 10
Russia. 133-7
Ruth. 19-20

S

Saiji-Franco. 171
Salkin-Harold. 199
Sammaciccia-Bruno. 170-1
Schneider-Phil. 273
Schmidt-Reinhold. 241
Schroeder-John.177
Sicily. 32
Siragusa-Eugenio. 32-3
Smith-Charles. 179
Smith-Wilbur. 77,143,205-11
South Africa. 27,137,160-4
Stanford-Ray. 45
Steckling- Fred/Glenn. 44,68
Stevens-Wendelle. 277
Stone-Fred. Chap.17, 64,66,69,106,113, 159-60,182,189,195-6,247-52,262,278
Stott-Murray. 262
Streeter-Lyman. 122,124
Sweden. 26,169

T

Tarnavolgl-Gyorgy. 240
Team of Independent Mars Researchers.78
Telepathy. Chap.12
Tesla. 120,212
Tomas-Andrew. 63,248
Toronto.15

U

Ummo. 1,201,203-4
United Nations. 146,182
Uvarov-Valery. 254,267

V

Van den Berg-Basil. 48
Van Tassel-George. 18,28-30,108

Vidal-Dr.Gerardo. 214
Villagrasa-Enrique. 203
Visani-Uberto. 170

W

W56. 171-2
Wales. 19
Wartena-Udo. 21-3
Watts-Carroll. 263-5
Wells-Alice. 46-7,53,59,68,70,76
West Virginia. 12
White-Fred. 164-5
Wilkinson-Wilbur. 124-5
Williamson-George Hunt. 30,45,47-8,77,122-4
Winchell-Walter. 46
Willisher-Pete. 258-60
Wisconsin. 23
Wood-Betty. 8
Wright-Dan. 179

X-Y-Z

Zigler-Ellen, 197
Zinsstag-Lou. 65,67,71
Zolotov-Aleksei. 267